The Orthodox Church and Civil Society in Russia

The Orthodox Church and Civil Society in Russia

Wallace L. Daniel

Texas A&M University Press

COLLEGE STATION

The paper used in this book meets the minimum requirements
of the American National Standard for Permanence
of Paper for Printed Library Materials, Z39.48-1984.
Binding materials have been chosen for durability.
∞

Poetry in chapter 4 is an excerpt from "Requiem" from *The Complete Poems of
Anna Akhmatova,* trans. Judith Hemschemeyer, ed. and with an intro. by Roberta Reeder.
Copyright © 1990, 1992, 1997 by Judith Hemschemeyer.
Reprinted by permission of Zephyr Press.

Library of Congress Cataloging-in-Publication Data

Daniel, Wallace L.
The Orthodox Church and civil society in Russia / Wallace L. Daniel. — 1st ed.
p. cm. — (Eugenia and Hugh M. Stewart '26 series on Eastern Europe)
Includes bibliographical references and index.
ISBN-13: 978-1-58544-523-3 (cloth : alk. paper)
ISBN-10: 1-58544-523-1 (cloth : alk. paper)
1. Christianity and politics—Russkaia pravoslavnaia tserkov'. 2. Christian sociology—
Russkaia pravoslavnaia tserkov'. 3. Christianity and politics—Russia (Federation)
4. Christian sociology—Russia (Federation) I. Title. II. Series.
BX510.D36 2006
281.947'090511—dc22
2006001537

To Karol, Zach, and Elizabeth

Lara started and stood still. This was about her. He was saying:
Happy are the downtrodden. They have something to tell about themselves.
They have everything before them. That was what he thought.
That was Christ's judgment.

—Boris Pasternak, *Doctor Zhivago*

Contents

Preface

This is not the book I started out to write or the chronicle I first tried to understand. I had wanted to focus on the Orthodox Church—how it fit into the larger social setting, how it attempted to address a people then emerging from the Communist state. I had returned to the Soviet Union in the summer of 1991 for a short visit after nearly a decade of absence. Gradually, it became clear to me that the most interesting stories lay not at the top, in the church hierarchy, but at the base of society, in the individuals and parishes struggling to find their way, endeavoring to regain certain aspects of the past and attempting to reconstruct their lives. They provided ways of viewing Russia's historic transformation that were personal yet also related to a much larger picture.

While primary and secondary materials comprised a substantial part of my research, interviews provided personal sources that were also extremely important. They were indispensable to my attempts to piece together a large and complex story, whose daily rhythms are not captured in the written records of the period under review. Much of this story is preserved in the memory of individuals whose struggles to find a new direction for their lives make up the core of my work.

In nearly all cases of the individuals cited in the text, I went back many times and usually over several years to get their stories, to fill in gaps, and, because these were dynamic times, to observe and try to comprehend the succeeding parts of their lives. Such interviews took various forms: some were brief conversations; others went for many hours; and still others took place over several days. I recorded most of the principal interviews on cassette tapes, and I have gone back to them repeatedly in order to listen to the nuances of speech and refresh my own memory about the emotions underlying their words. It is this sense of immediacy, this face-to-face interaction with one's primary materials, that often makes interviews such rich sources of information.

I made five extensive visits to Russia: the first in the summer of 1991, two months before the aborted August coup; the next three in 1992, 1994, and 1995; the final, and longest, in the spring and early summer of 1997, when I had the opportunity to observe the main subjects of my study over several months and interview most of them at length. People, of course, are always a part of communities of various kinds. And I have tried to place my interviewees within their communities, a process requiring close observation of the setting in which they worked and the other people with whom they interacted. The interviews conducted in this study were done in such a context.

I owe a large debt of gratitude to the main subjects of my research, who gave me a great deal of their time. I am also deeply indebted to several Russians who discussed my subject with me over many years, treated me with exceptional hospitality, and shared their knowledge and their insights with me. Like many others of their generation, they too have struggled to redefine themselves and their sense of Russia's present and future. They include in particular, Vladimir Salov, a historian and political economist, formerly of the Institute of Europe of the Russian Academy of Sciences and currently of the Ministry of Foreign Affairs. He took an early interest in my work, and his discussions with me, ranging over nearly a decade, have greatly deepened my understanding of Russia's heritage and current realities. Conversations with him, his wife, Vera, and other members of his family, have invariably been enriching to me, and this study could not have been accomplished without their generous assistance. Georgii Bovt, trained as a historian, who transformed himself into a journalist of the first rank, has also been of importance to this study. Originally a writer for the newspaper *Nedelia,* then for *Segodnia,* he became an editor of *Izvestiia.* He and his wife, Irina, have on multiple occasions offered friendship, hospitality, and insights into a society struggling to redefine itself. Much of the same can be said for Evgeniia Viktorovna Ivanova, formerly of the Russian Cultural Foundation, a scholar of Aleksandr Blok, Pavel Florenskii, and of Russia's silver age. She introduced me to Mother Serafima and to Maksim Shevchenko, and her strong interest in Russia's prerevolutionary philosophical-religious thought gave evidence of the continuing strength of this heritage.

I am thankful to others who provided considerable time and effort in my attempt to understand Russia's struggles—its challenges and hopes—since the demise of the Soviet Union. These individuals include Dmitrii Efimovich Furman, director of the Center of the Sociology of Religion, Russian Academy of Sciences; Sergei Borisovich Filatov, scholar in the Institute USA-Canada and the Center of the Sociology of Religion, Russian Academy of Sciences; Dmitrii Shusharin, journalist for *Nezavisimaia gazeta* and later *Segodnia;* Fr Vsevolod Chaplin, vice chairman of the Department for External Church Relations of the Moscow Patriarchate; Fr Andrei Il'ia Osipov, professor, Spiritual Academy of the Moscow Patriarchy, Sergiev Posad; Lev Niko-laevich Mitrokin, scholar, Institute of Philosophy, Russian Academy of Sciences; Elena Vladimorovna Panina, leader of the Russian Zemstvo Movement; Igor' Ivanovich Vinogradov, chief editor of *Kontinent;* and Evgenii Grigor'evich Mironenkov, director of the Institute of Europe, Russian Academy of Sciences.

This study could not have been accomplished without the generous support of various organizations and individuals. I am grateful for a Fulbright-Hays Fellowship for Faculty Research Abroad and for a grant from the Office of the Vice Provost for Research at Baylor University. Librarians and research assistants at the State Public Historical Library and the Russian State Library in Moscow have been unfailingly helpful, and they have always made it a great pleasure to work there. I have used extensively the materials of the church, the Russian periodical and daily press, and the rich collections of primary materials on Russian religious life at the Keston Institute in Oxford, England; I owe particular thanks to Malcolm Walker, the Keston Institute's resourceful and gifted librarian, as well as to Michael Bourdeaux, the institute's former director, and Philip Walters, editor of its journal *Religion, State, and Society,* for their research assistance, access to their collections, and their gracious hospitality. I owe much to Baylor University; the professionalism of the staff of the Moody Library and the J. M. Dawson Church-State Center at Baylor University; the European Division of the Library of Congress; the Davis Library at the University of North Carolina, Chapel Hill; the Perkins and Divinity Libraries at Duke University; and the Perry-Castañeda Library at the University of Texas, Austin.

I am grateful for the friendship of various other individuals, whose encouragement of this study was extremely important. They include the Russian and American participants in a roundtable discussion on Orthodoxy and church-state relations in contemporary Russia, held at the Moscow Patriarchate in July 2003; and the participants in the international conference on Orthodoxy and the construction of civil society and democracy in Russia, held at the Kennan Institute of the Woodrow Wilson International Center for Scholars, Washington, D.C., in March 2004. I am grateful to colleagues who gave valuable help during the writing and preparation of this manuscript; they include Christopher Marsh, Elizabeth Vardaman, Viola Osborn, Justin Miller, Michael Long, Stephen Gardner, Elizabeth Dell, Katherine Jeffrey, Lynnette Geary, and members of the Office of the Dean of the College of Arts and Sciences at Baylor University; and Mary Lenn Dixon, the talented chief editor of the Texas A&M University Press, Jennifer Ann Hobson, and Anne R.

Gibbons. In reading and commenting on the manuscript, all these individuals improved my work, saving me from many errors, and I am solely responsible for mistakes and flaws that remain.

It is a pleasure to acknowledge publicly my gratitude to Karol, whose support for me and my work has been unfailing. She has been an encourager, a critic, and always a joyful presence. She, as well as our children, Zach and Elizabeth, have been for me primary sources of inspiration not only for this project but also for many others. It is to them that this book is dedicated.

The Orthodox Church and Civil Society in Russia

Introduction

*Like the Imperial Eagle, the Russian Church had two heads, one representing
the ecclesiastical bureaucracy presided over by the Synod, the other the parochial
clergy and laity who were faithful to the Orthodox ideal of the Christian
community ('Sobornost''), guided and protected by the Holy Spirit. The contrast
between the external and internal life of the Russian Church was baffling. It
was the outcome of the peculiar history of Russian Christianity.*

—Nicholas Zernov

Since the collapse of the Soviet Union in 1991, Russia has struggled to regain
its sense of identity and purpose. This endeavor has witnessed the attempts of
many movements and groups, ranging from fascist to democratic, to provide
a vision for the future. A major player in the drama is the Russian Orthodox
Church, courted by the main participants, especially by the nationalist-
patriots and the Communists, but also by the proponents of an open, civil
society, who see the church and religion in general as key elements in the rebuilding of Russia. Historians and political analysts have primarily focused on
the Russian government and its political and military actions. But looking
beyond these traditional subjects and the official structures of power, one dis-
covers much that has profound implications for the future history of Russia.
In the monasteries and the churches and in the parishes connected to them
are found individuals and groups of people, who are quietly but surely defining the future shape of Russia's national life. Their struggles to do so, with
both positive and negative consequences, are the principal subjects of this
work.[1]

   As Russia attempts to rebuild and redefine itself after the fall of communism, one of the dominant questions is where it will find the basis for a civil
society and what the relationship of the state to that society will be. An often
overlooked source of values and models for a civil society is the Orthodox
Church. That model is not found in its most visible leaders and structures.
Rather one of the sites where civil society may emerge is in the trenches of

Orthodoxy, among a group the Russian scholar Dmitrii Sergeevich Likhachev has called the "tireless workers" of the church. What they are doing and whether they will succeed in building a new cultural infrastructure are questions of crucial importance to the Russia of the twenty-first century.

In this book, I have pursued answers to these questions, through in-depth looks at the experiences of four individuals, whose struggles demonstrate the role of religion in the Russia now evolving. Other studies have dealt with the broad outlines of religious policy and have taken a macro view of the Orthodox Church as an institution; few have looked closely at specific religious communities, exploring the way they operate, their efforts to rebuild parish life, and the individuals who have devoted themselves to such efforts. In my view, this is where much of the effort to reconstruct Russia, to revitalize its society, is taking place.

The United States' own role in the world is entwined with Russia's. Occupying the traditional heartland of Eurasia and possessing great natural resources, Russia should not be marginalized in the consciousness of the United States. Whether it devolves into chaos, develops a new nationalism, or evolves into a civil society will have a large bearing on America and its own role in a global context. Russian history has at key junctures intersected that of the United States'; in an increasingly interdependent world, it will continue to do so. But the significance of the subject addressed here goes beyond geopolitics. The individuals presented in this study have a great deal to teach us about struggle and survival, about the importance of ideals, about tradition and creativity, about Christianity and community, and about the recovery of cultural memory.

Beginning in the late 1980s, Russia experienced a religious renaissance that brought many formerly suppressed themes to the surface. Important among these themes was the rebirth and renewal of the Russian Orthodox Church and the church's struggle to rediscover its own place, both at the national and local levels of Russian life. "The fact that so many Russians seem to believe today that they cannot find their way unless they renew their spiritual roots makes that search a critical factor in all the processes now under way," wrote Serge Schmemann, the *New York Times'* Moscow correspondent, in 1992.[2] Schmemann's words addressed a theme deeply rooted in Russia's past that would resurface at the end of the Soviet period and that would continue to be a vital element in the next decade.

Released from government control and faced with the challenge of recovering its traditions, its historical memory, and its voice in a society searching for meaning, the Orthodox Church has had to look both inward and outward. This effort has raised several questions central to Russia's future: Will the church become a force that contributes to national stability, as the government has asked of it many times in Russia's past and asks of it today? Or will it be creative, speak to the community, offer a perspective on life that transcends the present, and provide a critique of the status quo? Will the church withdraw from the world or will it attempt to play an active social role, seeing in that activity a key part of its religious mission? And should it seek to play an active social role, what will be the consequences? Will it undermine or contribute to the development of a civil society? As the Russian historian James H. Billington has noted, "Whether the Orthodox Church can wrest itself from the state and become the conscience of the nation will be important in determining whether Russia can discover a new, democratic and civil culture or will return to a dark and threatening authoritarianism."[3]

Freedom, as the Russian émigré writer George Fedotov argued nearly half a century ago, is "a setting of limits to the power of the state in terms of the inalienable rights of the individual."[4] Setting limits to the power of the state enables a middle social sphere to flourish between the state and the individual—a civil society—where voluntary, civic associations operate. It is these civic associations and networks that cultivate freedom of thought, conscience, and assembly—the attributes and values that strengthen democracy. And it is these civic associations where individual interests are transformed into public spiritedness, where certain shared social virtues are cultivated—civility, cooperation, responsibility, solidarity, honesty, and love of neighbor. Voluntary networks are where civic skills are developed; they are the "schools of democracy." Such nonpolitical associations as families, neighborhoods, churches, and volunteer organizations develop what Robert Putnam has called social capital, the capacity to trust in the society and to work for a common purpose. In such a framework, Putnam has argued, the "cultural cement of the civic community" is created and the social values that underlie civil society are learned.[5]

The idea of civil society lies at the heart of the Western political tradition and relates to its central themes. Emerging in the seventeenth and eighteenth centuries during the breakdown of the old social order in Western Europe, civil society expressed a moral vision of the social realm, seeking both to achieve a new balance between the community and the individual and to redefine the relationship between public and private domains.[6] Civil society conceived of the person not as an isolated individual but as "part of a whole," a member of the community, who lived, Tocqueville would write about the United States, in creative tension between the self and the common good.[7]

While the networks and associations nurturing civil society are usually identified with Western Europe in the nineteenth and twentieth centuries, they were also present in Russia, although they have often gone unnoticed and unappreciated. They existed in several forms: in the circles of friends and family, in dissident groups, and in religious communities; all these groups encouraged independent thought and action, which they expressed in multiple ways. They made up what the Czech writer and political leader Vaclάv Havel called "the invisible realm of social consciousness."[8] In Russia, they drew from a rich, complex historical tradition containing many sources of inspiration, including the church. Such groups would come to the surface on many occasions, most especially in 1991, during the collapse of the Communist regime and the coup d'état that attempted to preserve the Soviet order, and they would continue to operate actively in the decade thereafter.[9]

Eastern European writers, in particular, have emphasized the moral and religious underpinnings of civil society. Instead of command, such underpinnings valued consent; instead of building walls and closing citizens in, they required tearing the walls down. They assumed a respect for the individual and a tolerance for different ways of seeing the world. To Havel, the deepest roots of civility and responsibility are moral, because genuine politics is a "responsibility, expressed through action, to and for the whole, a responsibility that is what it is—a 'higher' responsibility—only because it has a metaphysical grounding: that is, it grows out of a conscious or subconscious certainty that our death ends nothing, because everything is forever recorded and evaluated somewhere else 'above us,' in what I have called 'the memory of Being.'"[10] The development of civil society, to Havel, thus required connecting to this "memory of Being," recovering the memories that were lost or "airbrushed over," and seeking renewal of the moral dimensions that he claimed are "hidden in everything."[11]

In Russia, as several of her leading scholars have pointed out, the development of civil society will greatly depend upon the recovery of a sense of moral authority.[12] During the Communist era, the Soviet government tried to destroy or push to the margins individual responsibility for moral choices. Civil society necessitates restoring this individual responsibility. It is from there that a new system of laws, providing social justice, will evolve. It is from there, too, that a new political order can best be constructed. Historically, such a moral force had stood as a counterweight to armed power, the resolution of problems through violence, and the destruction of the natural world.[13] In Russia's past, the use of force "always required some higher legitimacy." Before engaging in battle, heroes in folk tales always sought the blessings of "older people and independent sources of moral authority," thereby "sharing with them a responsibility for the results."[14] Repeatedly, in Russia's cultural history, moral authority confronted material force, with the former proving to be superior. There were multiple origins of moral authority; primary among them was the Orthodox Church, with its liturgy and teachings about trust, compassion, forgiveness, responsibility, negotiation, and opposition to armed bloodshed. As I will argue, the rediscovery of these rich historical sources and memories and how they are incorporated into present-day Russian realities will have a large bearing on the prospects for developing a civil society.

"In ancient Russia," Likhachev has written, "one finds two main categories of people who were held to be sacred: princes or warrior-servitors and monks—founders and builders of monasteries, church activists on a national scale." Russian historians have written a great deal about the first category of people, the "defenders of the native land," but they have written little about the second, the builders of monasteries and church activists, those "tireless workers." Independent of government power, Likhachev has pointed out, they created many of the key structures—the buildings, meeting places, technological devices, and economic enterprises—that supported Russian civilization.[15]

The present study focuses on Likhachev's second category, the "tireless workers," who, often outside the official structures of power, made significant contributions to Russia's national story. My study takes seriously Likhachev's observation that "warrior-servitors" and agencies of the state comprise only part of its national experience and that much of Russia's history remains to be explored. Many important contributions came outside the official structures. The social activities of the tireless workers, and their impact on Russia, both in the past and in the present, warrant more attention than they have received: as Nicholas Zernov emphasized, the Imperial Eagle and the church have two heads.

The answers to the questions posed earlier about Russia's future direction are played out in the lives of four people who form the core of the present book. By telling their stories, I have taken a selective and somewhat personal approach to a very large subject. These individuals reveal separate parts of a complex and still developing mosaic; I have found all of them compelling. They include the priest of the former parish of the Troitskaia Church in Moscow, Fr Georgii Kochetkov; the leader of the parish at the famous Novodevichy Monastery in Moscow, Mother Serafima (Chernaia-Chichagova); the parish priest at the University Church of the Sacred muchenitsy Tat'iana at

Moscow University, Fr Maksim Kozlov; and the editor of the religion section of the newspaper *Nezavisimaia gazeta,* Maksim Leonidovich Shevchenko.

The son of members of the Moscow intelligentsia who were never avid Party members, Fr Georgii Kochetkov studied history and philosophy at Moscow State University before searching for a new career pattern for his life in the 1970s. After his seminary training, he worked his way up through the Orthodox Church until his assignment to several older parishes located in the center of Moscow in the early and mid-1990s. The second of these parishes was located in the church of the Dormition of the Mother of God in Pechatniki (Uspeniia Bogoroditsy Tserkov' v pechatnikakh) on Sretinskaia Street, east of the Kremlin, in one of Moscow's oldest neighborhoods. In those difficult times in Russia, when family life and communal ties had been shattered, he developed in the center of Russia's largest city a parish whose members supported each other, providing charity to the most needy among them and emotional help to those whose lives had been uprooted. The main focus of Fr Georgii's community, however, was on worship, through a new liturgy of the church, which he instituted among his followers. Fr Georgii used the vernacular to move his congregation in new, more direct, more personal approaches to worship. His reforms would make him one of the most controversial church leaders since the collapse of the Soviet Union, and they would lead him directly into conflict both with the Moscow Patriarchate and with Russian nationalist groups.

Mother Serafima's family roots lay in the Russian nobility, and her family history is entwined with one of Russia's most venerated old families, the Chichagovs. The granddaughter of a leading Orthodox priest who fell victim to the Great Purges in the 1930s, she carried his memory with her throughout her life. As a young woman, she studied chemistry, eventually becoming one of the country's leading synthetic chemists and managing one of the largest chemical institutions. Despite the successes of her career within the official establishment, however, she retained memories of the church and of her grandfather from her childhood and, in the 1990s, she had the opportunity to resurrect them and bring them back to the center of her life. In 1994, she was appointed director of Novodevichy Monastery, one of Russia's oldest and most renowned women's monasteries, whose reconstruction and restoration of its own memories she would lead. Her story is one of struggle, perseverance, courage, and hope.

Fr Maksim Kozlov was educated at a traditional center of theological learning, the Spiritual Academy at Sergiev Posad. The home of the Moscow Patriarchate before its move to the Danilov Monastery in Moscow in 1988, the

Spiritual Academy is among the church's most conservative theological institutions. In 1994, Fr Maksim was appointed head of the parish at Moscow University, the Church of the Sacred muchenitsy Tat'iana. Unlike Fr Georgii, he is not a reformer. He conceives of the church's main task as the restoration of its traditions, its religious mission, and its place in Russia's national consciousness, all of which were undermined by the Soviet government. His attempts to recover, rebuild, and re-create the church's historic voice as one of Russia's primary institutions of higher learning faced severe challenges. His struggles suggest both the opportunities and the limitations of Orthodoxy's efforts at renewal.

The final primary subject of this study moves away from the parish and takes a different direction but still focuses on the concrete realities of religion, politics, and society. Maksim Leonidovich Shevchenko is chief editor of the special religion section of the newspaper *Nezavisimaia gazeta*. Growing up in a village near Poltava, in Ukraine, Shevchenko came to see early in his life that much of both religious and social life took place outside the boundaries of official church and state institutions. In his village, unofficial, communal experiences defined most of his existence, as well as his consciousness, of the church. Well-educated, youthful, a former member of the Christian Democratic Party, and a friend of the social activist Aleksandr Ogorodnikov, Shevchenko is strongly committed to restoring the heritage of Orthodoxy and relating its teachings to society. In 1997, when the newspaper *Nezavisimaia gazeta* created a special monthly supplement on religion in Russia, Shevchenko was selected to be its editor. Under his leadership, the supplement has had several unique features: it has sought to provide a sympathetic voice, independent of the Moscow Patriarchy, for the discussion of Orthodoxy; it has aspired to give varied perspectives on important social and religious issues; it has emphasized that Russia had religious traditions other than Orthodoxy and they, too, needed exploration; and it has offered an extremely intelligent critique of the church and the state in the Soviet past. To Shevchenko, one of the dominant themes in the world since the 1970s had been the conflict between an increasingly secular society and the resurgence of religion. He wanted his newspaper to explore this conflict, in Russia especially, and to enrich public dialogue on its consequences.

The protagonists in this story are rooted in their own past, as well as in the history of Russia. Their beliefs and actions relate, in diverse ways, to this history, and the conflicts they exemplify belong to a larger historical framework than the previous decade only. The tension between warrior-princes and monks, between violence and a different way of relating to the world, and, in

Zernov's words, "between the external and internal life of the Russian Church" are found throughout Russia's history.

Kievan Rus' entered the Christian world shortly before the split, in 1054 A.D., of Christianity into Eastern (Orthodox) and Western (Roman Catholic) branches. Kiev had strong geographical and commercial ties with Constantinople, and both Greek and Byzantine missionaries for nearly a century had worked among the Slavs. In 957, Grand Princess Olga of Kiev, who ruled during the minority of her son Sviatoslav, converted to the Christian faith; her grandson Prince Vladimir embraced Christianity as the official religion of Russia in 988, a momentous decision for the future direction of the country. Vladimir's decision brought Kievan Rus', more firmly than before, into the cultural orbit of Byzantium, the center of Eastern Orthodox Christianity, and its theology, art, and ways of thought.

Kievan Rus's decision to embrace Byzantine Christianity would have great significance both in culture and in politics. Christianity entered a largely pagan country, in which power, force, and violence provided the chief means of resolving problems and settling conflicts. Before the introduction of Christianity, the Russian prince was primarily a military leader, a conqueror, who ruled through force. He brought his subjects into submission through his military retainers, his *druzhina,* who exacted tribute from them. Christianity did not eliminate these practices or the crudity of rulership, but it significantly changed the nature and character of the Russian ruler and the conception of "good order." "You have been sent from God to punish the wicked and to show mercy to the good," the bishops said to Prince Vladimir. Providing counsel to Prince Vladimir, Metropolitan Ilarion praised him, because he "frequently consulted very humbly with the bishops, whom he considered spiritual fathers, about establishing the law among people who had recently come to know the Lord."[16] The ideal of a just and ordered society in Russia had its roots in these prescriptions.

While the prince had the duty to protect the country and maintain good order, he entrusted the church with fostering civic order and morality. In Kievan Rus' the early Christian princes assigned to the church authority over family law, criminal cases, and immoral acts.[17] Throughout the entire Kievan period, the tenth to thirteenth centuries, the church had a significant impact on national welfare and self-consciousness. Teaching that torture was a sin, the church tried to temper slavery by appealing to masters to show compassion and mercy toward their subjects. The church sought to reduce the level of violence by opposing the custom of blood feuds and serving as a mediator between warring individuals and groups. Its role as mediator often was played out on a large stage, as it sought reconciliation between quarreling princes and tried to prevent civil war.[18]

Gradually, through the church, the great Russian historian V. O. Kliuchevskii emphasized, new ideas were imported and nourished, minds were changed, new standards were developed, and the people were prepared to accept these new standards. What the church did, Kliuchevskii showed, was to "deeply penetrate the legal and moral foundations of society."[19] The church's goal was to "construct a civil union in which the laws leaned on this moral sense and eventually would come to subsume it," thereby providing the foundations for a civil community based on law and legal standards, rather than on force and violence.[20] The church was not a "school of jurisprudence or legal codification," but in Kliuchevskii's words, it did establish the grounds supporting a moral sense and feeling, that would ultimately find expression in and be incorporated into the laws.[21] In family law, for example, the influence of the church transformed the relationship between husband and wife. In pagan Russia, extreme cruelty and even murder often characterized this relationship; under the teachings of the church, the wife's status changed from slave to the partner of the husband. In the laws of Kievan Rus', wives and widows had civil equality with males in the family. In legal affairs, the church set judicial norms and defined punishments for crimes, actions that also led to the abolition of the death penalty in Kievan Rus'.

The church had an additional important moral responsibility: it served as a social welfare organization, caring for the most unfortunate members of society and providing refuge for beggars, the poor, the homeless, the infirm, and slaves who had been freed.[22] The church's charity enterprises contributed greatly to the maintenance of "good order" throughout Kievan Rus'. The church nourished a sense of social connection and brotherhood that would become a key part of the notion of "good order." In this conception, each person had a responsibility to the entire social order and to each other. Such a conception would contribute greatly to overcoming barbarian practices and to the belief in individual dignity and worth. It was an idea that would later find additional expression in Russian thought in the teachings of Rev. Iosef Volotskii, the well-known religious leader, who late in the fifteenth century tried to convince serf owners to be merciful to their subjects: "They should remember that all are God's creation, one flesh with God, and all are blessed with myrrh. Everyone's life is in God's hands and all will stand before the Lord on the Day of Judgment."[23]

In politics, the church provided a significant constraint on the ruler's political power. In Kievan Rus' the prince did not exercise unlimited authority, but shared this responsibility with the head of the church, in *symphonia,* in harmony. *Symphonia* expressed a harmonious interaction between the political leader and the priesthood, a harmony toward which each should strive. In such a harmonious relationship, princes and priests each bore responsibilities toward the other—to support and respect each other and to interact in such a way that would work to the total welfare of all the people of the realm.[24]

In Byzantium, this notion of shared power and responsibility was defined in the famous sixth book of Justinian's codex as one of "God's greatest gifts." Whereas the head of the church had responsibility for the moral instruction of the people, the secular authority had the obligation to protect and serve the subjects of his realm. This shared ideal, this sense of each being part of a "greater unity, is well expressed in the *Epanagogue,* the imperial law book of ninth-century Byzantium: "Unity and concord in all things among the government and the clergy, therefore, mean peace and happiness for their subjects in spirit and in body." The secular authority had obligations—to nurture his subjects and to serve them well. According to the *Epanagogue,* "The purpose of the emperor is to do good, and therefore he is called benefactor, and when he fails in this obligation to do good, he forsakes his imperial dignity."[25] This political system, as the Orthodox scholar Fr John Meyendorff has stated, aimed to see the world as a whole and to make no separation between the secular and the sacred, the material and the divine, but to view them as continuous, as a symphony, in which church and state participated in "building a society based on charity and humaneness."[26]

In Russia, such a concept of political and religious authority the Orthodox Church would adopt in full. Political power, like the church, was answerable to a divine source and could not act with unlimited authority in civic affairs.[27] This view prevailed throughout the territory of Kievan Rus', which during the tenth to the thirteenth centuries stretched over an enormous territory, from the capital city of Kiev in the south to the great commercial cities of Novgorod and Pskov in the north. In this vast territory, princes were the heads of armies, political rulers, and supreme lawgivers, but they could not cross certain boundaries without violating the trust granted to them and facing retribution. In the northern city of Novgorod especially, the *veche,* or town assembly, ensured that the ruler did not abuse the political power entrusted to him. According to the *Primary Chronicle,* the main source book for ancient Russia, when the prince went too far and aroused the anger of the people, members of the *veche* would go to him and say "get away from us, prince, we do not want you"; the *veche* would proceed to consider a more worthy candidate.[28] Authority rested not only on legal and dynastic grounds but also on political and moral grounds, and in this relationship the church played the role of "supreme moral judge and critic."[29]

The Mongol invasion of Russia in 1238–40 destroyed Kievan political institutions, brought massive destruction, and dislocated nearly every aspect of Russian life. During the next three centuries, while under Mongol suzerainty, Russia nearly passed from existence as a country. In this difficult period, the church kept alive Russia's historical memory and its national consciousness. In the settlements and monasteries in the northern forest, monks preserved the historical records and extended the story into the present. "Rus' was united through its church long before it was united as a nation or state, and its religious unity was one of the powerful forces that provided its political unification," wrote S. M. Pushkarev.[30]

During this period leading officials of the church also worked for the reunification of the country under a strong Russian princely authority, which would throw off the infidel Mongol forces. The activities of Metropolitans Petr (1308–26), Aleksi (1353–78), and Iona (1448–61) are especially noteworthy in laying a foundation for the future and strengthening Moscow's national importance. Metropolitan Petr moved the seat of Russian Christianity from the south to the northern city of Vladimir, where he befriended Prince Ivan Danilevich Kalita, the prince of Moscow, then a backwater trading settlement. Metropolitan Aleksi served as guardian for the Moscow prince Dmitrii, who, as leader of the Russian army in 1380, inflicted the first military defeat on the Mongols at Kulikovo, an event that added greatly to Moscow's national prestige. Metropolitan Iona gave support to the principle of patrilineal succession of the Moscow prince as leader of Russia. As lodestar of Russia's national identity during the Mongol domination, the Russian Orthodox Church achieved a significantly enhanced political role.[31] As a supporting voice for national unification under the Moscow prince and as a chief repository of Russia's national memory, the church became a major contributor to shaping Russia's national consciousness.

While historians have often portrayed Muscovite Russia, the period from the late fourteenth to the end of the seventeenth century, as a complete break from Kievan Rus' and as a period of intellectual silence, Likhachev has emphasized its cultural connections.[32] Earlier political institutions were decimated, but the cultural and religious norms, themes, and ideas of ancient Rus-

sia—in literature, art, music, architecture, folk life, and religion—were preserved, forming what Likhachev called a "striking continuity" between ancient
Russia and succeeding periods, even into the twentieth century.

Civil society depends on a moral foundation that promotes social solidarity, trust, benevolence, and mutual obligation. In the writings of Adam
Ferguson, one of the early theorists of civil society, this moral foundation ultimately is what leads to community self-governance and positive forms of
individual action. Ferguson opposed civil society to militarism, with its pre-
occupation with force, command, violence, and conquest. When the "Tartar
[goes] to his prince," he promises "that he will go where he shall be commanded; that he will come when he shall be called; that he will kill whoever
is pointed out to him; and, for the future, that he will consider the voice of the
King as a sword."[33] During the violent Mongol assault on Russia, the moral
foundations and prescriptions of early Russia lay dormant, but, Kliuchevskii
argued, they continued to live in Russia's social consciousness and memory.
To Kliuchevskii, the Orthodox Church was the main agency that preserved
and developed this consciousness, that propagated freedom of conscience, the
responsibility of each citizen, and the moral habits associated with a sense of
community. The teachings and practices of Orthodoxy were among the chief
sources that promoted Russia's civil union.[34]

In the reawakening of Russia's moral consciousness, Kliuchevskii attributed a significant place to a churchman, Sergei Radonezhskii, Sergius of
Radonezh (?1314–92).[35] Russia's greatest national saint, Sergius founded a hermitage in the wilderness that ultimately became the Monastery of the Holy
Trinity, the spiritual center of Muscovy. According to Kliuchevskii, during the
most difficult period of Russian history, when the country suffered not only
physical but also moral destruction and "was plunged in the deepest despair,"
Sergius of Radonezh "inspired in Russian society faith in itself," renewing its
moral courage and reawakening "in it the feeling of spiritual strength."[36] As a
consort of Moscow princes, blessing Prince Dmitrii on the eve of Dmitrii's
historic battle with the Tatar force at Kulikovo Field in 1380, and an inspiration to people of all social classes, Sergius's example enabled Russia to get back
on its feet. Kliuchevskii considered this ability to recover after a period of intense suffering and despair to be one of the country's greatest strengths. Russia's moral recovery was a necessary precondition to its political recovery. That
was one of the most important lessons Sergius of Radonezh bequeathed to the
future. "If the icon lamps over [St Sergius's] shrine were ever extinguished or
the gates of the Sergievskaia Lavra were closed," Kliuchevskii maintained,

"then it would signify that our people would have squandered, would have cut themselves off, from one of their greatest moral sources."[37]

In Muscovite Russia, both the state and the church sought to maintain a balance of authority. The tsar had divine authority, and this power required him to be responsible for the people of the state, who were entrusted to him. The tsar's coronation oath especially underscored the obligation to protect the faith and the population. The metropolitan instructed him to "preserve the Christian faith of the Greek law, which is pure and unshakable. . . . Be a champion of truth, mercy, and justice. Take care of all Orthodox Christians."[38] This admonition established the fundamental principle of the tsar's authority, both to defend and take care of the people of the realm, and when he failed, church hierarchs had the right to reproach him, to call him to do his duty. Church leaders also had the right of *pechalovaniia* (intercession), which allowed them to intervene between the tsar and individuals they believed were wrongly accused or punished.[39] The tsar should not cause blood to be shed unnecessarily; when this happened, church leaders reminded him to cool his anger and show mercy. When Tsar Ivan IV (Ivan the Terrible) unleashed the *oprichnina,* his violent oppression on a large part of the country between 1565 and 1582, the church severely criticized his abuse of authority. Seeing the widespread suffering and fear, Metropolitan Filipp in 1566 reproached the tsar, first in private and then, when his admonitions failed, in public during a religious ceremony in the Kremlin, scolding the tsar for "shedding innocent blood." Infuriated by this criticism, Ivan violently flung his staff to the floor, ordered Metropolitan Filipp incarcerated, and in October 1568 had him deposed as metropolitan. A year later, one of Ivan's *oprichniki* strangled the former metropolitan.[40]

In refusing to listen and in taking such action, Ivan knew that he had crossed a line that he should not have violated. He was never able to obliterate the incident from his memory, nor would future tsars soon forget Ivan's transgression. Later, in the seventeenth century, Metropolitan Filipp was canonized; in 1652, Tsar Aleksei Mikhailovich dispatched a delegation to the Solovetskii Monastery to bring back Filipp's relics to Moscow. The prayer that Tsar Aleksei sent with the delegation to the long-deceased metropolitan bears citing, because it suggests the boundaries of the tsar's moral authority: "I beg and hope that you will forgive the sin committed against you by my great grandfather, tsar and grand prince Ioann. For it was inflicted irrationally and was a result of his inability to restrain his fury and envy. . . . I bow before your holy relics and subject all my power to you, in the hope that you will forgive us because you were offended in vain. . . . O holy father, holy bishop Filipp, our shepherd! We pray that you will heed our sinful prayer and will come to us in peace."[41] Such responsibility of the tsar and the church's right to criticize bear witness to the constraints on the tsar's political power. These constraints are essential to the development of civil society, for preparing the foundation in which social capital and reciprocity are nourished and for establishing a framework in which rights and responsibilities might evolve.

The *symphonia* between church and state was further strengthened in 1589, when, after the fall of Constantinople, Moscow gained its own patriarch. The Moscow patriarch was established to provide leadership and to articulate Christianity in an expanding Russian state. During the Time of Troubles (1598–1613), when Russia suffered a dynastic and social crisis and foreigners overran the country, the church responded and helped organize a national resistance. The church came to the aid of the state, supported the organization of a new government, and gave charitable assistance to those in need. In playing such a role, the political influence of the church dramatically increased. Under the first Romanov tsar, Mikhail Romanov (1613–45), Patriarch Filaret (1619–33) served not only as the head of the Orthodox Church but also as co-tsar, making policy and signing state documents along with the tsar. The father of the tsar, Filaret had the title of Great Sovereign and actually exercised a great deal of political authority during the fourteen years of his service. His work helped to restore the power and prestige of the tsar, which the Time of Troubles had greatly reduced.[42]

A significant turning point in the church's authority took place during the church schism in the middle of the seventeenth century (1666–67). The schism led to the subordination of the Russian Church to the state and the weakening of religious unity, processes that occurred gradually as the state tried to bring under control and to regulate all independent agencies. But it was Tsar Peter the Great, early in the eighteenth century, who sounded the death knell for the patriarch's privileged position and the church's independent status. In 1700, when Patriarch Adrian died, Peter did not call for elections for his successor. His frequent parodies of church officials and rituals, his travels abroad, his consorts with foreign church leaders, and his construction of the new and un-Russian "unholy city" of St. Petersburg seemed to many people acts of blasphemy. It was not that Peter disliked the Orthodox Church. He attended and participated frequently in its services; he loved the Orthodox liturgy; he often sang in the choir. He did not accept, however, the church's political position, its traditional view of its role in the state, and its potential opposition. He rejected the idea of *symphonia* and abolished the diarchy between church and state.

The final blow to the traditional concept of *symphonia* occurred in 1721, with the issuance of Peter's ecclesiastical regulation. The regulation, written by Feofan Prokopovich, Bishop of Pskov, was the culmination of a series of measures that covered Peter's entire reign and represented a key part of his attempt to create an absolutist state.[43] It placed the relationship between secular and spiritual power in Russia on a new basis; the church lost its independence. The ecclesiastical regulation abrogated the distinction made at the 1666 church council that "the tsar had preeminence in secular matters, the patriarch in ecclesiastical [matters]."[44] The state now assumed authority over many fields that the church had traditionally seen as primarily in its jurisdiction, including education, social morality, and family law. The regulation did not abolish the patriarchy but rather established in its place the Holy Synod, a branch of the civil government whose head, or "overprocurator," the tsar appointed. The underlying reasons for this change the ecclesiastical regulation spelled out clearly: "The fatherland need have no fear of revolts and disturbances from a conciliar administration such as proceed from a single, independent ecclesiastical administrator. For the common people do not understand how the spiritual authority is distinguishable from the autocratic, but marveling at the dignity and glory of the Highest Pastor, they imagine that such an administrator is a second Sovereign, a power equal to that of the Autocrat, or even greater than he, and that the pastoral office is another, and a better, sovereign authority."[45] The ecclesiastical regulation left little doubt who would be the sole authority in all matters concerning the state's interests. In the eyes of some people, Peter now became both the secular power and the "surrogate Patriarch."[46]

The ecclesiastical regulation established the political framework for the secular and spiritual powers that would last for nearly two hundred years in Russia, from 1721 until the 1917 Revolution. In this framework, the balance between the ecclesiastical domain and the political domain shifted dramatically. While it is an exaggeration and oversimplification to say that the church came under the domination of the state, the lines between these two authorities were significantly altered. The church's ability to influence national policy was greatly reduced, continuing a trend that had begun half a century earlier. Peter created the chief procurator, the Holy Synod's highest office, in 1722, to parallel the Governing Senate's chief procurator.[47] All high-ranking church officials—metropolitans, archbishops, and bishops—reported to the Holy Synod; they were required by law to obey its orders and instructions, "subject

to great punishment for resistance and disobedience, as with the other Col-
leges."[48] The overprocurator confirmed their appointments and had ultimate
responsibility for ecclesiastical assignments.

In giving birth to Imperial Russia, Peter the Great forced much more than
reform of its political structures. He imparted what the Russian historian
Evgenii Viktorovich Anisimov has called the cult of militarism and violence.
His achievement of progress through coercion would have a lasting impact on
the country's social consciousness.[49] This "Petersburg dreamer," this proponent of radical change through coercion, in Anisimov's words, made the state
the "main motor of progress" and the police the "soul of citizenry." In Peter's
system, a veritable cult of the laws was implanted, not laws in the sense of protecting the individual but laws designed to instruct and to supervise, to "beget
good order," and to subordinate all cultural values to the state principle.[50]
Peter implemented a social order that gave little scope to individual initiative,
and his "doctrine of progress though violence," would leave a legacy that
would strongly mark Russia's political and cultural evolution during the next
two centuries.

Peter's reform of the church administration comprised a central part of
his political agenda. His creation of the synod and his reorganization of the
church's internal structure integrated the church into the state system, and, in
Anisimov's words, made the church "the champion of a secular, or more precisely, autocratic ideology."[51] Beginning with Peter, the church pulpit became
the forum from which state decrees were read to parishioners, political criminals were castigated, and actions unsatisfactory to the state were publicly
criticized. The church hierarchy lost its position as a supreme moral authority; it became an apologist for the government's policies. Instead of a voice for
the downtrodden and oppressed, it often served as a defender of state coercion.[52]

Western historians have underscored the church's subservience to the
state and its docility as an instrument of state authority in the years following
Peter I's death in 1725. During the Cold War especially, Western writers generally described the church during Imperial Russia as obscurantist, inward
looking, cut off from the intellectual and social currents swirling outside, in-
capable of speaking to the educated elite, a relic of the medieval past, hostile
to all attempts at revitalization, and disinterested in its own theology.[53] The
church's insularity and rigid conservatism, it is said, repelled even its most creative religious minds.[54] Hindered by these weaknesses, the church was inca-
pable of nourishing civil society. It stifled independent social thought; church
schools made little contribution to public and higher education; the moral

underpinnings of society, for which the church had provided the foundation, eroded. The role of the overprocurator, the head of the Holy Synod, both symbolized and bore witness to the church's social isolation and indifference. Over time, the overprocurator's position became increasingly elevated in status and separated from the daily activities of the people serving under him. In 1835, the overprocurator was given status in the cabinet. In 1842, he was no longer required to hold regular meetings of the Holy Synod.[55] Not only did the authority of the church leadership steadily weaken during the eighteenth and nineteenth centuries, but the opportunity for dialogue over important religious and moral issues also declined.

Such views are prevalent both in the historical literature and in other writings on Russia, and they are partially accurate. This partial picture is displayed in the actions of Russia's last two overprocurators of the Holy Synod, D. A. Tolstoi (1865–80) and K. P. Pobedonostsev (1880–1905). When society greatly needed dialogue, they essentially turned their backs on it. Tolstoi had little personal commitment to religion, although he served as both synod over-procurator and minister of education; he later belonged to the Council of Ministers, a position the overprocurator normally did not hold and one that gave him extraordinary power over religious affairs. As a bulwark against what he perceived to be the growth of radical ideas and agendas in Russia's secular schools, he tried to enhance the conservative elements in the educational system, enlarging the study of theology, classical languages, and mathematics, subjects that he thought disciplined the minds of students.[56] Under such conditions, clergy in the seminaries and academies were isolated from the rest of society; the common cultural elements they might have shared were undermined by the overprocurator's policies.

K. P. Pobedonostsev presented, in many ways, a strong contrast to his predecessor. Unlike Tolstoi, Pobedonostsev was a devout believer and faithful churchgoer. He distrusted theologians, claiming that theology created too much sophistication and engendered doubt, in opposition to the simple faith that people most needed. He was, foremost, a man of politics, who viewed the church primarily as an instrument of the state and religion as an "agent of political stability and state security."[57] In his view, "all good Russian citizens should be Orthodox Christians," but in practice he placed much "more emphasis upon citizen," public order, and state security "than upon Orthodoxy."[58] Faith in such abstract ideas as democracy, parliamentarianism, universal suffrage, the sovereignty of the people—the concept of Liberal Democracy—constituted, to Pobedonostsev, the "great falsehood" of his times, which would lead inevitably to social anarchy and violence.[59] In such stifling conditions, the official church seemed like an anachronism; it could not have contributed to the development of civil society.

This generalized portrait of Orthodoxy's passivity and obedience to the state needs reexamination. The picture of a bureaucratic, archconservative, inward-looking, and marginalized Orthodox Church from Peter I's era to the early twentieth century tells only part of the story, represents only a piece of a rich tapestry that has other layers, many of which are yet to be uncovered. Most of what has passed in the literature about Orthodoxy's social role is based on preconceived notions, rather than on historical research. In the eighteenth century, the architect of Peter I's ecclesiastical regulation did not draw his ideas supporting autocracy from Orthodox tradition but from Western European sources.[60] In the early nineteenth century, Russian Orthodoxy played active roles in public and higher education, as well as in ecclesiastical schools; in both law and medicine, church schools made significant contributions.[61] Apart from its institutional structures, the "Russian Orthodox Church, especially in the imperial period," in the words of a twentieth-century scholar, "has been a woefully neglected field of scholarly research"; in studying Russia's political crises in the late nineteenth century, scholars have generally ignored the "strictly religious element—a cultural filter that not merely reflected but also configured social and political relations."[62]

Much of the life of Orthodoxy lay beyond the official boundaries of church-state relations—in the lives of individual parishes, in the service of bishops and priests, and in the long-neglected stories of men and women who devoted themselves to helping people in need. "To be sure, the church was under state control," noted Donald W. Treadgold. "However, it is obviously untrue to say that all or most of the clergy identified themselves with the state or the government, either before or after 1905–1906, when some possibility of legal political life and activity was created."[63] Beyond the boundaries of the state's bureaucratic structure, a different and multifaceted religious life also developed. There, social and religious traditions were nourished that led to trust, reciprocity, mutual responsibility, and care for others that fostered civil society and where freedom and responsibility existed apart from state controls.

Nineteenth-century Russia produced many outstanding individuals who exemplified such qualities. They included Filaret Drozhdov (served 1821–67), metropolitan of Moscow, a church historian, theologian, and, earlier, a leading reformer of ecclesiastical schools, whose work led to the creation of "student circles," where serious discussion of philosophy and theology began to take place; Evgenii Bolkhovitinov (1767–1837), metropolitan of Kiev, author of many church works, whose work with ecclesiastical schools also made them lively centers of learning and discussion; Margarita Tuchkova (1781–1852), founder of the Borodino community for women, widely recognized for its charitable activities; Fr Amvrosii (1812–91) of the Optina Pustyn' hermitage, who attracted intellectuals and writers, as well as people from all social ranks to the famous hermitage near Kozel'sk, in Kaluga province; Abbess Taisiia (1840–1915), educator and head of the Leushino monastic community for women in Novgorod diocese; and Fr John of Kronstadt (1829–1908), renowned for his service among the poor and the working classes of Kronstadt and St. Petersburg.[64]

The image of the church as servile, passive, insular, and lacking in individual action and initiative is further challenged by the research of D. S. Likhachev. His closely researched studies of early Russian literature, history, and folklore argue that the image of the Orthodox Church as docile, historically marginalized, and otherworldly would not hold true for much of Russian history, especially for the earlier periods, on which Likhachev's work is mainly focused. He is sharply critical of the view that Russian history essentially began with the reign of Peter the Great and that the long period preceding his reign served as a drab, featureless, backward-looking prelude. Likhachev's work disputes this view of the past. His writings on early Russian history; his scholarly studies of ancient Russian literature, painting, and architecture; and his research into the daily life and culture of that period emphasize its rich diversity and cultural depth. Most significant, he has elaborated the fundamental social ideals of early Russia; such ideals did not look inward, seeking to isolate Russians from the rest of the world and from each other, but gazed outward, trying to incorporate other experiences and connect with other people.[65] These broad vistas and expansive ideals, Likhachev argued, were later channeled into Russian literature, painting, and music, most especially into the creative works of Russia's greatest poet, Aleksander Pushkin. Likhachev emphasized two elements of Orthodoxy that have had a significant impact on Russia's national consciousness: the role of the church as a civilizing agent whose influence on social values and the daily life of the people was far greater, richer, and more permanent than historians have often acknowledged, and the effect of Orthodoxy's teachings extended much beyond the church's institutional boundaries.[66]

First, the ideals, self-sacrifice, and commitment to hard, diligent, and selfless labor were best modeled in the life of Russia's greatest saint, Sergei Radonezhskii, whose significance Kliuchevskii had elaborated earlier. Likhachev, however, focused on St Sergius's personal qualities, including his ethical choices and commitments. Like St Francis of Assisi, St Sergius went into the wilderness, embraced a life of poverty, lived close to nature, and befriended the animals of the forest. Both saints left legacies of asceticism and humility. But, in contrast to St Francis, who accepted gifts from admirers that sustained him on his journeys, St Sergius prohibited his followers from receiving presents; he commanded them to do hard labor and to receive their food and other provisions only by the work of their own hands. His monks carried water into the monastery, built huts, and tended gardens, and their self-sacrificing labor earned them the respect of the peasant population of all Russia.

In the monastery of St Sergius, work by its very nature was considered a form of prayer, a connection to the divine, and to Likhachev this ideal was brilliantly displayed in the life of St Sergius himself. His spirit of self-sacrifice, his kindness and devotion to serving others, his humility, and his acts of charity were elements he bequeathed to the future, aspects of his life that continued to instruct and inspire. Likhachev has pointed out that the love of honest labor and independent social activism of many different kinds are found repeatedly in the ideals of ancient Russia.[67] They were not missing in Russian history but they had rarely been emphasized. They needed to be uncovered and taught in the schools, because, Likhachev said, they "have a great deal to say to us" in the present.[68]

The second element that might provide a different perspective on Russia's past concerns the meaning of "church." In Russian Orthodoxy "church" signifies the entire "body of believers" and is not limited to the church's formal institutional structure. When employed as functionaries of the state, the clergy served poorly as spiritual leaders; uneducated, living in poverty, surviving by working in other occupations, they could hardly be distinguished from people in the lowest ranks of society.[69] In such a setting, spiritual inspiration did not typically evolve inside the state structure but rather developed outside it. This alternative religious culture relied on Orthodox Christianity for its main sources of inspiration, but it was not constrained by the church's physical buildings or its official representatives.

Religious feeling and practice persisted, even when there was neither church in which to worship nor clergy to perform the service. This continuity of faith outside the official boundaries of the church is a major reason Christianity survived nearly a century of relentless persecution by the Soviet government.[70] The "claims of conscience" and "living in the spirit of Christ" did not require official sanctions to be vital parts of daily life. Such beliefs and practices—self-sacrifice, compassion for others, and the search for truth— are brilliantly depicted in Russian literature. They are seen in the pilgrimages to distant monasteries in search of renewal; they are illustrated in the lives of certain "holy men," the *startsi,* portrayed by Dostoevsky's Father Zosima and Tolstoy's Father Sergius; and they are manifested repeatedly in the lives of people who showed compassion for the poor and the dispossessed.

To this alternative religious culture belongs another group of important figures: the "holy fools." They were revered by the common people of Russia for the antidote they provided to the sterile, highly structured rigors of official life. Wandering the Russian countryside, turning their backs on achievement of social position, disdaining the pursuit of material wealth, and eschewing formal social institutions, holy fools operated outside the framework that the state tried to impose. Yet kings and commoners alike believed they possessed unusual wisdom and listened to their advice. Likhachev attributed to them a great deal of significance in Russian culture: "one meets nothing like them in the West or the Near East and only in Russia did they receive such widespread respect." In Mussorgsky's opera *Boris Godunov,* the scene with the holy fool is one of the most powerful and beloved in the entire presentation.[71] "Claims of conscience," independent action, unwillingness to fit within the state-imposed system offered a different level of reality. As Likhachev pointed out, it is in this sphere that some of the most creative thinking and activity took place.

Operating outside government control and censorship, there was freedom to pursue one's own goals, to formulate new ideals, to seek different sources of inspiration, and to form groups and associations. In evaluating the Orthodox Church and its contributions to society, in exploring the church's struggle in the last decade to renew itself and redefine its social mission, such unofficial actions and ideals must also be considered. They provide materials that are extremely relevant to Russia's attempts to redefine itself and to reconstitute its national memory and identity. They also offer resources from which a civil society might be built, given that religion is a key component in the development of civil society, contributing core elements in the building of trust, civility, and social capital. The ideals emphasized by Likhachev for earlier periods of Russian history are precursors to ideals that will appear at later times. These ideals, in various forms, are exemplified in the lives of individuals portrayed in this book.

A few words are in order about procedural matters. While each of the following chapters includes historical background to the topics examined therein, the time sequences often cut across the Soviet and post-Soviet periods and, where essential, move back before 1917 to the tsarist era.[72] Beginning with Fr Aleksandr Men, whose life and murder suggest the tensions between the forces of change and tradition within the church, the first chapter surveys the changing relationship between the Orthodox Church and the state from the beginning of the Gorbachev period in 1985 until the end in 1991. The second chapter examines the church's struggle for renewal, its efforts to recover its voice and redefine its relationship to the state and society, from the abortive political coup in 1991 to the present, the period marked by the presidencies of Boris Yeltsin and Vladimir Putin. The church's attempts to reassert itself and the dilemmas it faced in that effort lie at the center of the chapter's attention. Both the first and second chapters establish the larger general context for what follows.

The succeeding chapters break the subject of rediscovery down to a more personal level. They change the point of view from the Moscow patriarchy to the perspective of the parish. They take a close look at leading individuals, all of whom have placed the struggle to redefine themselves and to rebuild Russia at the center of their lives. In reading about them, readers will get a glimpse of everyday realities, of a contemporary story still evolving, and of people whose lives are spent not at the top of the power structure, but in the parishes and on the streets. Hopefully, my readers will see in these people, as I have, the difficulties and the heroic qualities of their lives, their fight for survival, and their visions of the future. Their stories may well define the emerging history of Russia in the twenty-first century.

1 Religion and Politics at the End of the Soviet Era

In the early afternoon of September 10, 1990, a TASS news release informed the Russian public of a shocking event: "Archpriest Aleksandr Men has been murdered. His body was found not far from the house where he lived, near the railroad platform of Semkhoz of the Zagorskii district in the Moscow region. Doctors certified the death from the loss of blood inflicted by a severe blow to the head."[1]

The news bulletin cited only the bare details of Fr Aleksandr's significance. Age fifty-five, he had served as a leading dissident during the Brezhnev period of religious stagnation. But his chief importance had come in the middle and late 1980s, during the time of perestroika. Fr Aleksandr became the spiritual leader of reformers within the Orthodox Church. To these reformers, he served as the equivalent of an Andrei Sakharov in politics—challenging the old order and stressing the need for greater openness.[2] His books enjoyed a wide circulation, both among intellectuals and ordinary people; he appeared often on television; he gave many lectures on religious topics in Moscow, impressing a range of people with his words and his ideas. Boris Raushenbakh, the distinguished physicist, described Men's ability to connect the past with the present and to relate religion to a variety of topics. He recalled "a meeting held in the late 1980s in the Institute of Physics and Technology of the Russian Academy of Sciences. The Institute invited a senior official of the Church to a discussion about religious issues, including the role of the Orthodox Church in Russian society. I remember this meeting vividly, because my colleagues did not take the meeting seriously. Behind the scenes, they laughed at the senior priest; his style and language were completely inadequate for the audience. But I also remember a meeting in the Academy with Fr Aleksandr and the completely opposite effect he produced on my colleagues. Even now, they recall the depth of his words and ideas; he made an excellent impression."[3]

Fr Aleksandr also made many enemies: church officials who resented his growing popularity and his vision of the church; nationalist groups who disliked his Jewish roots; and members of the KGB who were offended that the agency's harassment of Fr Alexander, throughout his career, had yielded little results. As Fr Aleksandr's popularity increased, so too did the threats against his life and the lives of his wife and children.

On an early Sunday morning, September 9, 1990, Fr Aleksandr took his usual half-mile walk from his home in the village of Semkhoz near Sergiev Posad to the station to catch the train to his parish church. As he walked alone along the path through the woods, through the dense fog of that September morning, two men apparently approached him from behind. They probably showed him something to read, because his glasses would be found later lying by the path. As he bent his head to examine the paper, one of the men struck him on the back of his head with an ax, Russia's old instrument of execution. Critically injured but refusing to be stopped, Fr Aleksandr walked on to the railway station. There, with blood streaming from his wound, he understood the seriousness of his injury. He turned around, stumbled back along the path to his home, and reached the courtyard, before collapsing against the front gate. Several minutes later, the man who had symbolized renewal within the Russian Church was dead.

To this day, the police have not apprehended the murderer of Fr Aleksandr Men. Whether his death resulted from a random act of violence or a plot carried out by a group that disliked his work remains a subject of wide speculation. Convinced of the latter explanation, a young journalist wrote the following words underlining the main issues at stake: "Humanization and democratization are one side of our system. The other is murder. We have been freeing ourselves from fear, but the axe is an instrument to remind us of our fear. They are reminding us that we are defenseless."[4]

Fr Aleksandr's life, his teachings, and his death have an additional significance. In the years immediately following his murder in the Semkhoz woods, the political and religious situation in Russia would change dramatically. To Fr Aleksandr, the key elements that would greatly shape the future concerned whether the church would become more open, compassionate, and independent—all of which, he believed, required the separation of church and state. Although Men died in 1990, his writings would become even more popular after his death, particularly among those who wanted fundamental change. He would also inspire great enmity and suspicion among people who disliked his theological message and resented the challenges to church and state authority that he had represented. The Orthodox Church, as he had once emphasized, had to regain its own spiritual voice and project its unique vision to a people starving for fresh approaches to life. The questions he posed about the church's relationship to society and to the government would continue to attract much

attention and provoke heated discussion and controversy, both within and outside the Orthodox Church. These are the issues that, during a crucial period of
Russian history, from 1985 to 2005, are central elements of this book.

Fr Aleksandr's significance within the total framework of this study is
large. As the foremost Orthodox prophet of his times, he sought to reform the
church in order to make it more appealing to a population in search of deeper
answers to life and death than historical materialism, the Soviet vision of the
world, had provided. He well understood that the church had limited time in
which it might speak effectively to this population before other voices, less
compelling but more immediate, entered the fray. Most important, he saw a
population released from political subjugation, open to experiences different
from those offered by the Soviet past, dissatisfied with the shallow materialism of the long Brezhnev period and it successors, and able to examine history
and the primary sources of the church's rich heritage through fresh eyes. As
one of Men's leading disciples, Fr Aleksandr Borisov emphasized in 1988 the
liberation of the church from the tight control of the government gave it a rare
historical opportunity. The church had to seize this chance immediately; it
had to develop a new vocabulary and create fresh approaches to a population
craving spiritual direction. "Our society," Borisov said, "awaits today from the
Orthodox Church the Living Word of truth. . . . If it does not offer this Word,
then its spiritual poverty will be observed very quickly and it will be pushed
into the background."[5] Such longing and such openness would not be long
lasting. Men's dedication to his task, his frenzied efforts to use every available
moment, bore witness to his belief that this window of opportunity would be
short-lived. "It isn't easy to understand someone who for years has been tied
up on a leash," he wrote. "I am not complaining for myself, because God has
given me the possibility of doing something, even on the end of this leash."
He understood the dangers he confronted and the opposition his teachings
had engendered: "At the present time the wind is obviously stronger. . . . I
have to stand solidly on my own two feet, legs spread, in order not to be overturned. . . . I'm only an instrument that God is using for the moment."[6] After
Men's death, the wind would gather momentum.

FRIENDS AND FOES OF CHANGE

Before examining more closely the opening of the floodgates and the ensuing
turbulence, it may be helpful to take a brief look at several of the major assumptions and themes that characterized the tenuous status of religion and the

church-state relationship earlier in the Soviet Union. The Bolsheviks came to power in November 1917 aiming to develop a new social consciousness. Committed to Marxist ideology, they understood the world fundamentally in scientific and materialist terms, and envisioned a future built on these premises. Atheism served as a central component in their approach to human existence. To them, religion represented a key part of Russia's backwardness, the Orthodox Church a pillar of the Tsarist regime, and religion a system of belief that had to be eradicated in order to create the political and social order they envisioned.[7]

In 1917 the Bolsheviks found themselves in a hostile social environment. It was an environment greatly influenced by religious observances and practices: Orthodoxy shaped daily rituals, the main rites of passage, and the organization of the family household. The Bolsheviks' goal of creating a new social order required an intense struggle against these religious observances and the institutions that nourished them. Attempting to abrogate the church's authority and its social position, the Bolsheviks, as part of a general land decree, nationalized church property, and on November 2, 1917, issued the Declaration of the Rights of the Peoples of Russia, which formally abolished "all religious privileges in the country."[8] On December 11, the new government transferred all educational institutions under church control to state control. A week later, on December 18, the Bolshevik government decreed that the state would "recognize only civil marriages" and transferred the registration books on births, marriages, and deaths from religious institutions to state authorities. On January 20, 1918, the Bolsheviks issued the Decree on Freedom of Conscience, Church, and Religious Organizations, which fully separated church from state: the act reinforced what had previously been decreed; it attempted to further erode the church's economic and institutional bases; it removed religious symbols from public buildings, reaffirmed the separation of schools and church, prohibited religious groups from owning property, and abolished the legal rights of religious societies.[9]

In portraying Bolshevik policies and actions, historians have often described them as provoking war between the Bolsheviks and the church, in which the battle lines were sharply drawn. The conflict was a "two-sided confrontation" between state oppression and church resistance. According to this standard interpretation, the Bolsheviks created a "revolution from above," a violent assault on the foundations of Russian cultural life, including the church, and while the church attempted to defend itself, its opposition had little chance against this well-organized, vigorous, and single-minded opponent. In the revolutionary turmoil that gripped Russia, the church's resistance to Bolshevik coercion suffered tragic and fateful defeat.

Recent scholars have shown, however, that such a portrayal greatly over-simplifies the reality. While traditional accounts have accurately described some parts of the struggle, the "two-sided confrontation" overlooks elements that played a significant role in the conflict between the Bolsheviks and the church: the church's own internal disorder, the desire on the part of some leaders to seek accommodation with the new power, the widespread attempts to circumvent the laws, the many diverse understandings of Orthodoxy among the population, the intense internal conflict within local parishes, and what a leading Russian scholar has called the "parochialization of power"—the collapse of church administration and the transfer of power from the central church authority to local parish councils.[10] All these circumstances made for an extremely chaotic situation within the church, promoting rampant confusion over how to respond to the Bolshevik government.

In the early 1920s, Orthodoxy found it difficult either to resist or assimilate the demands of the new government, because the Orthodox laity viewed those who proposed to adapt to the new political system as heretics. In 1922, a group of church reformers who sought reconciliation between Orthodoxy and Bolshevism convinced Patriarch Tikhon (Belavin) to give them authority over church affairs and to abdicate his office. These reformers, or "renovationists," were convinced that the Orthodox Church was dying and the only hope lay in renovating it; they argued that the church either had to seek accommodation or face extinction. Most Orthodox believers refused such a compromise; they viewed it as heretical and those who advocated it as traitors to the faith. In 1922, the Bolshevik government placed former Patriarch Tikhon under house arrest and kept him there until June 1923. Upon his release, he announced his political loyalty to the Bolsheviks and reclaimed his patriarchal position. Later, he tried to back away from the public statement of loyalty to the state. But his successor to the patriarchal throne, Metropolitan Sergii Stragorodskii, on July 29, 1927, reiterated the church's loyalty to the Soviet power. Choosing political neutrality in exchange for the government's noninterference in church affairs, Metropolitan Sergii attempted to accommodate the Orthodox Church to the Soviet system. He accepted Bolshevik authority and the need to work within the law; he ordered adherence to the government's requirement for registering all parish and diocesan administrative bodies of the church. He placed himself in opposition to church reform. He abolished the liturgical and structural reforms passed by the church during the Revolution and in the early 1920s.[11]

The cultural revolution that followed, the Great Turn, from 1929 to 1932, brought severe repression to the Orthodox Church. It was part of a broadsided, devastating attack on religious belief, an attempt to remove the last traces of the tsarist regime and to transform Russia into a totally secular country. Led by the League of Militant Atheists, a state-sponsored organization, the assault came to include groups at many different levels—from Young Pioneers to workers' clubs—and would introduce a decade that witnessed the most violent persecution of religion in the Soviet period and one of the most violent in world history. Such persecution and violence would continue to characterize the relationship between church and state, although in subsequent decades government policy on religion did not follow a straight line.[12]

In a now-classic essay on Soviet politics in the mid-1980s, the U.S. political scientist Stephen Cohen wrote about what he called the "forces of reformism and conservatism."[13] These elements, Cohen argued, represented "'two poles' in Soviet political life," two fundamentally different approaches to culture, politics, and society. Cohen defined reformers as proponents of measured change who, while not wishing to overthrow the existing system, believed that it could be improved significantly, that it had not realized its potential, and that "change was progress." Conservatism, in contrast, did not resist all change but had a deep-seated fear that innovation could unleash disorder and create a future that would be worse than the present. Conservatism revered the past and defended the institutions, practices, and ideas that had evolved from it. "In times of profound crisis," Cohen maintained, "reformism and conservatism everywhere usually give rise to extremist trends and may even grow into their most extreme manifestations—revolution and counterrevolution. But apart from those extraordinarily historical moments, reformers and conservatives represent the great majority of mainstream political antagonists—the friends and foes of change—in the Soviet Union and elsewhere."[14] Conservatives sought to strengthen institutions and practices deeply rooted in the past; reformers were open to new ways of thinking about the past, about traditions, and about their applications to present circumstances.

While Cohen's essay dealt with Soviet politics, his categories of "reformism" and "conservatism" could also be applied to the Orthodox Church and its formal structures. To the conservatives, the original rituals and liturgy, preserved over time, were little open to change and experimentation. In the new conditions of freedom in the late 1980s and early 1990s, the original forms had to be reestablished, even in the Old Slavonic language, because they were the bearers of the Gospel and church tradition. To the conservatives, the hierarchy of the church, the caretakers of these forms, had to be respected, strengthened, and obeyed. Historically, the conservatives saw the church and state as partners, defenders of Russia's national heritage, and proponents of national interests, elements that, to them, went hand in hand.[15]

To the reformers, in contrast, the church's future strength, indeed its very survival, greatly depended on its ability to open up to fresh ideas. Moreover, they voiced respect for other religious traditions, and desired to see them flourish as well as Orthodoxy. The church should not fear what Men called "open spaces," nor should it seek to cut itself off from other traditions and ways of thinking. The open model of Christianity was "acceptable to those who are sure of their own grounds. Those who stand on shaky ground prefer a closed model because it is easier for them."[16] Reformers welcomed the dialogue with other religious traditions, believing that it could only sharpen and strengthen Orthodoxy's core convictions and its ability to articulate them clearly.

The leaders of reform within the church struggled to achieve a new concept of Orthodoxy, one squarely based on church tradition, especially on certain major themes within it that had stood up to power, challenged authoritarianism, and acted out of compassion and grace. In this tradition of the church, there were many independent voices and moral activists who had castigated violence and other abuses of power—Metropolitan Filipp, Vladimir Solov'ev, Pavel Florinskii, Mikhail Tareev, Nikolai Berdiaev, to name several examples. Their compassion, respect for the person, and openness to the world were grounded in and emerged from their religious beliefs.[17] Such beliefs had to be recovered and embraced; they provided some of the key principles for the reconstruction of Russian society.

The reformers wanted to revive Orthodoxy by transforming it, by making it more accessible and relevant to ordinary Russians. In some ways, their proposals parallel changes in the Roman Catholic Church arising earlier from Vatican II.[18] The emphasis on reform within the church, the desire to relate Orthodoxy's message to social needs, and the belief that the church had to be more open to the world correspond to similar claims for reform in the Catholic Church. As in Catholicism, such arguments could not fail to bring reformers into sharp conflict with the will of the church hierarchy, which saw the proposed reforms as anathema.

In assessing the impact of the struggle between the "reformers" and "conservatives" on civil society, one's sympathies lie with the "reformers." For the development of civil society, the break between "faith and power" was essential. Such a tight connection had hindered the encouragement of independent voices. Civil society, as Ernest Gellner has claimed, required breaking "the circle between faith, power, and society," separating religion from politics.[19] Equally important, severing this connection would encourage Russians to look above and within, to their own traditions for new sources of moral and political guidance. Maintaining the connection forced Russians to look not within but without, focusing on their enemies. The first approach, to borrow from Billington, fostered pluralism and hope; the latter, unity and fear.[20] Reformers advocated the decentralization of authority and a grassroots approach to religious life, which they believed lay squarely within Orthodox tradition and teachings and underscored the importance of the parish. By becoming less docile, more critical, and more assertive, the parish would be the stimulus for engaging in dialogue with the central authority, for rebuilding the local community, and for overcoming social inertia, all of which would nourish the growth of social capital.

The reformists would attract a large following in the late 1980s and early 1990s, and the influence of their ideas has continued to grow, both within and outside the Orthodox Church. To some church leaders, like Fr Andrei Il'ia Osipov, head of graduate studies at the Spiritual Academy at Sergiev Posad, their impact was minimal. "I consider Fr Aleksandr and his followers to exist only on the fringes of the Church and only among people who are discontented, who are always searching for new ways and new approaches, rather than [being] content with what is already proving its success," said Fr Andrei.[21] But Men had a legion of followers, and everywhere he spoke he attracted large crowds of people. His writings and lectures were published and reissued in large numbers of copies, a heavy demand that multiplied after his death.[22] While the influence of such religious activity is difficult to measure precisely, the large readership is evidence of his ability to reach widely diverse groups of people. The desire for reform can be found in Orthodox seminaries and academies among many young priests, whose theological and social views will eventually be heard.[23]

Moreover, among the church's top leaders are individuals who do not fall neatly and consistently into either category of "reformer" or "conservative," but rather, depending on the particular issue, exemplify one category or the other. Metropolitan Kirill (Gundiaev) of Smolensk and Kaliningrad is such a person. Like the conservatives, he took a strong stand against the incursion of Western missionaries. But he would advocate for the creation of a new social doctrine for the church, and later he would play a leadership role in the composition of such a document. Reformist ideas, reaching from Men to the philosophical-religious writers at the beginning of the twentieth century would inspire much of the discussion underlying the new doctrine.[24]

The reformers' struggles symbolize the turbulent, difficult, and contested experience of religious revival in the new Russia. Since the beginning of the Gorbachev period, the Russian Orthodox Church had many opportunities to move in the direction they advocated. Whether the church would do so, whether it would respond to the challenges that they defined, remained a large and troubling question. Men spoke from the core of a rapidly changing social context, in which a world was being turned upside down; the assumptions— political, religious, and social—that had dominated that past were severely challenged. "When Gorbachev opened the floodgates, reaction as well as democracy poured in. But reaction is always more aggressive," Men stated in his final interview before his murder. The last years of his life and his violent death, coinciding with the period of perestroika in the former Soviet Union, bear witness to the opportunities and hopes, as well as to the dangers and fears, that the changing social context unleashed.[25]

BEGINNING OF THE BATTLE

Mikhail Gorbachev's accession to power in 1985 and his program of perestroika had as one of its central features the creation of an active society. While his methods and style differed greatly from his famous eighteenth-century predecessor, Peter the Great, his aims had some similarities; like Peter, Gorbachev aspired to transform society, to awaken it from its lethargy and inward-looking vision, to make society more dynamic and less provincial. Like Peter, the church would occupy a large part of his program. But while Peter wanted to diminish the church's social influence and bind it to state authority, Gorbachev sought the opposite: he hoped to reinvigorate the church and loosen the political strictures that had crippled it. While this goal did not affect it at first, events that soon transpired involved the church dramatically. Gorbachev's reforms promoted the church's resurrection and, in part, instigated a spiritual awakening and a questioning that would cut across every facet of life in the Soviet Union.

The transformation that began with Mikhail Gorbachev would thus concern much more than politics and economics. It invoked the quest for a new reality, for new perceptions of life, for a different understanding of the world. Serge Schmemann, the *New York Times* lead correspondent in Moscow, emphasized the fundamental religious and cultural nature of this quest: "any attempt to understand what is happening in Russia today only through economics and politics, overlooking the yearning for new spiritual content . . .

would be incomplete."[26] Both the government's actions and the "yearning for new spiritual content" would give the Orthodox Church an opportunity it had rarely enjoyed in the twentieth century: the chance to redefine itself and its relationship with the government.

Changes in the relationship between the Orthodox Church and the Soviet government during the stormy Gorbachev period went through two distinct stages, the first from 1985 to 1987, the second from 1988 to 1991. Within these two periods emerged important movements that attempted to redefine the role of religion, that challenged in different ways the Soviet past, and that eventually would clash with each other. This confrontation provided a significant part of the political context for Fr Aleksandr's murder and for the revolutionary changes that soon followed. It also involved Russia's search for national identity, a conflict between different visions of the future. In this conflict, rival political groups attempted to use the church for their own purposes, seeing it as fulfilling differing roles and functions. In the collapse of Marxism-Leninism, some political groups viewed the church as offering a new ideology, a civil religion filling the moral vacuum that had opened up in Russian society. The struggle between these differing visions would sharply evolve and mark Russia's attempt to redefine itself.

Civil religion is a series of beliefs, practices, rituals, and ceremonies "which serve secular as opposed to transcendent or otherworldly ends."[27] It may overlap with a living, transcendent faith, especially when that faith is seen as a central part of a country's national heritage and identity.[28] Civil religion provides values that draw together the members of society, give them defining principles, and establish the moral touchstones of understanding and consensus. In Russia, various groups came to see Orthodoxy as the transmitter of certain cultural values deemed to be essentially Russian.

In the period from 1985 through 1987, following Mikhail Gorbachev's accession to leadership, the government's relationship to the church essentially remained the same as it had in the previous period; the government continued to exert tight controls over religious activities. But during these three years, reformers, taking advantage of the new political administration and its calls for more openness of expression, pressed strongly for changes in religious policies. Reformers, including key leaders of the intelligentsia, connected greater openness and democratic change in the Soviet Union to the rights of religious believers; the calls for civil liberties and freedom of speech, these leaders proclaimed, must include religious liberties and their protection under the laws. Such liberal publications as *Ogonek, Moskovskie novosti,* and *Literaturnaia gazeta,* leading heralds of Gorbachev's policy of *glasnost,* proclaimed repeatedly that these changes were essential to the transformation of Soviet-Marxism into the more open ideology that Gorbachev desired.[29] In December 1986, for example, the Soviet poet Evgenii Evtushenko published an article in *Literaturnaia gazeta* in which he called for the end to atheism as an official ideology. Critical of what he described as the shallow, crass nature of Soviet life, Evtushenko argued that the Communist Party had been wrong in its attack on the church; he praised religion as a source of both morality and creativity. He proposed to end the official censorship of religious publications and advocated that state publishing houses be encouraged to print religious books, including the Bible.[30]

In the meantime, the upper ranks of the Communist Party continued to speak about the virtues of an atheistic political and social order. In schools and universities, scientific materialism as the objective grounds of truth and morality held sway and gained even greater strength; in the mid-1980s, the teaching of scientific materialism actually intensified in Russian universities.[31] Moreover, the Central Committee of the Communist Party kept firmly in place the strictures against the church that former Bolshevik administrations had passed. The Moscow City Committee of the Communist Party played a major part in supporting such strictures. Boris Yeltsin chaired the Moscow City Committee, which did not tolerate religious belief. In 1987, on the eve of significant change in the Soviet Union, the Moscow committee that Yeltsin chaired rejected an appeal, made by members of a group who aspired to join the Party, on the grounds that they had taken part in religious ceremonies.[32]

During this period, what might be called the "conservative-patriotic" press said nothing about the rights of religious believers and displayed little interest in these questions.[33] To the traditionalists, the church held little importance. In past years, the leading publications of the conservative press— *Molodaia gvardiia, Moskva,* and *Nash sovremennik*—had supported the government in its hard-line approach to religion and the persecution of believers. Such publications had shown no sympathy to the church, the plight of believers, or religious rights. The introduction of *glasnost* did nothing to alter this stand or cause the conservative-patriotic press to reexamine its views of the church's role in the state, and it remained largely silent on religion.

In 1988, however, the situation changed dramatically. Such a shift not only led to the reawakening of the Orthodox Church but also instigated, both on the part of the government and the conservative-patriotic press, a fundamentally new direction.

Several key events precipitated the change. Mikhail Gorbachev never held militant, ideological views toward religion as did his predecessors, especially

Nikita Khrushchev, many of whose policies Gorbachev tried to rejuvenate. Raised by a mother who was probably a believer and married to a woman who expressed a warm interest in the Orthodox Church, Gorbachev was open to several possibilities that the church offered. He based his political program on the need to reawaken Russian society, improve its work ethic, and combat demoralizing social issues such as alcoholism, all of which required a change in its ethical and moral standards. He soon viewed the Orthodox Church as a potential ally in his campaign, because it was the repository of forgotten verities and because it offered the possibility of renewing certain ethical and moral standards that had been lost. As a promise of his intentions, in the last months of 1987, Gorbachev announced the return to the church of two famous monasteries, closed by the government in the 1920s: the Tolga Presentation of Mary Monastery near Iaroslavl' and the Optina Presentation men's hermitage near Kostroma, the latter serving as a primary source of inspiration for some of Russia's greatest cultural figures—Nikolai Gogol, Fedor Dostoevsky, Leo Tolstoy, and others.[34] Gorbachev did not act alone in promoting these important changes, but he certainly played a leading part in implementing them.

On April 29, 1988, Gorbachev invited Patriarch Pimen and five members of the Holy Synod to the Kremlin. Held in the Great Catherine Hall, this historic event marked the first meeting with the head of the Orthodox Church since the 1950s, when Patriarch Aleksi I had met with various Soviet leaders. The meeting with the patriarch and subsequent acts brought the church to the center stage of Gorbachev's political agenda. He rescinded one of the major goals of Marxism-Leninism—the obliteration of religious practices and beliefs. "Believers," Gorbachev told Pimen, "are Soviet people, workers, patriots, and they have the full right to express their convictions with dignity." In anticipation of the upcoming millennium of Russian Christianity, the Soviet leader emphasized that the church and the state had a common history and future.[35] Shortly afterward, in response to Pimen's request, the government returned to the church the Monastery of the Caves in Kiev, the site of the early Russian Church; gave permission to begin new training programs for priests and to open new seminaries; restored nine dioceses closed by Khrushchev in the early 1960s; revised the laws on regulating churches; authorized a large increase in the publication of Bibles and religious literature; and granted to the church permission to engage in charitable work—to aid the sick and infirm and open nursing homes for the old and disabled pensioners, acts of mercy that had been forbidden to the church since the early 1920s.[36]

An event more important in raising the religious consciousness of Russia took place that summer, in the celebration of the millennium of the adoption of Orthodox Christianity in Kievan Rus'. The celebration had been planned for more than five years but, because of the change in church-state relations, it soon became a much larger public spectacle than its original planners had intended or hoped. In the first two weeks of June 1988, in Moscow, Sergiev Posad, and Kiev, ceremonies drew religious leaders from all over the world. The Orthodox Church recognized nine new saints, the first to be canonized since the 1917 Revolution, including Andrei Rublev, Russia's greatest icon painter; Maxim the Greek, the venerated medieval theologian, translator, and philosopher who was especially revered by the Old Believers; and Dmitrii Donskoi, the Moscow prince and military leader who defeated the Mongol army in an epic battle at Kulikovo Field in 1380 and who occupied first place on the list of newly canonized saints.[37]

In addition to the deeply moving religious services performed throughout these weeks, the millennium celebrations held showings of artistic treasures from libraries, museums, and tiny archives from the villages of central Russia. Featured in the exhibits were also rare artifacts from Russia's religious and national heritage—Rostov enamels, icons, wood carvings, and ancient manuscripts. The exhibits and ceremonies drew huge crowds of both believers and nonbelievers, attracted to the spectacular events for many reasons— religious, aesthetic, patriotic—and to rituals and objects that lay buried in the national memory. The observance of the millennium served both as a religious and national ceremony. It marked the rehabilitation of the church as a social institution, and it underscored the large contribution the church had made to Russia's history, its representation of the common people.

Religious reformers had advocated a more open political system in which the church could operate more freely and had pressed for legislation guaranteeing freedom of conscience. Soon after the millennium events, however, reformers had to contend with another group that emerged in opposition. Until 1989, this group had paid little attention to church-state relations and had remained largely silent on the church's role in Russian history. In 1989, the conservative-patriotic forces began to rethink their position and shift their main focus to take advantage of a situation that was rapidly changing. Faced with a declining belief in Marxist-Leninist ideology, which national public opinion polls clearly showed, and with Russia's increasing openness to Western Europe and the United States, the conservative-patriots radically altered their views of religion. They saw an excellent opportunity in the Orthodox Church to strengthen both their own weakening political position and the legitimacy of authoritarian elements of the government. During the millennium celebrations, the bells in Russia's churches had once more begun to ring. The conservative-patriots heard in their peal not an ecumenical message, not the universal appeal of the church, but a nationalist theme, symbolizing Great Russia and an older conception of power. For these traditionalists, the unity of Tsar Bell and Tsar Cannon in the Moscow Kremlin would signify the unification of church and state.

By the middle of 1989, conservative-patriotic publications began to devote much attention to the subject of Orthodox religion. In general, the articles in the patriotic press played on a repeated theme, which it presented in extremely simple terms.[38] In his closely reasoned analysis of these articles, the Russian scholar S. B. Filatov noted that the conservatives saw the church as a major bulwark for protecting Russia against harmful "Western influences," namely democracy, pluralism, capitalism, liberalism, and ecumenism.[39] An article titled "Not by Bread Alone," written by one Fr Vladimir, is characteristic: "Russian people must not be assembled under such alien banners, which undermines for us eternal words: Orthodoxy, Motherland, national resurrection. We are obligated to build a Holy Russia, an eternal ideal of our historical life on whose wise and practical foundations the history of Russia has proceeded." And what was the essence of this identity? Fr Vladimir co-opted Dostoevsky's words in *Diary of a Writer* to make a political statement: "We are Russians to the degree that we are Orthodox. This is the central theme! It is the key to understanding our 'historical Golgotha,' our present crossroads and the future road of our people."[40]

As Soviet communism entered its decline, conservatives saw the church as an institution capable of filling the spiritual vacuum and identity. The emphasis on "Holy Russia," Russia as the preserver of a special culture, distinct from Western Europe, became the means of strengthening the spiritual fabric of the country. Conservative-patriotic writers often likened Russia's present crisis to the period of World War II, when Stalin, to strengthen the country's patriotic resolve, allied himself with the Orthodox Church.[41] Currently, it was assumed, Russia faced no less a crisis; to the conservatives, the renewal of the nation required resurrecting the image of Holy Russia, putting an end to the missionary expansion of non-Orthodox religions, and cutting Russia off from ideas and practices that would enslave it to the West.[42]

The conflict between conservatives and reformers was a battle between two very different views of government, society, and Russia's future. In that battle, differing political and social values were at war: nationalistic, authoritarian, extralegal personal values versus more cosmopolitan, less-authoritarian, legalistic perceptions of needs and goals.[43] The struggle directly related to the role of the church in society, and whether it would support the emergence of a civil society or an authoritarian one. Superficially, in their views of the outside world, the perceptions of conservatives and reformers bear certain vestiges of the classical Slavophile-Westernizer conflict, but, in fact, they relate more directly to the social crisis in the Soviet Union and the political struggle within the Party over reform and tradition. Whether Russia would evolve a civil society lay at the core of this conflict.

The Reformers and Orthodoxy

From 1988 to 1991, the reformers gained the ascendency. During this period the Russian government introduced social and political reforms, rethought earlier government policies, and opened Russia to Western contacts. Such processes would have a significant impact on the church. Several times Gorbachev spoke of the need to give the church a larger role in perestroika and the rebuilding of Russian society. To further emphasize his desire to reach out to the West and provide the church with a larger social role, he accepted an invitation to meet with Pope John Paul II in December 1989. On the eve of their historic meeting in the Vatican, Gorbachev said, "We have changed our attitude on some matters, such as religion, for example, which admittedly we used to treat in a simplistic manner." The Soviet leader emphasized the moral values that religion had fostered for centuries and that could now "help in the work of renewal in our country too." He noted that the Party had "abandoned the claim to have a monopoly on the truth. We no longer think that we are the best and that we are always right, that those who disagree with us are our enemies."[44]

The first half of 1990 also witnessed the emergence of a radical core group among Party reformers who aspired either to rethink socialist ideals or to reject such ideals altogether and embrace democratic ones. Inspired by the revolutions of 1989 in Eastern Europe, which showed that anticommunism had wide popular support and that political victories could be achieved not by taking a "half-way liberal socialist position, but by an uncompromising denial of socialism," the group searched for new ideals.[45] The radical group of reformers included Moscow mayor Gavril Popov, Galina Starovoitova, Boris Yeltsin, Oleg Rumiantsev, and Stephen Stankevich. They identified Russian society with Western civilization; they sought immediately to create a new society in Russia based on Western civic ideals, economic models, and religious values.[46]

A central part of their program involved emphasizing the Orthodox Church's legitimacy and its key role as a social institution. The increasing attraction of the population to the church, clearly shown in public opinion polls, induced their support. According to a national survey taken in June 1989, more people had confidence in the church than in any organization in Soviet society: 64 percent said they trusted most the Orthodox Church, 59 percent the armed forces, 18 percent the national-patriotic front *Pamiat'*, and 18 percent the Communist Party.[47] Given these results, it is not surprising that political leaders began increasingly to attend church services and to associate themselves with religious leaders.

Politically, therefore, an extremely curious situation had rapidly developed, and it amounted, on the surface at least, to a nearly complete reversal of seventy years of Soviet history. The Orthodox Church and religion in general, long victims of government policy, came to be seen as having a central role in the creation of a reformed political order. In large part, this impetus for change came from below: from the demand that Russian history be presented more truthfully, from political and religious dissidents who had for many years fought for the freedom of worship, and from a society hungry for approaches to life different from Soviet Marxism. By 1991, a sharp change had taken place. As the Russian sociologist D. E. Furman later wrote, it was a "transformation from official atheism practically to official orthodoxy, from the death to the resurrection of Jesus Christ, and from ceremonial party congresses to ceremonial public prayers."[48] The transformation would raise several major questions that Fr Aleksandr Men had earlier posed: how prepared was the Orthodox Church to respond to this dramatic reversal of its status in the Soviet Union? After decades of severe oppression and state control how deep in Soviet society was the momentum for these changes? In addition, how capable was the church of separating itself from the government and becoming a key institution in the development of civil society?

Renewal of the Orthodox Church?

In part, the answer to these questions greatly depended on the church's ability, its physical and mental capacity, to expand significantly its social activities and the scope of its mission. In January 1986, shortly after Gorbachev came into office, 6,742 Orthodox parishes were registered in the Soviet Union; in 1990 their number increased to 10,110. In 1985 the church had only about six thousand Orthodox priests and six functioning monasteries; in 1990 the number of priests in service grew to about seventy-two hundred and monasteries, by late 1990, to twenty-five.[49] By far the largest growth in these figures took place after the Gorbachev-Pimen meeting in April 1988, when the government encouraged the church to aid in the renewal of Soviet society and began the process of returning to the church buildings and other property that it had earlier confiscated.

In responding to these challenges, the Orthodox Church had two major problems, one among its leadership, another among its laity. Church leadership needed individuals who could provide sharp, critical assessment of the Stalinist past. But because of its affiliation with Soviet domination, recovering its own identity and restoring its spiritual mission presented enormous problems within the church. For nearly seventy years, the church had pledged its loyalty to the government, accommodating itself officially to Soviet power. Such an affiliation, as an Orthodox theologian has recently stated, resulted in the "gradual degradation . . . of the professional status of the church's ministers."[50] A government appendage, the church had neither developed its own reservoirs of talent nor educated within its own ranks a large corps of critically thinking individuals. Inside the leadership existed a group of church officials who still revered Stalin as the "savior of the people and wanted to restore Russian power."[51]

As the Orthodox Church sought to rebuild itself internally, it faced another major problem. In the 1980s, Russian dissidents had found in religion a vital source of opposition to Communist power, but in the late 1980s and early 1990s, the church lived in an environment demanding new and, in many ways, more complicated kinds of skills.[52] The church had to be more than an echo of the dissident past; to be effective, it had to play a constructive role, relating its message to a population facing chaos and hardship.

The times called for the Orthodox Church to be much more than a government office, to liberate itself from its past, and to recover its earlier traditions, especially its mission of education and service to others. To some leaders of the church, the new, more open environment was the best of times and offered unparalleled opportunities for spiritual leadership. But to many others, this was the worst of times, and they longed for a simpler, more secure environment. When the church was called upon in 1989 to reform itself, its challenge concerned not only overcoming seventy years of Communist oppression and its own collusion with an oppressive government, but it also involved carrying out an internal revolution, battling the old leadership style, facing the internal problems, overcoming the lack of direction, and dealing with the temptation to become again an ally of the government.

In late 1989 and early 1990, Viktor Popkov, a Russian writer on religion, published in the Paris newspaper *Russkaia mysl'*, a series of articles analyzing the internal life of the contemporary Orthodox Church. Popkov offered an incisive treatment of the situation confronting the church and its difficulties in adapting to the present political and social environment. He provided detailed discussion of the government organs, particularly the security police, that had for many years penetrated the church and forced it into submission. The primary function of the KGB in keeping such close watch over religious believers, he wrote, was to foster stability and to discover "elements within the church that might disrupt this stability."[53] This tight supervision encouraged an atmosphere of submissiveness in the church, making it difficult to act independently and to think critically. In such an atmosphere, the top leadership of the church echoed the thinking of the Central Committee of the Communist Party. The hierarchy of the church closely followed the directives of the Party; church leaders always knew what was expected of them, what decisions to make, and how they should relate to the population. Church leaders deliberately encouraged the status quo, because the political situation in which they operated demanded such a condition.

One of the most valuable parts of Popkov's treatment concerned his profile of the church leadership. While the leadership often appeared publicly to be unified in its outlook and monolithic in its approach to various religious and social issues, this apparently seamless exterior hid different identities and views within the church's internal structure. Popkov identified three main groups within the leadership. The first of these groups existed around Patriarch Pimen, whose primary commitment was to preserve the status quo in church life. Pimen had served as patriarch since 1971, and his tenure had been one of stasis. Around him existed a circle of close associates, connected not only by common views but also by blood ties, and they formed a tight circle at the core of the church hierarchy. Members of this group made few decisions and took little action without the approval of the KGB and the Central Committee. The KGB especially had played a large part in shaping the perspectives of the core group of leaders, providing them with patronage inside the church and, in some cases, had rewarded them with cash payments and social privileges, advantages the Russian press would later reveal in several sensational articles.

A second group within the church hierarchy consisted of a stratum of people who had considerable leadership experience. They had served for many years in such diverse activities as publishing and education, and they were more willing than the first group to take advantage of new opportunities. They had differences of opinion on theological and social issues; they wanted reform but not fundamental change. A large part of this group served on the Holy Synod and included Metropolitans Filaret (Minskii diocese) and Filaret (Kievskii diocese), Metropolitan Vladimir (Rostovskii diocese), Metropolitan Iuvenalii (Kratitskii diocese), Metropolitan Aleksi (Leningradskii diocese), and Archbishop Kirill (Smolenskii diocese).

Among the members of this group, Archbishop Kirill stood at the forefront, arguably the most impressive in erudition and demeanor. Later, in the mid-1990s, Kirill would temporarily become the church's most respected figure among the Russian intelligentsia, who saw him as a leading proponent of church renewal.[54] Popkov praised the archbishop's "courageous effort to restore the literary language of the services," his worries about the low educational standards among the clergy, his attempts to establish a training center in his diocese for priests, his work on a new internal statute for the church, and his important role in opening up for discussion the role of the Orthodox Church during the Soviet era.[55] Kirill's work, according to Popkov, had already left a clear mark on the church's own self-renewal.

Still a third group of church leaders had little active involvement in the political affairs of the upper administrative organs of the Orthodox Church. Representing an extremely large and diverse group, these bishops approached their roles in the church in widely different ways and capacities. They served as bishops in local towns and villages, in distant backwater places, routinely disconnected from politics and government intrigue and committed only to faithfully serving God. Many among them perceived service to the church simply as a way to make a living and saw their work as a career. Still others in this group devoted themselves with all their strength and ability to the service of God and the church and committed themselves quietly but wholeheartedly to helping the sick and destitute, bringing succor to those people in difficulty, bearing witness to the beauty and mystery of God's creation, and performing their service regardless of the heavy costs or pressures it involved. This latter group of bishops, Popkov lamented, were much too few in number but they offered a primary group on which the future might be built.[56]

While Viktor Popkov devoted most of his analysis to the official leadership of the Orthodox Church, he might have included, in terms of their significance, less official representatives of the church, who were also deeply interested in the spiritual revitalization of Russian society. Perestroika had encouraged the emergence of study groups and other "informal associations," some of which had existed illegally for years. These informal groups varied greatly in their character and purpose. Some of them had formed simply to

talk about literature or music; others took an active part in politics or in ecological movements; still others aimed at restoring Russia's spiritual heritage.
They provided alternative voices, sometimes critical ones, to the official views
of the church. In addition, the loosening of state control stimulated other
forms of revitalization that took place from below; such forms especially
included the re-creation of church parishes that, many church leaders believed, served as the key element in the revitalization of religion in Russia. If
the church offered the possibility of strengthening civil society, the parish
would have to play a major part in this movement. "The Church is separated
from the government," wrote Metropolitan Kirill in 1990, "but it is not separated, and by the nature of its task cannot be cut off, from the society or from
the people."[57] The church parish provided that essential connection, and in
1990 a new patriarch was elected whose life symbolized such a connection and
who would place the re-creation of parish life among the top goals on his
agenda.

THE NEW PATRIARCH

On May 3, 1990, Pimen, who had served in office since 1971, died, thus opening up the highest office of the Orthodox Church to the chance for a new direction. Rather than wait the traditional forty days of mourning, the Holy
Synod moved as quickly as possible, convening a meeting of the archbishops
on June 6, and setting the elections for the new patriarch for the next day. The
three candidates presented to the National Church Council on June 7 for the
first election were Metropolitan Vladimir (Sabodan) of Rostov, the highly respected chief administrator for the patriarchate and the rector of the Moscow
academy and seminary; Metropolitan Filaret (Denisenko) of Kiev, the senior
prelate and head of the Ukrainian Orthodox Church; and Metropolitan
Aleksi (Ridiger) of Leningrad, who had served successfully for three decades
as a bishop in Tallinn and for the past five years as head of the Leningrad and
Novgorod diocese.

Reformers within the church generally favored Metropolitan Vladimir
for the position of patriarch. Energetic, effective as an administrative leader
and educator, he was the youngest of the three prelates. His appointment to
the Holy Synod took place only in 1982; his associations at the highest levels
of authority thus did not extend very deeply into the past, and his connections
to the "period of stagnation" under Brezhnev were minimal. In comparison
with Vladimir, Metropolitan Filaret stood as the least reform-minded of the

candidates. Many senior officials thought that, since his elevation to head of
the Ukrainian Orthodox Church, he had poorly managed the Ukrainian-
Greek-Catholics, and his policies had exacerbated their resentment.[58] The last
person, Metropolitan Aleksi, served as a middle candidate between church reformers and traditionalists. While a non-Russian, a person of mixed ancestry
and Estonian nationality whose father had been a highly respected Orthodox
priest in Tallinn, Metropolitan Aleksi had a reputation as a conciliator, a "man
of peace," who could bring together the various groups within the church hierarchy.[59] Members of the council elected Aleksi, the compromiser, as the new
patriarch. On June 10, All Saints' Day in the Orthodox Church, Aleksi (II)
was enthroned as Patriarch of Moscow and All Russia, the fifteenth in Russian
history, the fifth in the Soviet era.

As one commentator wrote upon the occasion of Aleksi's election, "it
would be naive to expect the Russian Orthodox Church—after decades—
after seventy years of relentless oppression by the state, after decades of docile
silence and servile phrases—to express its will freely. It would be premature
to expect this now."[60] Members of the national council that elected Aleksi as
patriarch were traditionalists on most religious and policy issues. Aleksi II was
sixty-one years old; he had considerable administrative experience and many
years of seeking accommodations with state power. His appointment as
bishop had come during the Khrushchev period, one of the most oppressive
eras for the church in Soviet history; his rise to preeminence and his survival
could only have been accomplished by a willingness to cooperate fully or, at
least make it seem that way, to compromise many principles, and to make key
concessions to the government. Several documents from the archives of the
Council for Religious Affairs, published in 1987 in the dissident journal *Glasnost 13*, revealed that Aleksi had given information to the council about other
church officials and had, on occasion, reported to the KGB about the lives of
fellow clerics.[61] In the days preceding the meeting of the national council in
1990, Fr Georgii Edelshtein of Kostroma wrote a scathing article about Aleksi,
in which he accused him of having been a "professional informer" for the
Council of Religious Affairs and the KGB.[62] Edelshtein criticized the upcoming church proceedings and the haste with which the council was convened;
in describing the election, he used an old analogy, of the bereaved widow: "According to the centuries-old Christian tradition, a widow stays in mourning
for forty days, does not hold banquets or similar forms of entertainment, and
remains in an attitude of prayer and fasting." Edelshtein's point was that the
church had failed to follow its own decorum, thus rushing into a decision. He
had some sharp words of criticism about the outcome of the election: "Surely

the election of a hardened stool pigeon to the patriarchal throne will add a
sense of scandal to the current situation of the Russian Orthodox Church,
where practically every second priest is directly or indirectly linked with the
'competent organs.'"[63]

Another close observer countered Edelshtein's claims by pointing out that
the former Metropolitan Aleksi had had to cooperate in policies and engage
in many activities "that he could not avoid."[64] This same sympathetic supporter of the new patriarch recommended Aleksi on the basis of his outstanding personal characteristics that well qualified him for his new position:
"Aleksi stands out because of his energy, his readiness to review his values, his
ability to change and move in step with the times."[65] In reality, Aleksi had a
theological openness and a compassion for people, particularly the destitute,
that would soon be evident. He understood clearly that the church faced for-
midable tasks. Many times, Aleksi asserted, "the greatest wound inflicted by
the Communist dictatorship was lack of spirituality." "All the other evils," he
pointed out, "were the result of the systematic and total eradication from the
souls and consciousness of the people of the very notion of spirituality."[66]

In order to rebuild, the new patriarch knew he had to confront the past,
especially the blemishes on his own record. He was willing to admit his mistakes and accept responsibility for them. On the first anniversary of his election as patriarch, he officially apologized for his collaboration with the Communist Party and the Soviet government, and he sought repentance for his
earlier actions: "Before those people, however, to whom the compromises, silence, forced passivity or expressions of loyalty permitted by leaders of the
church in those years caused pain, before these people, and not only before
God, I ask forgiveness, understanding and prayer. We have to rebuild everything—charity, catechism. The new generation has forgotten everything—
the very word charity was barred from dictionaries. An immediate revival is
impossible, but the will is there."[67]

Aleksi is an ambiguous figure, caught between the past and the future,
unable to shake entirely old ways of thinking but aware of the need for fundamental reforms, for new sources of energy and initiative, and for reawakening and renewal. His ambivalence recalls that of his contemporary Mikhail
Gorbachev, whose path the new patriarch would cross many times at this crucial juncture in Russian history. As the Russian journalist Mikhail Pozdniaev
has pointed out in the popular journal *Stolitsa,* the two leaders displayed many
similarities: "these forgotten parallels bear remembering."[68] While the careers
of Aleksi Ridiger and Mikhail Gorbachev went in different directions, one
through the church and the other through the Communist Party, the two

leaders shared common features. Both came from solid, honest, hardworking families, who very early saw that their sons had special gifts; although Gorbachev began study in a tractor combine and Aleksi in a religious academy, both finished school at the top of their class. Unpretentious and modest, both men understood before graduation that they could not fully develop their talents if they remained in the provinces. They also knew that widening the scope of their service demanded that they enter the "corridors of power": for Aleksi, this road led to Leningrad; for Gorbachev, to Moscow.

Youth and charm, Pozdniaev writes, served both men well in their advancement through these "corridors of power." In their rapid accession, both developed close associations with a "wise teacher" and "powerful protector." In Gorbachev's case, Iurii Andropov played such a role; in Aleksi's case, Metropolitan Nikodim guided the future patriarch. Both men came to power as candidates who represented compromise, standing between other well-formed political factions in the Politburo or the Holy Synod; at first each man seemed the least threatening possibility. As general secretary, Gorbachev had to deal with former political dissenters, whom he tried to reintegrate; the patriarch reached out to the Orthodox Church abroad and sought to welcome it back. Each leader faced constant struggles within his own ranks: the Central Committee of the Communist Party displayed a unified exterior that masked its sharp internal conflicts; in similar fashion, the Holy Synod's public resolutions hid the conflicting views and rancor that marked many of its private sessions.

Publicly, each man's attempts to reach out to former dissidents and to the West would provoke strong reactions from ultraconservatives: President Gorbachev from the nationalistic Union of the Russian People, who saw him as betraying Russia; Patriarch Aleksi II from the Orthodox Brotherhood who, after his speech to Jewish rabbis in the United States, proposed to remove him from office. Like Gorbachev, Aleksi II was a contradictory person, who wanted fundamental reforms but faced sharp political constraints and social realities that limited what could be done. In such a context, politics and religion proceeded along parallel tracks, experienced similar conflicts, and suffered some of the same shortcomings.

One of the most important phenomena in the recovery of the church in 1989–90 concerned the attempts to revive parish and monastic life. In these two years, more than 4,000 new parishes were organized in the Soviet Union, nearly 1,600 in Russia and more than 1,700 in Ukraine.[69] The establishment of the parishes and the rebirth of monastic life held much significance to Aleksi, who had spent a large part of his church career as a parish priest and whose elevation as patriarch took place simultaneously with this revival. He saw the recovery of parishes and monasteries as a key to the restoration of spirituality in post-Soviet society. In an interview, he recalled the significance for his own spiritual journey of two pilgrimages he made with his parents early in his life to the Valaam Monastery on Lake Ladoga. He remembered his first trip in 1939, and his second a year later, on the eve of the Great Fatherland War that would devastate the region. The memories of these journeys were deeply engraved in his mind: "the striking beauty of the monastery left a lasting impression. The summer church had only just been restored and it shone with color and gold."[70] He recalled his sadness as he and his parents left the monastery that last summer, "sensing that it would be a long time before we could return." For many years, he said, he could not go back, unwilling to see the place despoiled by the war and fearing that such a sight would destroy one of his most treasured memories. These images from his childhood and his spiritual identity were bound closely together in his mind and shaped fundamentally his vision for the spiritual renewal of Russia.

Indeed, the monastery symbolizes the contradiction that would characterize Aleksi and his vision of the tasks that lay ahead. In Russian history the monastery stood for tradition and the close connection to the political authorities and the tsars who had fostered many of them, who often visited them, and who sent their families to reside in them. Monasteries played a significant role in the geographical history of Russia. They preserved much of what we know about the historical development of early Russia; they were the chief guardians and conveyers of historical knowledge. They were strongholds for defense, sites of exile, and places of imprisonment.[71]

But monasteries symbolized far more than these church-state connections. In Kievan Rus' their abbots often had a powerful independent voice in politics, and disputing princes resolved their differences through them. Later, from the fourteenth century, the Trinity Monastery, northeast of Moscow, aspired to become Russia's cultural center of Christian art and music. Founded by St Sergius, the monastery had emerged independent of political authority, and it attracted artists and pilgrims from distant parts of the country. Moreover, monasteries were visited by common people; most of the monks came from humble origins, not from the aristocracy. Russian monasteries offered the chief source of charity to the destitute, established the only hospitals for the sick, greatly influenced the economies of local regions, and helped local culture flourish. In contrast to Western Europe, monks and nuns were not secluded, but were closely connected to the people and social life. Monasteries were national repositories, but to Aleksi they also were places where the high and low could meet. They were places of reconciliation and redemption. They embodied the spirit of hope; this image, embedded in Aleksi from his early life, promised to bring something new out of a destructive past.

Such an image shaped Aleksi's views of the principal tasks that lay ahead. As patriarch, his two primary goals focused on strengthening education and revitalizing parish life, and he saw them as fundamental to the future well-being of the church. His first official statement after becoming patriarch proclaimed the need for the church to become a public teaching institution. He revived a great many of the church's publication activities, and he played an extremely active role in the rebirth of the Russian Bible Society in October 1991.[72] Education, he maintained, meant not only passing on knowledge but also bringing "out a certain image in people," encouraging the element of the holy that lay within every human being.[73]

As a former parish priest, Aleksi also saw the importance of revitalizing the grassroots organization of society, and he placed the renewal of local communities at the center of his vision. While his public pronouncements did not deal with civil society, his emphasis on the importance of rebuilding Russia's moral strength and its nongovernmental organizations and institutions aimed in that direction. Russia had to reconnect with the spiritual, activist sources of its tradition, which offered models of mutual aid, reciprocity, and acts of reaching out to others. He lamented the deep chasm separating the church from the people and the problems that were engulfing it from all sides. "It seems that we have willingly distanced ourselves from the sick, the elderly, the disabled, the orphaned, the poor, the imprisoned and all who suffer," he said. He believed that the church had to focus immediately on organizing religious education and opening workshops, temperance societies, hostels, and orphanages, activities in which the church had been traditionally involved. "But today," he said, "we are starting from nothing and are making only the very first steps in this direction."[74]

In character, the new patriarch differed from another protagonist in this unfolding drama, Fr Aleksandr Men. Fr Aleksandr was a true reformer, a proponent of the new. Aleksi stood between competing voices, between the old and the new, and sometimes moved from one side to the other. He existed between change and tradition, between political action and inaction, between silence and speech, between the church as a mediator and as a participant in the life of the people. The monastery displayed all these elements, these dichotomies that existed together, both in Russian society and in Aleksi himself. Such ambiguities would come to mark his tenure as Russian patriarch.

Rebuilding the parish communities and engaging in social activities to

Aleksi, as to Aleksandr Men, required the church's independence from the government. Beyond asking for a repeal of the 1929 law on religious associations that forbade the church to engage in charity and to educate children and calling for removal of government-appointed *starosti* in the parishes, Aleksi did not develop in detail the subject of the church's relationship to the government. He focused instead on the present and future tasks facing the church. He stressed the importance of the 1990 draft law on freedom of conscience and religious associations, then in its first draft and under consideration by the Congress of People's Deputies. To the reformers, aspiring to redefine Russia and develop a civil society, the law represented a preeminent achievement.

On October 1, 1990, the Soviet parliament passed the long-awaited Soviet Law on Freedom of Conscience and Religious Organizations. The law, which applied to all Soviet republics, turned upside down values that lay at the heart of the Soviet Constitution of 1977 and many previous enactments of the Soviet government; it represented a significant victory for the reformers, who connected religious liberty to the building of a democratic political order. The framers of the law saw religious freedom "as the linchpin of all liberty" and proceeded to define the rights and interests that would protect this freedom.[75] The law left to the citizen the right to decide his own views of religion, express his views publicly, and spread religious ideas, either alone or with others. It declared citizens equal under the law in all political, social, and cultural activities "regardless of their attitudes toward religion." It gave religious organizations the right to publish freely, participate in charitable activities, disseminate religious materials, and engage in economic pursuits for their own purposes. The law rescinded the view that the Party represented the most enlightened, leading group in society. It abrogated the previous conception of "freedom of conscience" that, in practice, had meant primarily the freedom to propagate and spread atheistic ideas.

While the new law contained elements that the Orthodox hierarchy did not like, it nevertheless significantly widened the church's opportunities to act in Russian society. The legislation removed the onerous legal requirement that forced religious communities to register with the government. The 1929 Soviet Constitution had forbidden the church to own land, had confiscated the buildings of religious organizations that had not registered with the government, and had even cut the church off from participation in charitable activities. The 1990 law "On Freedom of Conscience and Religious Organizations" permitted religious communities to engage in charity work and print materials for religious services. The new law overturned long-held practices; it forbade atheistic organizations from using government money to propagandize against religion. The law authorized religious instruction for children in private facilities, thus removing one of the most restrictive features of the laws on religion in effect since the early 1920s.[76] This law, along with other legislation issued in 1990, restored to religious organizations rights to own buildings and other facilities necessary to their activities. The church's status and role in society, therefore, underwent a significant reversal. It now had unprecedented opportunities for service that it had lacked during the entire Soviet period.

In establishing educational and political rights, the new law also fundamentally differed from the Soviet past. It made legitimate the religious instruction of children of any age, and it gave religious organizations that were registered the right to set their own educational requirements and to engage in religious education. It affirmed the separation of church and state; it prohibited religious organizations from taking part in or providing funds for the activities of political parties, but it allowed for individual participation on an equal basis with all citizens. The law authorized religious institutions to own property.[77] It gave students training in religious establishments the same deferment from military service as students in state-supported institutions.

Symbolically, also, the new law represented the growing status of religion in Soviet society and confirmed the resurgence of religion in Russia. This status was displayed in the large numbers of people who now flocked to the churches to take part in religious ceremonies. In 1990 and 1991, concurrent with the increasing status and popularity of the church, another unexpected phenomenon took place. Political figures, some of whom had previously been antagonistic to religion, now became much more sympathetic to the church or even embraced it. In 1991, Aleksandr Iakovlev, one of the principal architects of Gorbachev's political reforms and a person well known for his harsh attitudes toward religion and his dislike for the church, went on a pilgrimage to the newly reopened monastery at Optyna Pustyn'. There he made an emotional speech about the large contribution the church had made in the history of Russian culture.[78] The reformist mayors of St. Petersburg and Moscow, Anatolii Sobchak and Gavril Popov, frequently had their pictures taken with bishops of the Orthodox Church, with whom they now wanted to be associated.

Perhaps the most significant example of a political figure aligning himself publicly with the church occurred in June 1991, in Boris Yeltsin's inauguration as president of Russia. Paying homage to the dramatic shift in public sentiment and also seeking to connect himself to the Russian past, Boris Yeltsin had a spectacular inauguration ceremony in the Kremlin, carried nationwide on television. Yeltsin had Patriarch Aleksi II with him on the stage in a service resembling that of tsarist Russia. Yeltsin's inauguration can be interpreted both as the politicians' effort to reclaim institutions once renounced under communism and as the church's effort to show support for the new president. The patriarch's presence alongside Boris Yeltsin symbolized the church's new position, and it greatly elevated its political status. His presence also held political meaning for Yeltsin; it gave the new president additional political legitimacy, a purpose opposed to Patriarch Aleksi's stated view that the church's chief role lay in the "regeneration of souls."[79] To the reformers, who had emphasized the church's need to separate itself from the government, the ceremony suggested a different phenomenon—the church's affinity for political power and service to the government.

Whether the relationship between the church and the leaders of the Russian government, as witnessed in the president's inauguration, had only momentary significance or whether it represented the first step of a longer and deeper process could not be determined in the summer of 1991. But this evolving relationship between church and state was very important to Russia's present and future development, and it would gain further significance in the circumstances during and after the August coup of 1991.

2 The Church's Struggle for Renewal

"Every historical crisis is an epoch of doubt and searching; for the fallen idols were once upon a time objects of veneration," the historian A. Karpov has written. "The seeking of new criteria during epochs of crisis is not the peaceful creative impulse of a sound organism, but resembles more the feverish nightmares of a patient struggling against disease."[1] The frenetic search for these "new criteria" is difficult, often moving forward and then backward before settling on a new course, overcoming the illness and restoring the patient to health. From such a perspective, Russia's pursuit of these new criteria would continue throughout the 1990s and beyond, and a central part of the quest would involve the church and its relationship to society.

THE AUGUST 1991 COUP AND THE AFTERMATH

"The central tension in the Soviet Union today is neither a political one between personalities nor an economic one between programs," noted the historian and librarian of Congress James H. Billington in 1991. "The key conflict is rather an elemental struggle for legitimacy between two very different, rival forces—primeval moral forces that compete within, as well as among people—forces that can be best understood by reading the long novels rather than the short histories of Russia."[2] This struggle for legitimacy pitted political power against moral authority, the military and police strength of the state existing above against the popular grassroots voices coming from below. These grassroots elements were propelled in part by anger and disillusionment with the current government structure and ideology. But they were also looking for sources of meaning and guidance within their own cultural traditions. The next decade would witness a search for legitimacy and authority different from the ones used in the Soviet past.

The historic events that began in the summer of 1991 Billington has called Russia's "fever break" with totalitarianism, and these events brought the Orthodox Church to center stage. On the first day and night of the attempted "putsch," as government troops ringed the parliament building, Patriarch Aleksi II remained silent, content to observe the face-off of these two irreconcilable forces. On the second night, just before the storming of the White House (as the Russian parliament was popularly known) was set to begin, the patriarch shifted his position from disinterested silence to social action; he asked members of the military not to shed the innocent blood of their countrymen. In a prayer broadcast to troops surrounding the White House, he told them that whoever uses violence "against his neighbor, against unarmed people, weighs down his soul with the heaviest of sins, cutting him off from the Church and from God," and he prayed that the "Lord deliver us from this terrible sin of fratricide."[3] That night of August 20, as crowds gathered to defend the parliament building, two Orthodox priests organized resistance around the White House. Both had been close friends of Fr Aleksandr Men: Fr Gleb Yakunin, who had been released from prison in 1987 and was an outspoken member of the Russian parliament, and Fr Aleksandr Borisov, who worked nonstop around the White House, praying, baptizing, counseling, and distributing Bibles, nearly two thousand of which went to youths manning the tanks.[4] These church officials, as well as the many priests and women in the crowds at the barricades and in other cities, contributed to the nonviolent outcome and the inability of the large and powerful Leninist political machine to dispel the forces intent on building a new Russia. The widespread sense of exhilaration, which had gathered momentum the preceding spring and summer, enveloped much of the country.

In the euphoria that followed the collapse of the August coup, Boris Yeltsin and his supporters aspired, they said, to put into place in Russia the "liberal-democratic" principles that had aided their victory over the Communists: equality of opportunity, government by law, civil rights, and what they called "general human values." The articulation of these much-needed ideals had promised a quick victory over the Communist Party; now, however, they needed implementation, a task that required the building of a moral and ethical framework different from the previous Soviet one.[5]

The concept of "general human values" entailed the revival of Russia's spiritual heritage, so assaulted by the Communists. In late 1991 and 1992, President Yeltsin gave several public demonstrations of the important role he intended the church to play and of his support for the current religious leadership, including his visit to the Sacred Danilov Monastery in Moscow. On June 14, 1992, the feast day of the Holy Trinity, and on the eve of his trip to the United States, he traveled to the Troitse-Sergieva Monastery at Sergiev

Posad, attended a service with the patriarch, and then, with the patriarch standing by his side, spoke from the balcony of the patriarch's courtyard.[6] "Tomorrow I am going to the United States," Yeltsin said. "I think that the signatures by the President [of Russia] and the President of the United States will put a final full stop to ensure that we will never be enemies again. We will eliminate nuclear weapons altogether." He maintained that he had come to the monastery seeking blessings for the trip.[7] By word and deed, the president had revived an old Russian tradition in which the political leader sought out the head of the church prior to his engagement in a major historical event. President Yeltsin's audience with the patriarch suggested his intention of using the church as a main participant in the quest for legitimacy and in the construction of a new political order.

In seeking to define its proper course of action, the church spoke with more than one voice. While they represented only a small minority, reformers within the church expressed the desire to reach out, to extend the boundaries of thought, to confront the most pressing social issues, and to play a more active role in society. The desire for reform can be detected in Orthodox seminaries and academies among many young priests whose theological and social views coalesced and found expression in the 1990s, planting the seeds of popular dialogue that would increase in richness throughout the next decade.[8]

The aspiration toward active social service can best be found at the local level, in the parishes, whose church members energetically tried to respond to Russia's social crisis. An example of such a response can be found in the Moscow parish of Evgeniia Viktorovna Ivanova, then a director of the Russian Cultural Foundation, who described her own parish's service to the elderly and the poor:

> I personally am involved in many programs of humanitarian aid; in this city the Church has been the most effective and reliable source in giving and distributing help for the destitute. The Church also provides a great deal of aid to old people who are suffering; this is extremely important work because elderly women were the first to be affected by the social crisis. People from my parish went to their homes, brought food, medicine, and other necessary things. In our parish, for example, priests have organized collections of secondhand clothes and distributed them among the elderly of the community and among people recently released from prison, who also needed these clothes and came to the Church asking for them.[9]

Since 1992, on the local level, the Orthodox Church has greatly expanded its social activities in an effort to restore practices that many parishioners see as part of its fundamental mission. In Moscow, the church established child-care homes for orphans and street children, providing them with food and clothing and teaching them spiritual values. As the church's financial resources improved, plans were to greatly expand this program, thus recovering one of the church's main social activities in prerevolutionary times. In addition, the First City Hospital of Moscow, the Pirogovskaia *bol'nitsa,* contained a special section organized by the Orthodox Church. It established in the hospital a major training school for Sisters of Mercy, who have already become well known and admired for their skills, compassion, and sense of responsibility. Fr Andrei, the priest who organized this special section, used as his organizational model a Roman Catholic hospital in Italy. Thus the Orthodox Church in the aftermath of the 1991 coup looked both to its past and to other contemporary churches for ways to implement social responsibility.[10]

Unlike the reformers who concentrated on social activities, the primary goal of the conservatives focused on the full recovery of the church's ancient religious heritage, a part of which is the recovery of physical property. The new government considered this property part of the church's legal inheritance and instructed leaders of the church to prepare inventories of churches, buildings, monasteries, and museums, which the Soviet government had illegally confiscated and which the government expressed its intention to return. It is important to note that such a transfer of property did not take place to any other institution or person, and it set in motion a whole series of dilemmas that would, perhaps unwittingly, impel the Orthodox Church into a new association with the government.[11]

The return to the church of its former extensive holdings that began on a large scale in early 1992 might seem fully justified, given the massive assault on religious institutions that occurred in the Soviet period and the government's desire in the 1990s to rebuild the society. But the transfer of property, as the Russian sociologist S. B. Filatov has written, was fraught with difficulties. In a new way, it tied the government to the church bureaucracy, since the transfer of property took place exclusively through this hierarchy. In the case of monasteries, the return of property led to a particularly anomalous situation. The renewal of the monasteries did not emerge from the grassroots level of society, arising around the energetic activities of a certain monk or association of spiritual mentors, but arose again because of the government's transfer to the church of monastic buildings and properties. Monks did not have an organically close connection to their followers, and they did not achieve their positions because they had responded to the organic needs of the members of their community. Rather they held their positions because the government

sought to re-create an earlier monastic setting.[12] While the church in the Soviet period had been part of the government machine and was now set free,
circumstances like the transfer of properties operated against this independence and pulled the two entities, in subtle ways, back toward mutual dependence, economically and psychologically.

In addition, the transfer of property gave the Moscow Patriarchate a privileged position over religious organizations and bodies that lay outside the
church's jurisdiction. Orthodox groups that had originated within the church
but had broken with it over its cooperation with the Soviet government did
not regain rights to their former property. Moreover, many Christian religious
minorities—Russian Catholics, Old Believers, Baptists and other Protestants—existed in Russia and had known constant persecution in prerevolutionary Russia. Shortly before the 1917 Revolution, these minorities had
gained full legal rights to own property and to build on it. The legislation issued in 1993 did not return their property, and this fostered a situation that
reverted to old discriminations. To receive their property, religious minorities
had to pay a large sum of money, a requirement that the government did not
make of the Orthodox Church.[13] The government gave the Orthodox
Church a privileged position and that, in itself, created a dependence and a
servility that the church found difficult to reject.

Still another problem relating to the transfer of property concerned the
plight of museums that held many of the historic treasures of Russia's national
culture. Some of the museum complexes were located in monasteries and
churches. During the Soviet period, when religious activities had been closed,
the museums had continued to operate, often under the dutiful eyes of men
and women who devoted their lives to preserving not only religious objects
but also the precious artifacts of Russia's artistic heritage. The hierarchy of the
Orthodox Church wanted these museum complexes transferred to the church
as part of its domain.

In many cases, the government complied, closing many museums from
public view as, for example, the museum of architecture in the Donskoi Monastery in Moscow; museums of popular culture in Kostroma, Novgorod, and
Sergiev Posad; the literature museum in Vysokopetrovskii; and small museums throughout the country.[14] The government transferred the museum
complexes to the central control of the church, which used them for its own
displays and to suit its own purposes. The reasons underlying the transfers of
these national treasures did not come from idealism or generosity on the
state's part. Superficially, such actions signified the "return of a rich inheritance," enabling the church to restore its identity. But from another point of

view, the transfer of the museums gave the church the privilege of controlling the display of national treasures, and it presented a major temptation to control Russia's national memory. The transfer of the museums fit a larger pattern of circumstances that, for political reasons, drew church and government together. The timing of the change suggests a great deal about the underlying motivation. President Yeltsin signed the orders calling for the transfer of these museums on the eve of the presidential referendum in April 1993, a move that assured him of the church's support in this and in subsequent elections.[15]

Through the transfer of property, the leadership of the Russian Orthodox Church gained and consolidated a privileged position in religion and society. Having achieved a special status, church leaders now faced the problem that they had not had to confront earlier under the Soviet system. They had to deal with the question of religious toleration. In the atmosphere of greater freedom, Roman Catholic and Protestant denominations had also rapidly gained supporters and had enthusiastically campaigned for new converts. The alternative voices greatly disturbed Orthodox leaders and raised the question of how tolerant they should be toward these different perspectives. Earlier, Fr Aleksandr Men had maintained that in "our church there had always been" both conservative and open traditions, and "between both trends had often taken place a very sharp struggle."[16] Such a clash reoccurred in the 1990s, during a time when all religious faiths were trying to adjust to the new political context in which they found themselves.

Conservatives saw Orthodoxy as Russia's central cultural force, the foundation of its national heritage, and the force that historically unified the country, in spite of Russia's ever-changing political structure. They did not like what they called Catholic and Protestant "spiritual expansion"—"proselytizing," saving souls, and serving their existing communities. High-ranking members of the patriarchate in Moscow demanded that President Yeltsin "make a correction" in the laws that gave Catholic and Protestant religions the privileges to operate in Russia, and they threatened withdrawal of their support if he did not comply.[17] They argued that Russia needed, especially during this difficult time of adjustment, to reconnect "the broken threads of its own traditions," to reconcile with its own story and heritage, after decades of severe repression. The Orthodox Church should not have to face, in its present weak position, another onslaught from religious groups also wanting to gain religious privileges.

In late 1992 and 1993, when these demands increased, some corrections were made; the authorities restricted various religious groups' rights and property. For example, in Arkhangel'sk, district local authorities had granted to

Baptists a piece of land on which they had asked to build a house of worship. But in the fall of 1993, local officials reversed their decision, asking the local Baptist leader whether he had heard about the new law and telling him that this "land we cannot give to your congregation, because by tradition we must first think of our Orthodox people, and evangelical Christian Baptists do not represent our people."[18] In Serpukhov, the head of the city government early in 1993 "willingly" gave to Seventh-Day Adventists an allotment of land on which they wanted to build a place of worship, but in the summer he reversed his earlier decision, telling them that, because of protests from the Orthodox Church, he had "reconsidered the offer."[19]

Such acts of discrimination against minority religious groups were carried out for two main reasons, both of which related to the larger political and cultural context in which the Orthodox Church operated. These reasons were financial and ideological. First, needing to rebuild the moral and spiritual foundation of society, the government financially supported the church. The new legislation gave the church the opportunity to develop fresh spiritual and social visions for society. To fulfill its tasks, the church needed to restore and operate the buildings and monastic complexes that the government had returned, open new training centers, educate its priests, and deal with a population hungrily, persistently seeking spiritual guidance and wanting to explore what the church had to offer. Such needs created not only opportunity but also a great deal of pressure.[20]

The 1990 law "On Freedom of Conscience and on Religious Organizations" called for the return of church buildings and other properties but said nothing about the financial resources to operate these properties; in allowing for moral justice—the freedom to worship—it failed to provide for economic justice.[21] The church, therefore, had few financial means of dealing with the tasks that it had to confront. Having insufficient funds, church officials turned to the government for immediate help and asked for grants and subsidies to cover the costs of restoring church buildings. Paradoxically, the church came to rely on the institution from which it most needed to gain independence. Practical financial reasons tempted church officials to move in that direction.

The second reason is closely connected to what S. B. Filatov has called the "ideology of the Moscow Patriarchate" and its conception of "patriotic service." According to Filatov, this conception was the creation of Joseph Stalin at the end of the Second World War, although its roots lay in earlier periods of Russian history, when the Holy Synod was established as a servitor of the state. In September 1943, with German troops on Russian soil, Stalin's government eased its relentless persecution of the church. Rather than seeking to obliterate the church, Stalin sought its renewal: he restored the patriarchate, reopened monasteries, and revived several religious publications. While historians have generally attributed the decision as Stalin's desire to engage the church in the struggle against the Nazis, some Russian scholars have reexamined this explanation and have seen different underlying reasons. Stalin's renewal of the church took place not during but shortly after the worst of the Nazi threats to the Soviet Union had passed; the church's revival, therefore, had causes other than immediate military ones. The fundamental reasons were ideological.[22] By the late 1930s and 1940s, when the large gap between Communist ideals and social realities was clearly visible to all Soviet citizens, Bolshevik ideology lay in shambles. The Bolshevik Revolution's "eschatological message"—its belief in world revolution and the dream of building an earthly utopia—had clearly not been accomplished.[23] Soviet ideology, Furman claims, underwent a significant change: nationalistic replaced original eschatological ideals. The concepts of Great Russia and Holy Russia were revived; images of Russia surrounded on all sides by enemies were re-created. During the war, the worst imagined fears were realized, as the Soviet people experienced firsthand the horrors of invasion. In such a setting, Stalin resurrected the Orthodox Church because it fit into the need to redirect the former grandiose expectations of the people with nationalistic goals. A crude form of Orthodoxy, a nationalistic mission tied to the service of the state, replaced Marxism-Leninism. Orthodoxy functioned as a civil religion, whose ceremonies and rituals essentially served secular ends.

In its actual operations, the church resembled the role it had previously played, particularly in the period of Tsar Nicholas I (1825–55), when it promoted political stability and state power. As under Nicholas I, the church glorified Russian history and the military deeds that had contributed to the power and glory of the state. As in this earlier period also, the church saw conformity as a distinctive feature of loyalty. It viewed sectarianism as seditious, maintained tight censorship over the discussion of religious subjects, did not tolerate spiritual dissidents who used religion as a basis for criticism of the state or the church, and joined the government in persecuting such spiritual dissidents. The most creative spiritual dissidents were driven into exile and could only publish their works abroad. In its close connection to the government, the church hierarchy contributed to the spiritual sterility, conformity, and oppression Soviet citizens had endured. By cooperating so closely with the government, by making so many concessions, both in belief and practice, the church had promoted a "bureaucratic mentality" among its leaders that stifled independent thought. Such a mentality had made the leadership unresponsive to fresh religious and philosophic ideas, even within the Orthodox tradition. A vibrant, living, ever-renewing faith had become ossified, rigid, and closed.

Under Stalin and his successors, the church's alliance with the government bred among church officials a servile attitude toward political power, as church leaders took an active part in ceremonies in the Kremlin and participated in the struggle against foreign enemies. But this alliance with the government in the 1940s differed in one significant way from the past. Earlier in Russian history, the church had supported a tsarist government committed to the same religious principles. The alliance under Stalin and his successors, however, amounted to a unique and contradictory historical phenomenon: of a religious institution supporting an atheistic autocracy that officially aspired to destroy religion.[24] While Stalin's successor, Nikita Khrushchev, began in 1957 a vigorous campaign to destroy the church, his sharp, crude assaults on religious institutions did not obliterate church attitudes toward state authority that had developed earlier.[25] The church continued to act servilely and deferentially on behalf of the ruling power. In subsequent decades, this servility persisted in church leaders' attempts to expand their international contacts, to take part in peace activities on behalf of the government, to flatter political authorities, and to overlook the cruelty and hypocrisy they did not wish to see, accepting uncritically the privileges this power conferred.[26] It would have been "necessary to possess unusual intelligence and spiritual qualities," the Russian sociologist Dmitrii Furman has written, "not to give way to the temptation and the seduction of serving the various causes of the political power."[27]

The conception of "patriotic service" persisted after the collapse of the Soviet government in 1991, continuing to exert a strong influence on the church hierarchy. The repeated calls for "national unity" and "solidarity" and its invectives against foreign religious faiths replicated statements that church leaders had made in the past.[28] During the presidency of Boris Yeltsin, the political relationship between the government and the church grew even closer, as the Russian president sought to consolidate his power and turned to the church for assistance in his quest for political legitimacy. His public appearances with the patriarch, his symbolic use of the church in political ceremonies, and his appeals for national unity—appeals that the church strongly endorsed—bore witness to this alliance. But such a relationship between politics and religion, between state and church, and between political and moral authority was fraught with ambiguities and uncertainties that would soon be put to the test. As church leaders struggled with the renewal of the church, with recovering a voice in the period after the fall of communism, they had to confront these ambiguities and uncertainties.

The Crisis of 1993

In the autumn crisis of 1993, the church intensified its efforts to play a larger role in Russian politics. In September of that year, the Congress of People's Deputies and the Supreme Soviet clashed with President Yeltsin over the proposed budget and the appointment of ministers to the government bureaucracy. The government submitted to the Russian parliament a state budget much lower than it had wanted to enact; the parliament believed it had to increase social welfare payments to provide for those suffering from extreme economic difficulties. Also to offset the recent economic downturn, some members of the parliament wanted to provide more credit for state industries that were threatened with bankruptcy.

In late September, a group of radicals who wanted an outright confrontation with the government gained the upper hand in the parliament. President Yeltsin had several times expressed contempt for vocal members of the parliament, and in the previous year he had threatened to close parliament. In late September he announced that he had begun to make "artillery preparations" for carrying out this act. He placed the parliament building under siege, surrounded it with his troops, and in a major televised address announced that "the security of Russia and its people is a higher value than formal observations of discrepant norms."[29] On two earlier occasions in Russian history, in 1906 and 1918, the government had disbanded by force Russia's national parliamentary institutions. To repeat this action was perceived as extremely serious. Both sides refused to compromise, and the situation rapidly moved to a deadly confrontation.

As the crisis unfolded, top officials of the Orthodox Church tried to play a direct role in seeking a resolution. Members of the church were found on both sides of the conflict; several priests, strong supporters of the opposition to President Yeltsin, remained inside the legislative building during its encirclement.[30] On September 21, when Yeltsin issued his decree disbanding the parliament, Patriarch Aleksi II was on a trip to Alaska. Upon hearing of the presidential decree, he flew immediately to San Francisco, and from the airport there issued his own proclamation, which was carried on radio and television in Russia. He implored all branches of the government, their institutions, the military, law enforcement agencies, and all Russians not to engage in a bloody solution and plunge the country into "civil war" but to seek a peaceful resolution. He spoke of the importance of redemption and healing, echoing themes similar to those expressed earlier by Russian religious leaders. His words drew from the incarnational theology of the Russian Orthodox Church; they connected the sacred and the material and argued that the key concerns were not the secular issues of political power but the fundamental needs of harmony and reconciliation. His appeal called for patience, dialogue, and good will on both sides. He announced that he was cutting short his American visit and returning to Moscow at once.[31]

In the following week, as tensions mounted both inside the executive branch and the parliament, the patriarch proclaimed his political neutrality in the confrontation. He offered himself as a mediator, thereby attempting to insert the spiritual world into this political conflict. The alternative approach, he said, would lead to bloodshed. He warned, "Russia is on the brink of a precipice. In these days we have an option: either to stop the madness or to bury the hope for a peaceful future of Russia. If events continue along the present path, the Russian state will disintegrate and the results will be felt for decades, perhaps for as much as a century."[32]

Assisted by Metropolitans Kirill and Iuvenali, Patriarch Aleksi began negotiations with the leaders of the parliament in order to seek a settlement between the opposing forces. On September 29, they met with the chairman of the Constitutional Court, V. D. Zor'kin, and the patriarch expressed his desire to mediate negotiations between the conflicting parties. On the same day the patriarch asked Iu. M. Luzhkov, the mayor of Moscow, to provide medical and food supplies and drinking water to the deputies inside the besieged White House.[33] As the tensions escalated on September 30 and October 1, information circulated that the several hundred deputies blockaded in the White House had weapons and intended to defend the building should it be attacked by government forces. Cognizant of these escalating tensions, the patriarch and the Holy Synod of the Russian Orthodox Church threatened excommunication for those people who first used weapons in the conflict: "We declare that whoever lifts up his hand against the powerless and sheds innocent blood will be excommunicated from the Church and will be anathematized."[34] In these actions the patriarch inserted the Orthodox Church directly as a mediator but also as a participant in the conflict, whose stakes in the outcome, for the church and the state, were extremely high.

The confrontation between the government and the parliament was resolved in the bloody events that began in the evening of October 3 and lasted for nearly a week. Patriarch Aleksi and Metropolitans Kirill and Iuvenali continued to try, until the last moments on October 3, to mediate the conflict, calling for national unity, solidarity, and reconciliation. The leading role in creating this unity, as the patriarch's words and actions suggested, belonged to the Orthodox Church. This was an old cry of the church, justifying its national mission and its "service to the state." But the cry also bespoke of the church's incarnational theology and its desire to harmonize the opposing political forces. In the ensuing days it continued to offer its services; in all Orthodox places of worship and monasteries the patriarch ordered a day of national mourning and prayers for the people who had died during the tragic events in Moscow and, to aid the reconciliation of the country, conducted joint funeral services for the dead.

It was also fitting that Friday, October 8, was the holy day of Saint Sergius of Radonezh, one of Russia's greatest conciliators. On that day the Holy Synod of the Orthodox Church, its top ecclesiastical body, held a special meeting in St Sergius's church, the Troitse-Sergieva Lavra, at Sergiev Posad. At that service, Aleksi II spoke movingly about the country's present condition. He saw the calamity primarily in spiritual terms, as devastating the spiritual conditions of the country, as the mark of Cain on the conscience of all those who participated in the shedding of blood: "Today we all lie under spiritual ruins. And we must help one another get out from under them, to clear them and to resume building our house in peace and harmony. All that has happened to us in the last tragic days is an indication of our spiritual and moral degradation."[35] He claimed that "without the spiritual renewal" of the Russian people, "it is impossible to heal the sickness of our society." As he looked at the question of what must be done immediately, the patriarch asserted the need "to return to peaceful life, ensure human rights and civil freedoms, and establish a lawful order in the country as soon as possible. We should abandon all discord and build the life of our Motherland."[36]

Aleksi II's actions during the crisis and his reconciling words at the conclusion recall the ambiguity and the dual image of the church's role in post-Communist Russia. The first image sees the church's primary mission as the bearer of an essentially moral and spiritual message, as above the fray or an objective observer, as an agent of mercy and healing, as a reminder of the Christian fundamentals relating to the home, the family, the sick, and the destitute. The second image relates to the world of privilege and to the power structure. This concept leads to the church's isolation and separation from the physical and spiritual needs of the society. In the words and deeds of the church and its leaders since the collapse of the Soviet Union, both images found powerful expression.

The church's behavior during the fateful Black October days lend themselves to different interpretations. To some analysts the patriarch's offer to mediate the crisis was admirable and provided a possible way out of a dangerously escalating political situation. His words were aimed at reconciliation and at trying to prevent the shedding of blood and the descent into civil war. He took the only course of action he had: to offer the church as a negotiator and peacemaker and to seek resolution of the conflict, regardless of the consequences that the church might suffer. As Metropolitan Iuvenali cried out on October 3, "Today, as many times in history through the ages, the fateful moment is repeated when people look to the Church and its Primate as a force which reconciles and eliminates discord in the Russian land."[37] The patriarch has since then talked about times when the church cannot stand back from politics and has to enter that arena. For the church, Black October presented one of those times.

But the church did insert itself strongly into politics. To some critics, the church's mediation bought time for parliamentary forces to prepare for the assault on the Ostankino television tower on the night of October 3.[38] Still other critics have argued that the actions of the patriarch hardly amounted to a neutral political role. The patriarch's threat of excommunication was aimed at members of the church involved in the conflict, and it also sought to establish his own moral expectations for their behavior. He tried to neutralize the weapons of the parliamentary forces. He offered these forces bread and water, threatened excommunication, and told them to give up their weapons. His message, in essence, supported Yeltsin's government and the "united opposition" to the parliament.[39]

What stands out in the church's role in the October crisis is the readiness of both the presidential and parliamentary sides in the conflict to accept the mediation of the church. Such readiness testifies to the moral authority the church commanded in the eyes of both protagonists. Leaders on both sides very much needed the church's support and, symbolically, the church could bestow this moral authority. Both parliament and Yeltsin were seeking another source of power, and the church offered it. Reflecting on the events of October, the Very Rev. Vsevolod Chaplin, secretary of the Department of External Church Relations of the Moscow patriarch, recalled the passionate rush to violence and the church's role in quelling it: At the most intense moment, "it is quite possible that without the dialogue in the monastic calm everything would have ended in greater bloodshed."[40]

A key element in the October crisis also concerns the failure of politicians on both sides to reach a compromise. Many observers have commented that this failure is one of the most disturbing features of Russian politics and its lack of democratic experience. The rejection of compromise, the desire to crush opponents by force, rather than to seek accommodation, has repeatedly characterized Russian attitudes toward political opposition. Analyzing the political consequences of the October crisis, the journalist Liudmila Tiulen' found that the main victim was the principle of compromise.[41]

During these tumultuous events, the leadership of the church was trying to find its voice, one that would speak effectively to a new community. This attempt was fraught with great difficulties, partly because of the oppression the church had suffered for many decades and partly because of the bewildering circumstances that now engulfed the whole society. As a close observer of the October events noted hopefully, the church's actions in these events contained signs of learning once again to "plea for the people" in confronting secular authority.[42] Certainly, such a place for memory and redemption marked the words of the patriarch on October 8, at Sergiev Posad: "The Lord Pantocrator and the All-Holy Virgin will work in this world through us, powerless and unworldly as we are; what will happen to Russia depends on us. If we take the path of revenge, violence, and chaos, the country will fall into a precipice. If the rulers of the country yield to the temptation to persecute those who are weaker than they are, they will ruin both themselves and our people."[43]

The events of 1993–94 set the stage for the next decade of Russian history and the early context for the main subjects of this book. This next decade witnessed an ongoing struggle to define the new political and social order, to develop new institutions, and to overcome the legacy of the Soviet past. The quest for legitimacy and authority would continue, as would, on an even deeper level than before, attempts to rediscover Russia's spiritual and cultural traditions. "Whither Russia?" and whether Russian society had the aspirations and the will to develop a civil society and to redefine its own commitments and values remained open questions. As Russia sought to rediscover and restore what Fr Aleksandr Men called its "lost and forgotten values from the past," Orthodoxy played a vital role in that process, simultaneously rediscovering its own "age-old values." What precisely was this changing landscape of social and religious attitudes and values to which Orthodoxy had to relate, and how did such attitudes and values manifest themselves during such a dynamic time of transition? In the 1990s, among Russian scholars these questions produced diverse answers.

To Dmitrii Efimovich Furman, one of Russia's most distinguished sociologists of religion, the "social pendulum" had swung dramatically from atheism to religion, a trend that originally began with Soviet dissidents in the

1960s and now embraced a large proportion of society. As codirector of the Institute of Sociology in the Academy of Sciences in 1996–97, he had completed two major surveys of religious attitudes and ethical values in present-day Russia. In the early 1990s, he believed, the pendulum had reached its apex, and had begun slowly to move back in the opposite direction. The social data in the second survey, conducted in 1996–97, showed 7 percent of the Russian population to be "traditional believers," who attended church services regularly, and 5.5 percent of the population to be atheists. The large group of people in the middle, 87.5 percent, is difficult to categorize, but it is the most intriguing. In the survey materials, they described their lives as characterized by great flux, the quest for new experiences, and the revolt against older ways of thinking.[44] They are the people who will essentially be constructing the future of Russia. "The major question," Furman thinks, "is what kind of society can be created from this social base?" He finds stability in the short run to be very unlikely, because "our data show little evidence of such stability, of a solid core of beliefs, of a consistent system of ethical values."[45]

To Furman's former student Sergei Borisovich Filatov, director of the Sociological Center of the Russian Sociological Foundation, the picture looked different. Filatov's sociological data were gathered by his institute in 1993–94. While he agreed with Furman that the present surveys of social values reveal little discernable pattern, he found in them elements of hope that did not stand out in the past. They suggested a reaction against previous Communist ideas and assertions, but he saw in them not a "pendulum swing," as Furman had characterized this reaction, but a movement toward something new, which was now taking shape but whose eventual construct was far from certain.[46] He saw reflected in the surveys a fundamental shift in attitude toward government and a lack of faith in its ability to solve social problems. But at the same time, especially among young people, from those in their late teens through their early thirties, the survey materials revealed a strong belief in the need to "serve people," to "serve society," even a sense of "higher calling" to "serve God," and to be part of a mutual aid society or a charitable organization. In a sense, the traditional theme of service to the state has been transformed and has taken on new meaning, which, to Filatov, exhibited the seeds of a nascent civil society.[47]

To Iurii Leonidovich Vasilevskii, doctoral candidate in psychology, the psychological process under way in Russia went beyond the capacities of political and religious institutions to respond to them. Vasilevskii's data came from surveys taken between 1992 and 1996 of ten thousand people in Russia and Ukraine. His study found that during this period Christian beliefs had increased but, surprisingly, non-Christian belief had grown even more, most dramatically among the young. The development of individual talents and personal relationships ranked as the highest aspirations among young people, and less than 10 percent claimed these aspirations were served through the church, through "Christian commitment," or through politics.[48] Such trends were confirmed by the work of Boris Vladimirovich Dubin, head research fellow at the Russian Center for Public Opinion Research (VTsIOM). In data collected in Moscow in May 1997, Dubin found that 41 percent of men and 58 percent of women in the capital city considered themselves Orthodox. More than half the individuals (54 percent) who identified themselves as Orthodox never attended church services and still another third (34 percent) went to church only several times a year. A large part of the people, particularly among the youth, were "searching for their place in life or experimenting with values that cover the range of possibilities," which generally did not fall within the boundaries of the official church.[49]

From Boris Yeltsin to Vladimir Putin

Boris Yeltsin had come to power in 1991 aiming to turn his back on the Soviet past and showing his disdain for the principles underlying the Soviet political order. His embrace of reformist ideas and perspectives, his advocacy of the need for a fresh start, aspired to cleanse Russia of the dogmatic thinking that had characterized the Soviet period. But in implementing reforms and opening up Russia to Western ideas and perspectives, he had also opened the doors to social chaos, to a cacophony of competing voices. Questions of how to rediscover and reconnect to traditional sources of renewal were often overshadowed by perspectives offering a multitude of answers to such questions as how to organize a democracy, how to privatize an economy, and how to accommodate diversity. The confusion and discomfort exhibited in social surveys in the mid-1990s were evidence of this social disorder, this lack of a moral and political center. "We have fallen into a condition of permanent historical catastrophe," wrote Igor' Volgin, the literary critic and Dostoevsky scholar, in 1995. "In this country the state has committed suicide." According to Volgin, "we exist in some kind of ill-defined, fantastical, artificial world, and the more it shows signs of being doomed, the louder its disciples try to convince us that it is completely the reverse."[50]

In 1996, Boris Yeltsin was reelected president of Russia. He owed much of his electoral victory to a powerful group of Russian multimillionaires—

media giants, oilmen, electricity magnates, and bankers—known as oligarchs, who gave their allegiance to him in return for wealth and influence. The oligarchs weathered the devastating financial collapse in August 1998 by engaging in property deals and manipulating the capital markets to their own advantage. The last three years of the twentieth century saw Yeltsin's popularity decline precipitously, his political image weakened by his inability to deliver economic miracles, his deteriorating physical condition, and his failure to fulfill the goals he had promised to reach.

The tension between a pluralistic society and state order had existed throughout the 1990s. In religious affairs, as Russia sought to rediscover its own unique heritage and traditions, the tension between these two forces was especially sharp. Church officials argued that the 1990 law "On Freedom of Conscience and on Religious Organizations" had opened the doors too wide to religious groups seeking to undermine Orthodoxy and replace it with "foreign proselytizing faiths." Such proselytizing faiths, church leaders claimed, showed little respect for Russia's own cultural and religious traditions; these officials proclaimed that foreign missionaries, with their large financial resources and their media expertise, "have started fighting with our church, like boxers in a ring with their pumped up muscles, delivering blows." The Moscow Patriarchate expressed resentment against the "massive influx" of foreign missionaries who started "a crusade against the Russian church, even as it began recovering from a prolonged disease, standing on its feet with weakened muscles."[51] The opening of the country had brought a perceived powerful assault on Russian religious and cultural traditions that Orthodox officials found extremely disturbing and ultimately destructive.

The conflict over the 1990 law, as the American legal scholar John Witte Jr. has pointed out, was both "a theological war" and "a legal war."[52] Western and Eastern missionaries viewed Russia as a great field for new converts; they saw a historic opportunity to proclaim their theological message and win Russian souls. By 1997, it is estimated that 5,606 foreign missionaries were active in the former Soviet Union, representing at least twenty five denominations and agencies.[53] Understandably, this rapid foreign incursion threatened the Orthodox hierarchy during a time when it was trying to recover its own theological voice and reestablish its spiritual leadership.

The controversy over the 1990 law also represented the struggle to develop "a new legal culture," to define the rights and privileges of religious organizations, while giving special privileges to those groups considered the preservers of the country's national heritage and repressing the rights of others, namely Western evangelists, mainline Protestants, and Roman Catholics.[54]

The government increasingly came to view the Orthodox Church as the fundamental source of Russia's moral authority, whose central tenets should not be left up to competition with foreign organizations. As a moral authority, the church greatly contributed to social stability. "Which Russia will be inherited by our grandchildren depends on us," said Aleksi II in April 1997. "Russia came to exist as a state on the basis of the Orthodox religion," the patriarch maintained, "and it is only on the basis of the Orthodox religion that the Motherland can regain its magnificence."[55] Earlier, in July 1993, the Russian parliament (officially still known as the Supreme Soviet) passed a new comprehensive law "On the Introduction of Changes and Additions to the RSFSR (Russian Soviet Federated Socialist Republic) Law on Freedom of Religion." President Yeltsin refused to sign the law, returning it to the chairman of the Supreme Soviet, Ruslan Khasbulatov, arguing that it "violated the Russian Constitution and international treaties." His letter to Khasbulatov sharply criticized the attempts to compromise the "equal rights of individuals to enjoy freedom of conscience and religion in the territory of Russia, regardless of their possession of Russian citizenship."[56]

Despite his earlier strong stand, President Yeltsin reversed his position and, on September 26, 1997, signed the new law "On Freedom of Conscience and on Religious Associations." The new law was enacted after four years of intense pressure brought in the Russian parliament and on the president by the Orthodox Church and by nationalist groups protesting the activities of foreign missionaries. The new law virtually repeated the proposed 1993 law. Pushed hastily through the working groups of the parliament in 1997 by Viktor Zorkaltsev, the Communist Party chairman of the committee on public organization and religious associations, with little opportunity for discussion and debate, the new law sought to limit religious liberty.[57] It confirmed in law a situation that already existed in reality in some of Russia's provincial regions.[58] The 1997 law, for all its inconsistencies, might also be seen not as a long-term but as a short-term pronouncement, part of the "birth pangs of a new political and legal order struggling to come forth in Russia."[59]

In contrast to the 1990 USSR law that prohibited religious discrimination, the 1997 law defined three different groups of religions in Russia, to whom it gave different privileges: the Russian Orthodox Church and its members, who would enjoy full legal privileges and certain financial, material, and other benefits from the state; various "traditional Christians," Jews, Muslims, and Buddhist groups, who would have full legal privileges but fewer benefits from the state; all other religious groups and individuals, who would in theory have freedom of worship and of conscience, would receive no state benefits, and would be required to register each year.[60] The preamble to the 1997 law "recognizes the special contribution of Orthodoxy to the history of Russia and to the establishment and development of Russia's spirituality and culture." The preamble also "respects Christianity, Islam, Buddhism, and Judaism, and other religions and creeds which constitute an inseparable part of the historic heritage of Russia's people."

A further contrast with the 1990 law is the 1997 law's contradiction of Russia's own constitutional structure and the "generally recognized principles and norms of international law."[61] Unlike the earlier law, the 1997 law imposed harsh restrictions on religious and, therefore, on human rights.[62] In essence, the 1997 law underscored a conflict that ran all through the 1990s: the clash between liberal principles and state stability, between freedom of conscience and civil rights and the preservation of the nation's heritage and moral values. To proponents of the first set of principles, civil society and democracy depended most of all on "freedom of conscience" and the ability of all citizens to choose freely their own beliefs, rights that the laws would protect in full. Recognition of "freedom of conscience" and acknowledgment of the "individual's ultimate accountability to God" provided the philosophical underpinnings of civil society, and the laws had to sanctify them.[63] In contrast, to proponents of the second set of principles, civil society in Russia could not be developed apart from the country's national heritage and traditions. Civil society required boundaries and ideals that flowed from these traditions. Following the most violent assault on such boundaries and ideals in modern history, they had to be rediscovered and renewed before Russia could move forward. Civil society did not emerge from a marketplace of competing voices and interests, but from re-creating the country's moral center. It was from this moral center—promoting social justice, respect for all the members of society, the dignity of the individual, the rights of each person in the community—that the future ought to be built.

The tension between these elements would become especially sharp during the tenure of Yeltsin's successor, Vladimir Vladimirovich Putin. On New Year's Eve 1999, Boris Yeltsin announced his decision to retire and allow Putin to become acting president, until a new election could be held within the constitutionally determined period of three months. In this presidential election Putin won by a large majority.[64] A tough-minded former KGB intelligence officer, Putin proved to be a pragmatic, extremely competent, and nonideological leader, well aware of Russia's deficiencies and its needs. He inherited the chief problems of Yeltsin's administration—its crime, corruption, threats to its territorial integrity, and the disorder in its legal system.

Putin immediately set about to strengthen the state, sometimes using ruthless and authoritarian tactics to accomplish this task. But he also sought to continue the reforms begun by Gorbachev and Yeltsin—the privatization policies, the political architecture, the attempts to nurture civil society, and the efforts to attract foreign investment and promote domestic entrepreneurship. "Our position is extremely clear," he said; "it is only a strong, an effective—if somebody does not like the word 'strong'—it is only an effective state and a democratic state if it is capable of protecting civic, political, and economic freedoms."[65] Among his greatest challenges, then, was finding the right balance between the power of the state and the power of society, between building the state's authority while also developing civil society.[66]

Putin knew that he needed the church, and not for reasons of personal faith but for reasons of state. The church offered a bridge to the rebuilding of national unity, as the guardian of national values and religious traditions. "The time of disunity is over," Patriarch Aleksi II announced in December 1999, in supporting the unification of Russia and Belarus.[67] In January 2000, he stated, "the Church has preserved its unity" at the end of a decade when regional authorities had proclaimed their independence and centrifugal forces threatened the disintegration of the former Soviet Union. "We took a firm stand," the patriarch recalled, thereby promoting the "centralization of church authority."[68] He favored the unification of territories of the former Soviet Union not through Marxist ideology but through the principles of the Orthodox Church.[69] The church would provide the civic values and the moral center that Russia lacked and greatly needed in order to restore its identity.

In his message to Aleksi II, congratulating him on the tenth anniversary of his patriarchal service, President Putin underscored this civic role: "The Russian Orthodox Church plays an enormous role in the spiritual unification of the Russian land after many years of life without faith, [of] moral degradation, and atheism. . . . The church is recovering its traditional mission as a key force in promoting social stability and moral unity around general moral priorities of justice, patriotism, good works, constructive labour and family values. Although it fell to you to lead the church in a difficult and confusing period, the past decade has become a unique time for the real regeneration of the moral foundations of society."[70]

As the Very Rev. Vsevolod Chaplin has emphasized: "The Church's abstention from participation in the political struggle should not entail its self-isolation from what is happening in the country and the world." The church spoke out on social and economic matters, questions of social morality, international relations, and the "development of general and European processes."

According to Chaplin, "the Church also is firmly prepared to promote a dialogue of public forces and their leaders in the interest of uniting its forces in service to the fatherland and the nation."[71] This dialogue the church had promoted in the 1993 crisis; as a mediator, a bridge between competing forces, a contributor to dialogue, and an aid to internal peace and reconciliation, the Orthodox Church stood ready to act.

From the beginning, Putin viewed the church as a main bulwark of national reconciliation. In his 2000 Christmas Eve address to Orthodox believers, the president wrote: "Orthodoxy has traditionally played a special role in Russian history. It has been not only a moral touchstone for every believer but also an unbending spiritual core of the entire people and state. Based on the idea of love for one's neighbor and on the commandments of good, mercy, and justice, Orthodoxy has largely determined the character of Russian civilization. . . . It is my firm belief as we are entering the third millennium today that its ideals will make it possible to strengthen mutual understanding and consensus in our society and will contribute to the spiritual and moral rebirth of the Fatherland." While there is little evidence in him of any personal faith commitment, Putin emphasized the church's role in building trust within society, in strengthening "mutual understanding and consensus in our society."[72] Public opinion surveys early in the twenty-first century showed that the Orthodox Church more than any other institution enjoyed the highest level of trust in Russian society, a perception the president used for his own pragmatic purposes.[73] Putin paid a lot of attention to Patriarch Aleksi II, requesting, as Yeltsin had, the patriarch's participation in his inauguration ceremony in the Kremlin and in visits with him at Peredelkino, the Solovetskii monastery, and Sergiev Posad. The president's veneration of holy sites suggested a strong commitment to national unity. It also showed his strong desire to distance himself from Russia's revolutionary past.[74]

Politically, he could hardly have made a better choice.

There are many ways to tell the story of the church's struggle to renew itself after the collapse of the Soviet state. The perspective of the Moscow patriarchy presents one side of a multifaceted tale. Recounted from that viewpoint, however, the story misses much of the day-to-day encounters, the challenges and dilemmas met on the ground floor, and the successes and defeats, the hopes and the frustrations, and the men and women in the parishes who aspired to rediscover and to rebuild. To these encounters, the next chapters now turn, and to the multifarious efforts to rebuild life in the parishes and local communities, where, it might be said, civil society must begin.

3 Father Georgii Kochetkov and the Politics of Memory

The Orthodox conception of community is central to its teachings. The concept of *sobornost'* or "conciliarity" has long been one of Orthodoxy's main strengths; it means to be imbued with the practices and traditions of the church, to experience oneself as part of a larger society, and to understand one's connections to the whole of creation. *Sobornost'* does not imply that the individual should renounce all self-expression or that individual ideas and talents are little valued, but that each person is inescapably part of a larger body—including the holy fathers, the saints, the great teachers, and the current members of the church.

It was this concept of conciliarity, sustained by love and freedom, that the nineteenth-century Slavophile theologian Aleksei Stepanovich Khomiakov defined as one of the keystones of Orthodoxy. In his view, the church was not an authority, but a union of free believers who were organically connected. "In the fullness of its divine doctrine," Khomiakov emphasized, Orthodox Christianity "propounded the ideas of unity and freedom, indissolubly joined together in *the moral law of mutual love.*"[1] Religious experience thus had meaning primarily within the church, "amidst the faithful assembled in prayer."[2]

As a theological conception, *sobornost'* was related to many of the central values of Russian society, especially the belief that all members of the community were united in a common bond. Such solidarity was a central ideal of the old peasant community, the *mir*. The *mir* offered a supportive community that helped the sick and old, gave mutual aid to the needy, took care of all its members, and provided a warm and supportive atmosphere. Although the *mir* was officially disbanded by Stalin in 1929, this spirit of camaraderie would later become transplanted into the urban world in the Soviet Union; workers who themselves were uprooted from their villages tried to re-create similar networks at their workplaces or in their apartments.[3] Something of this community spirit could be found within the intelligentsia in the cohesive little circles that met for discussion and, often, spiritual support. The search for spiritual support had marked religious dissidents in the 1970s and 1980s. Disillusioned with Soviet Marxism, looking for what they called a "more honest view of the world," they had not found this community in the Orthodox Church because of its inability to develop an active parish life.[4]

The same ideas were to resurface during and after the collapse of Communist rule. Seeking to regain its identity and its own traditions, the Orthodox Church now faced a crucial question: how to define its relationship to the people flocking in such large numbers into its sanctuaries. In the early 1990s, as the Orthodox Church began to recover its voice and its own sense of identity, church leaders focused on the parish as a central part of this process. In 1990 Orthodox participants in a roundtable discussion in Moscow "acknowledged the special significance of the parish" for rehabilitating Russian society and transforming the role of the Orthodox Church in that society. The spiritual and moral resuscitation of the Russian people, participants in the discussion claimed, depended heavily on the rebirth of the parish. It was there that the church touched most basically the life of the people.

While these church leaders emphasized the importance of the parishes, they also saw clearly the challenges facing them. As Fr Vladimir Rozhkov, who served in one of Moscow's largest parishes, pointed out, the chief difficulties were not physical and material, but mental and spiritual. The parish, he noted, "is not a territory, but is essentially a people and is, therefore, extremely hard to reconstruct."[5] When a very large percentage of the people living in a given district "rarely take an active part in parish life or come to the Church only accidentally or on Easter," Fr Vladimir asked, "how can we meaningfully call this territory a parish?" The renewal of parish life, in these terms, heavily depended on the church's ability to overcome the people's indifference and speak to their needs.

Yet addressing these needs presented special difficulties. Church leaders had to understand what such needs were and how they had emerged. Church leaders, Fr Vladimir emphasized, had to draw much closer to the people they served; they had to "know well the lives of the people who resided in their parish." Church leaders too often lived outside their parishes, related poorly to the people, and came to their parishes only to direct church services.[6] Such leaders rarely met their parishioners outside the formal, officially scheduled church services and rituals. In rebuilding the parish, participants in the roundtable discussion emphasized, it was important that church leaders break through these formal structures, meet with parishioners in unofficial locations, and overcome the general inertia that had long characterized parish life.[7]

As a disappointed convert in the 1980s had complained: "In the Church there is almost no Christian interpersonal sociability, no activity in fulfillment of the second commandment. How many lonely old people are too weak to leave their homes for bread or medicine, and the people with whom they have prayed together for years don't even know of their plight?"[8] The need to re-build the spirit of community, which the church had once seen as one of its greatest resources, was a paramount challenge and concern.[9]

In the early 1990s, Metropolitan Kirill addressed the subject in his attempt to define the most pressing issues facing the church. He spoke in detail about the revival of parish life in Russian towns and villages, especially where a sense of community hardly existed and "people did not know each other." These conditions created a moral and spiritual vacuum, a feeling of isolation, and the "lack of any center." Metropolitan Kirill especially underscored the importance of rediscovering *miloserdie* (compassion) and charity. "We must have," he said, "a revival of these elements; they are essential characteristics of a Christian community," qualities that had to be implanted at the center of the parish.[10] Children, the elderly, and the infirm were among the most vulnerable people in Russian society, and in re-creating the parish community, Metropolitan Kirill believed, concern for them ought to be the organizing principle.[11]

In articulating such principles and needs, Metropolitan Kirill and other church leaders expressed what might be called a rudimentary social doctrine of the Orthodox Church. Their principles also related to the development of civil society; the charity, compassion, energy, community, and social action they proposed to nourish and encourage are key elements in the creation of social capital. But whether the theoretical statements and goals these leaders voiced could effectively be put into practice remained open questions. In the decade following, how were such goals demonstrated in reality? In the practical circumstances of parish life, did these modes of religious discourse bear fruit or were they repelled or circumvented by other elements?

The large number of people flocking into the churches in the late 1980s and early 1990s came for various reasons: many were curious and wanted a firsthand taste of what had long been discouraged or even forbidden; still others came to gain spiritual strength through the liturgy, to be nourished by the contemplative tradition of the church's teachers and holy men, and to experience the unforgettable beauty, warmth, and fraternal spirit of the service itself. This spirit is beautifully evoked by Serge Schmemann in his portrayal of the Easter service in his ancestral village of Sergeevskoe (Koltsovo), near Kaluga: "In the great images of the Holy Week services, the horror of man's sin and the suffering of the Creator leading to the great triumph of the resurrection, I suddenly discovered that eternal, indestructible beginning, which was also in that temporarily quiet spring, hiding in itself the seed of a total renewal of all that lives."[12] To many worshippers, the quest for this spirit of renewal related to the social and personal needs they saw all around them following the collapse of the Communist state. They wanted to become part of a larger and different kind of community than they had previously experienced.

A key part of the perceived detachment from the real needs of parishioners concerned the use of language in the service. The church hierarchy insisted that the entire Orthodox Church service continue to be performed in the traditional language of the church, whereas others desired an accessible vernacular liturgy. But the fundamental issues behind this conflict of opinion related to much more than the use of words. They involved the whole conception of Christianity: the relationship of priests and other leaders of the church to their congregations and the ability of the church to relate its message to the present, to "translate" the Gospel to people whose background and previous exposure to the teachings of Christianity had been minimal.

For traditionalists, the old language of the church posed no more than a fleeting problem to the worshipper, because the sights and sounds of the service held the greatest meaning; with patience, one could gain access to the divine word and experience the great beauty and sense of wholeness that the Orthodox service provided. To change the language, they felt, would be to change the essence of the church's message. It would be "to give in to the Church as entertainment, to make its members too lazy to participate actively, and to take away from the service the sense of struggle, the need to involve one's entire mind and soul," as a young priest at the Orthodox theological academy at Sergiev Posad said.[13] The traditionalists see the reformers as undermining sacred elements of the church, and they wish to keep these elements intact. Additionally, traditionalists are suspicious of any reforms that are implemented too hastily, especially at the present time, when the urge to discard earlier practices is everywhere evident. As a literary critic and scholar of Russian culture, Evgeniia Viktorovna Ivanova, warned: "For modern culture, it is typical to consent to progress, to accept the new trends uncritically, as a movement forward, as progressive, positive developments. Everything new is considered superior to the old. The Church, however, is one institution in our society that should not support this approach; not every new word or idea is better than the old."[14]

Reformers, on the other hand, contend that unless the church presents its theological message in language that is understandable, the message will remain incomprehensible to the majority of the people, and the church will lose an unusual opportunity to relate its message to a population hungry for spiritual substance in their lives. As the reformers like to point out, this is not a new issue. Modernizing the language of the church service was discussed at length in ecclesiastical conferences early in the twentieth century, before and during the Russian Revolution of 1917.[15] The issue resurfaced in one of the last church conferences in the Soviet period, held during the millennium celebrations of 1988, conferences attended both by clergy and by Russian philosophers and philologists.

At that meeting, convened in Leningrad, a debate developed between two distinguished scholars, Gelian Prokhorov, who argued for retaining the old church Slavonic texts, and Sergei Averintsev, who proposed their translation into modern Russian.[16] Prokhorov argued that it is through the language that the person comes to know God; language explicates the essence of the service—the liturgy, the singing, the reading of the scriptures. Language, he said, holds everything together, and through study of the old church Slavonic language, the worshipper comes to understand the divine service. Averintsev, who had previously made several superb translations of texts for the divine service, disagreed. He maintained that the church had to overcome its distance from the people; while preserving its traditions, it had also to make its message understandable to a population yearning for spiritual meaning. It had to bring directly to them the spiritual benefits that Orthodoxy offered, in contrast to the shallow doctrines of historical materialism that the Soviet state had promulgated.

The clash over the two different visions of Orthodoxy and over the outer forms of worship would generate a great deal of conflict. While outwardly the church may have appeared calm, inside the church leadership and in its seminaries, the question of reform, centering on the language issue, sparked heated debate.[17] The controversy particularly centered on Fr Georgii Kochetkov and his community at the church of the monastery of the Presentation in Moscow, where the language reforms had been put into effect. Kochetkov's parish community served as a living model for the reform effort; its existence, as well as its growing strength, threatened traditionalists, both within and outside the church, who saw in Kochetkov's actions a dangerous, misguided effort to undermine sacred forms. The controversy would quickly spill over into other concerns, leading to charges of "heresy" against Fr Georgii and of undermining the Orthodox Church.

The conflicts that were brewing inside the church in the 1990s in some ways mirror the issues that led to the Great Church Schism in the seventeenth century (1666–67). Both conflicts began over the problem of reform, including the modernization of liturgical language and of the forms to be used in worship, reforms that many saw as tampering with the essence of Christianity. Both disputes emerged over seemingly local, specific matters that quickly escalated in intensity and appeared to threaten the church's identity.[18] Both controversies originated within the church but, as passions on both sides became more heated, attracted the attention of social and political forces outside the church. The 1667 church schism was one of the defining moments of Russian history and marked what the historian James H. Billington has referred to as *perelom,* a sharp division, the culmination of a fever, whose effects would have lasting consequences.[19] The Kochetkov case in the 1990s clearly does not have such historical magnitude, but the problems it raised have long-lasting implications. Fr Georgii's activities and the responses they provoked would intersect with other fundamental issues: the development of parish life and community, the problem of violence, and the moral education of the citizenry.

Fr Georgii

A slim person of medium height, Kochetkov's demeanor suggests considerable energy and passion for his parish ministry. He speaks softly, though with a great deal of expression, and he is clearly a person of much warmth, as evidenced by his constant presence with people, including small children, who approach him with confidence and ease. He is a priest who clearly does not distance himself from the members of his parish. The services he conducted expressed a quiet reverence, a genuine caring for people, and a seriousness but also joy at being part of this community.

Born in 1950 in Moscow to parents who were not members of the Communist Party, Kochetkov learned early to be disciplined and self-directed. "My father and mother had their own principles and beliefs," he said; "they had some difficulties in dealing with the rigid Soviet system, but they always felt they were free internally and they never made compromises with the Soviet government or the police." His parents taught their children to preserve their own inner life and not to submit to the outward authority of the state or the party. Growing up in the 1950s and 1960s, Kochetkov experienced the questioning and the political turmoil of the Khrushchev and early Brezhnev periods, when certain cracks and strains in the system were already becoming apparent. These were times of idealism and hope, but also of growing disillusionment—of Khrushchev's utopian dreams of Soviet communism but also his denunciation, in 1956, of the recent Communist past, when, in his "secret speech" to the Twentieth Party Congress, he denounced the crimes of Stalin. In 1962, he extended his criticism of Stalin's misdeeds, moving beyond Stalin himself to the Soviet system and to the conditions supporting these crimes. They were years, too, marked by important literary events—in 1957 the publication abroad of Boris Pasternak's *Doctor Zhivago,* in 1962 the publication of Aleksandr Solzhenitsyn's *One Day in the Life of Ivan Denisovich,* and in 1967 of Mikhail Bulgakov's *The Master and Margarita.* These novels evidenced new ways of looking at the world and were works of considerable philosophical and spiritual depth. Young Kochetkov was doubtless sensitive to the social, intellectual, and religious ferment percolating all around him, questioning the past and the authoritarian structures that had shaped it.

Kochetkov decided to become an Orthodox priest in the late 1970s. At the university, he had studied economics, then entered the graduate program at Moscow State University in 1974, where he spent the next four years studying political economy. His evolution toward the priesthood seems to have occurred gradually, the product of his own increasing sensitivity to Christianity as a way of life and his increasing cynicism about the Soviet state. In 1978 he changed the course of his life, committing himself to the church; two years later he was admitted to the Ecclesiastical Academy in Leningrad. Thus he began a journey that would take many turns, both difficult and exhilarating, provide him with an excellent education, and connect him to the world outside the classroom.

During his years in Leningrad, Kochetkov met with several other religious groups, engaging in discussions, exploring theological works in much depth, and meeting and engaging with foreign religious groups from whom he learned approaches to the church and to religious activity different from the Orthodox and from his experiences in the classroom. His encounters with these different faiths, these diverse worlds, would remain with him for many years and sharpen his understanding of their views and their contrasting techniques and approaches to worship. At the Ecclesiastical Academy, his academic performance earned him high marks; he ranked near the top of his class. Despite his academic record, however, Kochetkov's extracurricular activities, his contacts with dissident religious groups and with foreigners in Leningrad, attracted the attention of the police. Shortly before his scheduled graduation from the Ecclesiastical Academy in 1984, he was expelled. In the mid-1980s, his degree unfinished, in difficulty with the authorities, unable to find a job either in the church or in the workplace, he entered an extremely difficult time in his life. He relied on his friends to sustain him. He moved from place to place, living on the edge of life in Leningrad, experiencing the city in all its diversity, trying to survive. All the time he was reading widely and studying, preparing himself for what he would later describe as his own religious journey into the priesthood.

When the renewal of the church came in 1988, Kochetkov's life changed dramatically. As a member of the church trying to expand its activities and re-open formerly closed churches, he received an assignment as priest in a small town near Moscow, named Elektro-izba, whose local church was in extremely sad condition. The church building had not been repaired for many decades; the walls were crumbling, and grass was growing through cracks in the floor. Several years later, Kochetkov would recall these humble beginnings both with joy and incredulity: "I started my ministry at the bottom level in this small town; only the walls of the local church were standing. The church had neither windows nor doors, and in the winter, during the service the temperature in the church sometimes reached minus fifteen degrees and snow blew through the open windows and fell on our heads."[20]

Yet this experience taught him how to reach out and to build from the lowest possible level and it gave him exposure to people's circumstances at the end of the Soviet period. He served in this local parish for more than a year, prior to his transfer, in 1990, to Moscow and to the church of the monastery of the Presentation. That is the position he held until conflict erupted over his methods, and he ran into difficulty with the Moscow Patriarchate.

In describing his journey from university to theological seminary to his expulsion and his private studies, then to his appointment in the church, Kochetkov recalled the experiences and encounters that had shaped his own personal vision. He recounted his association with non-Orthodox groups in Leningrad in the late 1970s, particularly with Baptists, associations that eventually led to his troubles with the police. Kochetkov remembered these unofficial contacts with Baptists as being extremely helpful to his own spiritual development, because, he said, "they raised questions that I had never thought about before, and they stimulated my friends and me to study and to look at our own faith in new ways." Such questions related to the nature of the church service, to the interpretation of the Scriptures, and to certain theological issues concerning the relationship of the church and the community. According to Fr Georgii, he and his friends had paid little attention to such questions prior to the contacts: "We didn't need the answers before. No one had cared, since we had never raised these questions. The contacts we had sharpened our vision and helped us to become better Orthodox believers. Such experiences enabled us to understand better our own religious commitments and to deepen knowledge of our faith."

To Fr Georgii, as to Aleksandr Men earlier, the contacts with other religious denominations were essential to the Orthodox Church, especially at a time when the church sought to reestablish itself. He believed the church had to open itself to a dialogue with different kinds of traditions, because such dialogue would enable the church to recover its own traditions and beliefs and sharpen its ability to articulate them. Open discussion with Protestants and Catholics, he claimed, would not weaken the church but would resolve what he called "the contradictions in its own practices."[21] But his emphasis on dialogue did not extend only outward; he believed the church also had to look inward, to find guidance in parts of its own history, and it was from that source that he discovered the historical justification to support his reforms.

When he discusses these subjects, Fr Georgii's demeanor is serious, but he also exhibits a lot of emotion and passion. He has not led a comfortable life nor have his intellectual explorations always had successful endings. He is a person who has read a great deal, who has immersed himself in Orthodox history and theology, as well as the history of Russia. "In my view," said a member of the religious intelligentsia, "Kochetkov has read more history and theology than anyone [else] in our Church leadership."[22] Both of his parishes in Moscow attracted members of the Russian intelligentsia and, following the death of Fr Aleksandr Men, became major centers for their gathering. His appeals to them lay not only in the reforms that he boldly advanced but also in his theological teachings and in the kind of parish community that he organized. His actions displayed a great deal of courage. As a person, both in his appearance and in his actions, he is constantly questioning, probing, pushing accepted boundaries, and looking into church traditions for ways of dealing with some of his country's most pressing problems. He is a passionate believer that the renewal of the parish is central to Orthodoxy's future well being.

In 1995 he described his parish community as follows:

> As I look at the last two years, I think that we have entered the open sea. The actual life in our community has achieved a quality that was lacking in the Orthodox Church in the last seventy years. When everything we aspired to develop in our spiritual life was blocked and everything was closed, this quality could not exist, much less could it thrive. Presently, our community is adrift in the sea, with nowhere to cast our anchor. According to the old symbolism, the Church is the anchor of salvation, the place where one finds peace in one's soul, the place where one meets God. And yet it also faces enormous problems and feels intense pressure from many different quarters.

Since 1991, a large number of people have entered the Church but they have continued to view the Church through either the prisms of ideology or national patriotism. According to both prisms, if you are Russian, you are automatically an Orthodox believer. But we take the opposite view: if you are Orthodox, you may or may not be Russian. When the nationalists look at the Church, they see national identity to be the principal feature. When we view the Church, we see it as universal, embracing the world, reflecting God's trust. The Church represents love and freedom, and they cannot be limited to Russia's identity. . . . In the last year, we lost our main cathedral, were forced to close our kindergarten, and suffered a large cut in funds, but at the same time we have gained much by our experience of functioning in an open sea. We have developed a large number of contacts with other religions denominations; we have communicated with theologians of different schools, Orthodox and non-Orthodox, and while we had such relationships earlier, they were never as many or as rich as they are now.[23]

How did he seek to reconstruct his parish and on what principles? In the harsh conditions of Russia in the 1990s, what were the concrete realities in which his parish operated, and with what results?

Rival Visions

Built in the seventeenth century, the church of the monastery of the Presentation is one of Moscow's most venerated and beautiful churches. Located near the Kremlin, the monastery stands in Kutchko Field, the former place of execution for criminals and political rebels, but here also, on the site of the cathedral, the Vladimir Virgin is said to have ascended into heaven in 1395. This is, therefore, a mystical site, offering the possibility of redemption and reform, but it is also a political place, symbolizing bereavement and protest. The case of Fr Georgii embodies both these elements.

In the neighborhood of his parish, Kochetkov created a new kind of community where people worked and worshipped together. In those difficult times in Russia, when family life and communal ties had been shattered, he developed in the center of Russia's largest city a congregation whose members supported each other, providing charity to the neediest among them and emotional help to those whose lives had been uprooted. But the main focus of Fr Georgii's community was on worship, through a new liturgy of the church, which he instituted among his followers. Rather than using the old Slavonic liturgy, he performed it in modern Russian. The texts and prayers were skillfully translated by Sergei Averintsev, the philologist, stylist, and poet, who became a member of the parish. Using Averintsev's translations, Fr Georgii employed the vernacular to move his congregation in new, more direct, more personal approaches to worship.[24]

The attempts to render in Russian some of the texts of the service began in the church of the monastery of the Presentation in 1991, in the months preceding the collapse of the Soviet state. Concurrent with the use of vernacular Russian, Kochetkov introduced other reforms in his parish as part of his renewal efforts. He established a school for children, a higher Christian school for adults in the community, and a journal titled *Orthodox Community* (*Pravoslavnaia Obshchina*). He published the journal six times a year, serving as its chief editor and viewing it as a means of binding together his parishioners and engaging in discussion with them. *Pravoslavnaia Obshchina* contained Kochetkov's writings, as well as articles written by leading members of his parish, literary essays, and reprints of theological/philosophical essays written at the beginning of the twentieth century.[25] In addition, he created an adult organization named the Preobrazhenskoe Brotherhood (*Preobrazhenskoe bratstvo*), and it too served as a multiheaded center of leadership and a means of organizing his parish.

Kochetkov explored the chief organizational principles of the parish in an essay originally written in 1988, near the beginning of perestroika in the Soviet Union. The essay remained for several years unpublished, until it appeared in the first issue of *Pravoslavnaia obshchina* in 1991. In the article, Fr Georgii discussed several dilemmas facing the church and society in present-day Russia, and he outlined his views of parish life and what had to be done to revive and enliven it. He criticized the church's present administrative structure for its failure to promote the spirit of community, arguing that this structure encouraged the opposite development, isolation. The parish, he pointed out, is part of a diocese under the supervision of the bishop or archbishop. In most cases, such an official had little connection with or interest in the daily problems confronting parishioners, because the appointment came from the top of the church hierarchy. Consequently, the bishop's and archbishop's fundamental allegiance and attention were not directed to the community but to the upper echelons of the administrative structure. Church officials were isolated from the major social issues that confronted parish priests and members of the parish community every day. Until the church hierarchy and the parish community bridged their separate worlds, they would be unable to truly create the "symphony" that the church officially affirmed in the new church charter issued in June 1988, which formally recognized the parish as the fundamental self-governing unit of the Orthodox Church.[26]

Kochetkov viewed the general framework of the church as anachronistic. Its centralized, inflexible, hierarchical organization fit the needs of a much earlier time in history, but it could not deal effectively with the complexities of present-day Russia and the religious and moral needs of the people. Kochetkov criticized a litany of psychological and social qualities that had resulted: the church's lack of adaptability, its absorption with nourishing its own power, its debilitating tendencies to turn inward, and its failure to connect to the daily concerns of the people who lived in the parish. The leadership of the church had little connection to its main body but operated in some preposterous realm of its own, in disharmony with the body, like the "Tom-Cat" in E. T. A. Hoffmann's fantastical tales or the "Nose" in Gogol's short story.[27] Rather than create unity, such a structure had provoked disunity.

To Kochetkov, the church had devoted its attention primarily to restoring the "old forms." It had, therefore, become inaccessible to large numbers of people who needed its teachings and who were searching for meaning in a society turned upside down. Like other reformers, he believed that, for the church to be effective, it had to concern itself first with correcting its own internal weaknesses, beginning with asking forgiveness for its "sins" and "historical mistakes." Such acts of humility and contrition would set the stage for the church to become more credible, would lay the foundation for it to become more dynamic and creative, to narrow the gap between the hierarchy and the people, and to direct its attention at the local level.[28]

While Fr Aleksandr Men had focused on recovering the church's independent voice, Kochetkov extended this recovery further, to the parish. He saw the key to the church's renewal in re-creating the community and reviving *sobornost'*. To achieve the renewal of community life, the parish had to gain greater independence from the hierarchy of power. The church, he believed, would work more effectively as a local community, responsive in language and methods suited to local circumstances and to the spiritual needs of its people, rather than as a hierarchical organization. Fr Georgii saw aspirations for community everywhere ascendant in Russian society—in the informal organizations and associations—that now needed further encouragement and cultivation. Many of these "informals," *informalnye,* had started as circles of friends, gathering for reading, for study, for making pilgrimages to monasteries, for discussing sacred writings, for working together and engaging in social service, as well as for many other purposes.[29] To him, the *informalnye* bore the hope of the future.

From the beginning, Fr Georgii sent to the Moscow Patriarch reports, materials, examples of translations, and descriptions of activities taking place at the monastery. "We requested [the patriarch's] blessings on our school, our journal, our practices toward children, and the use of the Russian language in some of our religious texts," recounted Aleksandr Kopirovskii, one of Fr Georgii's close associates. But during all of 1991, 1992, and most of 1993, the patriarch did not respond to the activities taking place at the monastery. Fr Georgii's organization did not hear anything from the patriarch's office, negative or otherwise, Kopirovskii said; "we were given to understand that none of the reforms we were making was forbidden to us."[30]

In the fall of 1993, however, these circumstances changed. Fr Georgii was summoned to an audience in the patriarch's office to answer a series of questions about his monastery's activities. The discussion that took place there, Kopirovskii recalled, was extremely difficult, but Fr Georgii responded to the questions clearly and in detail, and he left the meeting feeling that he had alleviated the misgivings that church officials had expressed. But, within a week, an article in the archconservative newspaper *Russkii vestnik* appeared, written by members of an organization called the Union of Orthodox Brotherhood, accusing Kochetkov of heresy and conspiracy against the church.[31] The letter writers viewed Fr Georgii's reforms as an attack on the church itself and on the core of Russia's cultural identity. Instead of continuing the conversation with Kochetkov about his activities, the patriarch now chose to terminate it and, yielding to pressure from traditionalist groups, called Fr Georgii to appear before the bishop's council. This meeting took place on January 31, 1994, and the bishops categorically demanded that Fr Georgii cease using the modern Russian language in his services.

Rather than ending the conflict between these two visions of Orthodoxy within the church, the decision of the bishops' council escalated it. At the meeting of the bishops' council, Fr Georgii told church leaders that, while he submitted to their decision, as he was canonically obligated, he respectfully disagreed with them. At a time when Russia needed spiritual enlightenment, he argued, such teaching had not come forth, and a wide gap continued to separate the church and the people. These assertions apparently angered members of the bishops' council, who again ordered Kochetkov to comply with their decision; they threatened to close his parish and "fence him off from his flock and his flock from him." Fr Georgii's answer to this statement could only have further angered church officials; he accused them of threatening violence in resolving internal church disputes: "I simply named things," he said later; "I called their actions by their proper names."[32] Immediately after the meeting, Fr Georgii sent Aleksi II a petition, expressing his dismay at the bishops' decision and requesting a reexamination of the facts. His request was denied.

At the same time that these events were taking place within the church hierarchy, other kinds of pressure were being brought to bear directly on Fr Georgii and his followers. Ultraconservative groups outside the church began to engage in the dispute and to seek out church leaders who had sown "heresy," as writers of the letter to *Russkii vestnik* had termed Kochetkov's reforms. During the Christmas holidays, in January 1994, the monastery received a series of threatening telephone calls. One of the calls urged a meeting with a priest, Fr Tikhon Shevkunov, who had close ties with ultraconservative political organizations. We have only Kochetkov's account of the conversation. At the meeting, Fr Tikhon threatened his dismissal: "If you do not do as we say, then we will see that you will soon be serving the liturgy on the street, rather than in the church," he said. Fr Tikhon was very firm in his demands: he promised to bring in security forces should Kochetkov and his followers refuse to comply, and then, should that not be enough, he threatened to call upon some of his acquaintances in the Russian Mafia.

Kochetkov and his associates understood these remarkable statements to be provocations, which would soon lead to some kind of action. To prepare for such circumstances, they closed the doors of the main cathedral where they had conducted services in Russian, and moved into a smaller church within the monastery. On a late January evening in 1994, the threatened violence that Fr Tikhon had mentioned became a reality. Fr Tikhon and his people, who numbered about one hundred, gathered in the streets outside the gates of the monastery. According to Kochetkov, the crowd included a mixture of soldiers, street criminals, and members of the Black Hundreds—the latter an ultraconservative, anti-Semitic organization. Fr Georgii and his associates remained inside the church throughout the night, discussing what they should do and eventually deciding, when the morning came, that they would throw open the doors of the church. Repeatedly, they heard members of the crowd outside question Fr Tikhon about when they were going to strike, how they were going to force open the doors and "deal with the Jews inside."

When the morning came, Fr Georgii opened the doors, as he had planned, and began to perform the liturgy. The effect on the crowd was one of great surprise. Aleksandr Kopirovskii heard one of the soldiers say, "Where is the enemy? Where are those we have come to oppose?" Still another expressed his bewilderment, "This is an Orthodox Church." When members of the mob saw that they were witnessing an Orthodox service, their mood quickly changed and, soon afterward, they began to leave the courtyard. Violence, on that occasion, was averted, but the comfort Fr Georgii and his followers might have felt would be short-lived, because several days later they received orders from the patriarch to leave the church of the monastery of the Presentation and move to a much smaller church in a nearby neighborhood of Moscow.

The issues dividing Kochetkov and the bishops' council represent their differing visions of the church's mission and social role. Kochetkov's reinterpretation of church tradition, his use of the vernacular in the services, his refusal to bend to the hierarchy's admonitions, and his outreach to diverse faiths provoked the hierarchy's ire. But these differences do not fully explain the passionate emotional responses that the events inflamed nor convey the depth of the antagonisms that Kochetkov's circle inspired, either within the church or within certain traditionalist social groups. As Igor' Vinogradov, chief editor of the journal *Kontinent,* asked, "Why did Kochetkov and his associates arouse so much heat and enthusiasm, on such a scale, and what religious and social nerves had they touched to cause such violent opposition?"[33]

These were issues that greatly troubled Fr Georgii. One explanation, he believed, lay in the different approaches that the Moscow patriarchy and he took to the restoration of Christianity in Russia, efforts that involved a whole range of reforms, in addition to changes in the language. As the church struggled to resolve issues important to its own identity, problems lying dormant for many years and brought quickly to the surface in the 1990s became explosive. In looking back at periods of church reform in Russia's history, Fr Georgii pointed out that the most successful "reforms had evolved organically, within the Church itself, over an extended period of time."[34] Early in the twentieth century, he maintained, the church council had instituted basic changes in religious practice and resolved its disputes peacefully within. Church resolutions took place following a long period of preparation and did not inspire heated controversy that spilled out into society. But in the 1990s, the church was unprepared, in essence, to confront the dilemmas of speaking to a postcommunist society. For nearly a century, it had not been allowed to engage with the larger culture around it.

A second explanation lay within the church itself, not with its theology, but with those who interpreted that theology and the tendency, expressed repeatedly in the twentieth century, to view the world in simplistic terms. Kochetkov admitted his own difficulties in understanding why the search for external enemies had occupied such a predominant place in Russian thought. Part of this tendency had come from the desire to create internal cohesion, a fatal weakness in the church's perspective. Even before the Bolsheviks came to power, Kochetkov observed, "it was considered a mark of loyalty in the Church for members of the higher orders to demonstrate unity with the Russian people and identify certain 'enemies of the people.'"[35]

This need to express unity with the people historically had produced dangerous trends, and while church officials might not formally have joined ultranationalist groups, they were often sympathetic to their ideals, including the ideals of the Black Hundreds, the ultranationalist group that had operated early in the twentieth century and had now reemerged. There is a tendency within the church, according to Kochetkov, especially "when it is frightened, when something it regards as threatening confronts it," toward hysteria, which causes "mirages, with accompanying phantoms, to take shape in the consciousness of our people." The church has had an unfortunate tendency to view itself as under assault—from Catholics, from Muslims, and from other faiths—and this perception had also bred hysteria, the claim that such religions are "anti-Christ." Russian Orthodoxy, Fr Georgii argued, had to grow beyond such tendencies; it had to identify the psychological causes of this hysteria, which had fostered violence and shaped its own tragic history in the twentieth century.[36]

Third, in speaking of the church hierarchy, Kochetkov was severely critical of its lack of creativity. "The processes within the Church," he said, "resemble the standards and norms of the eighteenth century."[37] While these standards were based on religious principles, they were principles "of the most conservative kind": they focused on ritual, prized ceremony, sought cooperation with the absolutist state, and turned away from the concrete problems of the world. What the church ought to be, Kochetkov maintained, quoting the distinguished Russian cellist Mstislav Rostropovich, was a window, a spiritual *fortochka,* that provided ventilation in the house and brought "fresh spiritual wind into an ordinary day."[38]

Reconciling memory with current needs and realities, restoring the ecclesiastical order of the past with the present, and reclaiming traditions in a situation in which they were dimly or selectively remembered can create great opportunities; they can also produce sharp conflicts. In such a context, the words of a leading Russian authority on church history at the beginning of the twentieth century, Vasilii Bolotov, bear recalling: "I think there is no greater mistake than the attempt to restore the ecclesiastical order of a distant past. Only a reform that really responds to the needs of the present time, accompanied by the improvements resulting therefrom, can be regarded as truly canonical, even if it is without a single historical precedent. Church history is only a useful record; it is in no way a code of laws. The Sabbath was made for man, not man for the Sabbath."[39] Fr Georgii Kochetkov acted in such a spirit, seeing Orthodoxy as a living tradition, not as something malleable, but as a faith that is profoundly relevant to the contemporary situation. Rather than trying to break the connection between religious experience and social life, he embraced that connection.

Still a fourth explanation relates to the circumstances in which the church found itself after more than seventy years of Bolshevik rule. As the church struggled to redefine itself and renew its mission, it also sought to restore its memory and its tradition, and this task was extremely difficult, presenting a whole range of conflicting options and impulses. How could the church hierarchy embrace Kochetkov, who seemed to challenge the church's unity and its authority, at a time when it was trying to recover its memory and tradition? In the words of the French sociologist of religion Danièle Hervieu-Léger: "How can religious institutions, with their prime purpose of preserving and transmitting a tradition, reform their own system of authority—essential for the continuity of a line of belief—when the tradition is thought of, even by believers, not as a sacred trust, but as an ethico-cultural heritage, a fund of memory and a reservoir of signs at the disposal of individuals? All religious institutions, whatever the theological notions of the religious authority they deploy, are faced with this question."[40]

To the members of the church hierarchy, Kochetkov represented the danger of fragmentation. Should he continue in his reform efforts, moving toward a more individualized, more decentralized system of belief, he threatened to split the church at a time when the hierarchy saw unity as a primary goal. The Kochetkov conflict essentially involved the kind of community Orthodoxy aspired to be. It centered on what Hervieu-Léger called the creation of a "living collective 'chain of memory' as a fund of meaning."[41] Russia had long suffered from a kind of collective amnesia, and the ecclesiastical authorities now hastened to reawaken memories of Orthodox tradition as they defined it. But part of that tradition, about which the church was willfully forgetful, lay in the late nineteenth and early twentieth centuries, a period that Kochetkov found to be among the most creative and instructive in the entire history of the church.

The church council of 1917–18 had passed several resolutions in which Kochetkov found inspiration and to which he tried to connect to his own reform endeavors. The resolutions made during this period, before the Bolshevik maelstrom against the church, warrant a brief review. They are aspects of the historical tradition that Kochetkov has attempted to recover and to extend, features that, he claims, justified the actions of his parish brotherhood.

The Chain of Memory

The period from 1905 to 1918 was remarkable in its attempts to reform a traditional autocratic social order and to bring tsarist Russia into the modern world. Following the humiliating defeats by the Japanese army in the Russo-Japanese war of 1904–1905, the Russian government made many significant changes in the relationship between the rulers and the ruled. Among these changes were efforts to put religious groups, Christian and non-Christian, on a new basis, to remove the restrictions that the state had imposed upon them and to give them greater freedom and initiative. In the spring of 1905, Nicholas II's talented prime minister Sergei Witte wrote a memorandum titled "Contemporary Situation of the Orthodox Church" in which he proposed a "return to the canonical form of government"; only such a change, the prime minister said, could reenergize the church and renew its sense of mission among the people. Witte evidently believed that the government's control of the church that had existed since the time of Peter the Great had undermined the spirit of Orthodoxy, that it was harmful both to the church and the Empire, and that only the abolition of this control could restore the people's commitment and trust in the church.[42]

The proposal concerning church renewal produced a vigorous discussion among members of the educated public that would last for more than a decade. Opponents, led by the powerful procurator of the Holy Synod Konstantin Petrovich Pobedonostsev, denounced Witte's proposal. They argued that it would lead to the rule of monks and bishops and that this, in turn, would produce chaos. But proponents of the new relationship between church and state believed strongly that church administration had to be decentralized, that the church had to be liberated from the procurator of the Holy Synod, and that parish priests had to be released from the obligation to serve as agents of the state. Proponents also argued for the revival of *sobornost'*, the ancient principle that called members of the church to "loving and responsible participation in Church life." In a questionnaire sent out by the synod to sixty-two bishops throughout the country in 1905, sixty stated they wished to see the church rebuild on this principle of *sobornost'*.[43] The bishops' responses, opposing every form of exclusion and domination by a single person, were surprising; they contradicted the widely held assumption of the clergy's political docility and indifference to self-government.

In the next decade the synod appointed two major church commissions to continue the discussion and prepare the way for a church council. Several themes ran through these deliberations about the church's role in the state, leading to recommendations to strengthen the vitality of the church. The first theme was the renewal of the parish, a goal that would require the decentralization of ecclesiastical administration. Another was the belief that church life could be greatly improved by being freed from the synodal bureaucracy, which had overseen it since Peter I's ecclesiastical regulation had made the church an ecclesiastical department of the state. "Nothing could be more harmful to the State than to obstruct the development and free manifestation" of Orthodoxy, this "great force among the people, by trying as they [officials] do now, to press it into the framework of dry bureaucratic principles," Witte wrote in 1905, a view that would continue to be expressed in the commissions' work.[44] An additional theme concerned the desire to restore the patriarchate and to make the principle of conciliarity once again central to the life of the church. By violating the conciliar principle established by the church's canon, the state had erected a barrier between the church and the people. The commissions' proposals aspired to remove this barrier.[45]

The work of these appointed commissions, however, failed to change the position of the Orthodox Church at the end of the Old Regime. Tsar Nicholas II did not convene a church council to act on the commissions' recommendations, and the centralized church administration remained firmly intact. The vision of autonomy, strongly endorsed in much of the commissions' materials, existed only on paper as the monarchy persisted in its control of the church. "Reaction triumphed over reform when reform was most needed," a recent scholar has written. But even if reform, as it was then conceived, "had been left to run its course," it would have found success difficult to achieve; "its social and geographical base, and its intellectual foundations, were too precarious for that."[46]

In February 1917, when crowds of workers and soldiers poured into the streets of Petrograd, bringing an end to the Old Regime, the church was greatly affected. The collapse of the tsarist government broke the church's connections to the state and provided an opportunity for leading church spokesmen to advance their case for self-government and to assert freedom from state control. The provisional government, set up in early March 1917, granted freedom to religious bodies, while recognizing the Orthodox Church as the preeminent denomination and preserving many of its privileges. In April 1917, the synod announced plans to convene a church council (*Sobor*) of bishops, lower clergy, and laity; its intention was to establish self-government and to redefine the church's role and status in the state. This council, which opened in Moscow in mid-August, faced an enormous challenge. With the

country disintegrating around it and revolutionary turmoil engulfing all seg-
ments of the population, the council tried to construct a new order for the
church, to rebuild the core principles on which it would operate in the future,
and to establish a new form of ecclesiastical government. In late October, following a spirited debate and as violence was spreading throughout Moscow,
the council voted to restore the patriarchate. Nearly a week later, on November 5, 1917, in the Cathedral of Christ the Savior in Moscow, the election of
the patriarch was held. The Bolshevik government was by then already in
power in Petrograd. The church's opportunity to reassert itself was thus
greatly tempered by the nearly simultaneous emergence of a government hostile to it and to the claims of religion in general.[47]

This tension between the Orthodox Church and the Bolshevik government became evident almost immediately after the Bolsheviks seized power.
On December 4, 1917, less than a month after the Bolshevik accession, the
government passed a decree nationalizing all land, including the land belonging to churches and monasteries, an act that undermined the church's economic interests. On December 11, all ecclesiastical schools were nationalized
and, shortly thereafter, closed. On January 23 (February 5), 1918, the government passed a decree separating church and state. The decree represented
much more than a separation of powers and an affirmation of freedom of conscience; it was a thinly disguised effort to strip the church of its legal rights and
to give legal sanction to persecution. Acts of violence and pillage, including
armed attempts to seize the monasteries, increased, their victims having little
recourse through the courts.[48]

The church responded to the new government by throwing down the
gauntlet, excoriating the Bolsheviks and reaching out to the people. On January 19, 1918, when the church council was on Christmas holiday, Patriarch
Tikhon repudiated the government's actions, which, he said, "aim at destroy-
ing the work of Christ, and, instead of Christian love, sow everywhere the
seeds of evil, of hatred, of fratricidal struggle." He called Bolshevik repression
"the work of Satan for which you deserve eternal fire after death and the ter-
rifying curse of future generations to come in this life." He entreated the faithful "not to enter [into] any communion whatsoever with such monsters of the
human race."[49] His direct appeal to the people was met enthusiastically. In
May 1918, Patriarch Tikhon rode in his carriage from the train station in Petrograd to the Aleksandr Nevskii Lavra, blessing large crowds who knelt by the
road along the way. This Accession Day procession amassed outside the Kazan
Cathedral—"a sea of humanity, which did not disperse until four o'clock in

the afternoon."[50] The leaders of the church assumed Lenin's regime to be only a temporary phenomenon; its acts, they thought, would not be permanent, and it would soon be replaced by a legitimate government of Russia.

For these reasons the church could take such a courageous stand against the Bolsheviks. In 1917 and until its dissolution in September 1918, the council continued to meet, working under the most chaotic conditions and preparing a new foundation for the church's future. These months witnessed a remarkable series of legislative acts based on canonical forms, restoring conciliar, self-governing principles to the church's governing structure. What is striking about this reorganization of the church, from top to bottom, is the council's attempt to apply these principles to the entire structure of the Orthodox Church. The council made use of the materials of the previous commissions and discussions. In the new order that it proposed, the supreme legislative and judicial authority in the Orthodox Church was to be the council, which would be convened periodically and would be composed of bishops, priests, and laypeople. The council would appoint two supreme bodies, presided over by the patriarch, the senior bishop, to govern the church between its meetings: the Holy Synod, which would deal with matters of church doctrine and religious education; and the High Commission of the church, which would take charge of the daily administration.[51] The diocese would be presided over by the bishop, assisted by a diocesan council of priests and laymen; the council would be elected by a diocesan assembly, itself chosen by parish assemblies.[52]

The council's work on the parishes produced results of even greater significance. In April 1918, the council passed the Regulation of the Parish, which established the parish as an autonomous unit. The regulation gave priests greater personal security, making them no longer servitors of the state but servitors of the local people. The regulation further stipulated the duties of the associate laymen, attempting to give the parish more unity and stability and to establish it on the basis of *sobornost'*. The council's intent was to bring the church closer to the people, an effort that required translation of doctrine and instructions to them in language that could be readily understood. To make services more comprehensible, the Regulation of the Parish allowed the use of the Russian language in the reading of the liturgy and in other parts of the service. Additional acts, previously denied, were admitted into practice, including reading the Psalms in Russian and opening the tsar's gates in the iconostasis, innovations aimed at making the church's message more accessible to the people.[53]

Fr Georgii, more than seventy years later, was thus able to claim that he stood firmly in the tradition of this early twentieth-century council and, as such, in the tradition of Russian Orthodoxy. He was no innovator or "heretic": his parish had simply carried out resolutions the church had already passed but that the Bolshevik government had curtailed. In recovering this part of the "chain of memory," in reclaiming the spirit of earlier councils, he was enabled, in fresh ways, to confront the social and spiritual dislocation of a post-Communist, urban world whose daunting challenges, he passionately believed, demanded creative approaches.

Speaking to the City

In 1988 the Russian journal *Nauka i religiia* (*Science and Religion*) published a special essay on Harvey Cox's book *The Secular City: Secularization and Urbanization in Theological Perspective* (1965). Cox's book, controversial and provocative nearly a quarter century ago when it was first published in the United States, had not been issued in Russia. But Russian readers could easily recognize the problems it raised as having relevance to Russia's current problems.[54] *The Secular City* had argued that we do not live in cities very well, but our future is dependent on our ability to learn to do so. As Leonid Stolovich, the author of the article in *Nauka i religiia* pointed out, we live today without the moral compass that our ancestors had, and everywhere we confront a more fragmented, technological, urban world. Stolovich, as had Cox earlier, called for religious people to seek out the complexity of the city rather than to flee from it. Rather than cut themselves off, such people ought to involve themselves in the city, become acquainted with its diverse ways of life, and relate to the downtrodden and the outcast—in short, they ought to heed Dietrich Bonhoeffer's admonition from his prison cell that human beings must "share the suffering of God in the world."[55] Drawing upon Bonhoeffer, Cox argued that God was present in both the secular and the religious world, and he maintained that we "limit the Holy by trying to divorce it from the rest of human life and confine it to a separate realm of existence." This argument Leonid Stolovich similarly advanced. He maintained that religion had much to offer urban individuals increasingly alienated from the world around them, isolated from their fellow citizens, and in need of bringing the secular and sacred more closely together.[56]

Fr Georgii Kochetkov shared these ideas. He strongly believed that the church must not turn its back on the secular world but must connect itself to this "suffering humanity." He echoed the earlier views of Fr Aleksandr Men and the desire to speak to a secular society. But his views also related to deeper themes within Orthodoxy's tradition, especially to its conception of grace. In the Western church, grace is conferred on those of the faith, on the virtuous, on the ordained. In Orthodoxy, grace is part of creation; it is extended to all human beings; it has the capacity to draw into it all people in the Lord's created order. "When you see your brother, you see God," said Clement of Alexandria (d. 215).[57] In this conception, anyone who stands at the door and knocks is invited in, and the grace of God extends to this person. Such a belief requires an opening up, rather than a closing off, a vision of the harmonious whole, rather than the establishment of rigid boundaries. This conception would be especially relevant in Kochetkov's new surroundings.

Despite their expulsion from the church of the monastery of the Presentation, Fr Georgii and his associate Aleksandr Kopirovskii maintained that the core of their message was preserved. Fr Georgii understood that many obstacles still lay in their way and that their enemies would not be satisfied. "But we have made our choice," Fr Georgii said, "we do not expect to be frightened, go into exile, or be silent." His congregation wanted "to be open without clamor, but open to do that which is demanded of our conscience before God. We aspired to be authentic Orthodox people and nothing else."[58] He strove to speak not only to a people searching for new meaning in a post-Communist society but also to people of the city, an educated public looking for a moral compass to their lives. Drawing on the experiences of his previous parish, Kochetkov would continue to develop his message and his approach.

The parish to which he was moved in 1994 is located in the small Church of the Dormition of the Most Holy Mother of God in Pechatniki (Uspeniia Presviatoi Bogoroditsy Tserkov' v Pechatnikakh) on Sretinskaia Street. The church lies just east of the Kremlin, in one of Moscow's oldest neighborhoods, which in the sixteenth and seventeenth centuries housed the special suburb of printing guilds. At that time, this suburb was part of the "wooden city," separated from the inner "white city" by a stone wall. The printing masters who lived here provided the skilled specialists to the state printing office, which was established in 1553, and they served in this capacity for the next 350 years.[59]

Today, this neighborhood is the location of bakeries, bookstores, sewing shops, crowded apartment buildings, and the many nooks, crannies and small courtyards that characterize the center of Moscow. The Dormition Church in Pechatniki stands in one of these courtyards. Built in 1695, during the reign of Peter the Great, the church was plundered and its interior burned during Napoleon's invasion in 1812, was restored soon thereafter, and then was fully renovated at the end of the nineteenth century. Under the Soviet government, the church fell on hard times; for many years it served as a museum for the navy of the Soviet Union.[60] Its cracked, dilapidated structure, and the worn, unpainted casing of its belfry clearly testify that the main cathedral had for many years been left untended and unused. Reopened in 1994, its occupants had much work to do to make it serviceable.

Ironically, diagonally across the street, on the corners of Sretinka and Rybnikov pereulok, in 1995, stood the campaign headquarters of the supranationalist politician Vladimir Zhirinovskii, newly opened to support his upcoming campaign for the Russian presidency. This building had been completely remodeled, and across its entrance was mounted a large, iconlike portrait of Zhirinovskii, fringed in red and black.[61] Zhirinovskii spoke of power, especially of Holy Russia, and ostentatiously proclaimed the need to "recover Russia's faded glory." Fr Georgii's church across the street from Zhirinovskii's headquarters expressed a different set of commitments. These different commitments and interests were revealed in several ways—in the church's environment, composition of its membership, the manner of its services, and its conception of community.

Upon entering Kochetkov's church for an evening service shortly after the move, the observer immediately experienced an assault on the senses. The entire atmosphere bespoke a subdued and sacred place; the church bells pealed their rich sonorous sounds, and the lights were low, with only thin shafts of natural light coming in the narrow windows providing visibility. The smell of burning candles and the lingering aroma of incense enveloped everyone who came through the doors. Along the back walls of the church, members of Kochetkov's parish had been hard at work, scraping and freshening the paint and attempting to restore the interior. These efforts had a long way to go, and the scaffolding and workmen's benches stood in full view, expressing both symbolically and actually the process of renewal and reconstruction. In one of the back corners of the church stood a large table where candles, small icons, and church literature were being sold, in addition to the publications of the church brotherhood, essays of Russia's early twentieth-century philosopher-theologians, and essays of contemporary Orthodox writers, including Fr Aleksandr Men.

Several aspects of the service bear description, because they are different from practices in many Orthodox churches and because they provide a window into the ethos of Kochetkov's parish.[62] First, the nature of the worshippers was distinctive. Most of the people present that evening were young; 80 to 90 percent of the approximately three hundred people in attendance were between twenty and forty years of age; a few people were older, and about

Church of the Dormition of the Mother of God in Pechatniki. Built in 1695, the church existed in one of Moscow's oldest neighborhoods and, beginning in 1994, was the parish of Fr Georgii Kochetkov.

twenty children were present. As in other settings, women made up a large percentage of the worshippers, approximately 65 percent of the people who had come that evening. While some of the young women covered their hair, most of them did not, in contrast to female attire in the typical Orthodox service. In scarce attendance were the babushkas who, for many years, served as the bedrock of the Russian Church. Socially and intellectually, most of the people present in the service clearly belonged to the intelligentsia; their dress was not working class and a large number of them carried either sacred texts or theological works. Many of the members knew each other. Before the services began, they stood in groups of three or four talking. As they greeted each other, members often embraced, such acts of welcome including both men and women. These people had already created a bond; they participated as members of an urban community; they were not the isolated individuals of Cox's *Secular City,* but were united by their gathering and their outward displays of friendship.

A second striking feature of the service concerned the members' visible participation. While the choirs' singing of the liturgy is one of the most beautiful parts of the Orthodox church service, in Fr Georgii's church, the ministers conducted the singing differently. Members of the community joined in the activity, reading the words and music from printed materials that they had brought with them. The sense of belonging and of *sobornost'* was demonstrated in the singing; it was the church at prayer. The ministers conducted most of the service in modern Russian. The use of language understandable to the community gave a much different tone and feel to the entire service than one might ordinarily have experienced; the impact of the liturgical music expressed itself joyfully and profoundly among the worshippers. One could not help but reflect on the contrast with Zhirinovskii, competing for adherents in the same neighborhood. If the nationalist leader exemplified bombastic rhetoric and aggressive self-promotion, the accent here was on simplicity, humility, and the sense of shared joy and peace.

A third distinctive quality lay in the preaching of the Word. Orthodox priests are not commissioned to preach their own private views, but base their teachings on a fixed point of expression, the Gospel of Jesus Christ, and "they are committed to this sole and perennial message."[63] The preaching of the Word of God is generally not something that should be accommodated to the fleeting circumstances of a particular time but should speak to every generation and to all circumstances.[64] Fr Georgii spoke twice, for fifteen to twenty minutes each time. He began by reading the scriptures, then proceeded to discuss their meaning and how they were not static but dynamic. In the first segment, Fr Georgii focused on the importance for life of compassion, kindness toward others, and love. Speaking of love as the foundation for the other two virtues as it was the foundation of the teachings of Jesus Christ, he explored these three qualities in depth, saying that love, the extension of the self to other people and the practical care for them, formed the bedrock of community.

In the second segment, Fr Georgii talked to his parishioners directly about the community. He told them that the spirit of tradition transcended their church and their community, but that coming together in this place enabled them to enlarge their vision of the self and its relationship to the rest of creation and to deepen their sense of responsibility—in essence, to nurture their humanity and their relationship to tradition. To understand tradition, he said, the person must live within the Christian community. He maintained again that love was universal and encompassed human beings everywhere, drawing them together on a spiritual level in a kind of universal brotherhood. Through the Trinity and within the community, they were enabled to show love mutually toward each other; indeed, through the triune relationship within the godhead, they were bound together in a love that was truly revolutionary.

Fr Georgii then discussed the present circumstances of the parish. He knew that living conditions for many people "had become increasingly worse," and he pointed out how difficult the experience of the parishioners had been. But, in response to these hardships, he also insisted that the spirit of God was present in this church and their community, and that this spirit would give strength to endure and to find regeneration. His words spoke of concrete realities and the sense of struggle, of a constant battle with difficult physical and emotional circumstances. He addressed directly the isolated individualism of the secular city; he stressed the need to rebuild a communal structure, whose members were committed to living sacrificially and for each other, bound together and to the holy father in mutual love.

To Fr Georgii, for the church to break fully from the Soviet past, decentralization and greater independence had to be coupled with a new vision of society and the world. He found the sources for such a vision in Orthodoxy's own theology—in which the workshop, the school, and the parish are icons of the Trinity, and in which, through the Trinity, all forms of oppression and injustice are opposed. Russia now needed this commitment more than ever, he wrote, beset, as it were, by nihilism, loss of community, extreme individualism, internal devastation, alienation, lack of respect for human life, the crushing of all traditions, and trampling down of "refined and higher values." The church could not ignore such conditions. It had to counter this nihilism, this "flight from life," with values that lay at the core of the Orthodox faith.[65]

In his parish at the Church of the Dormition, Fr Georgii had tried to establish the connection between vision and concrete action in several specific ways, all of which responded to problems found in the parish's urban setting. First, Fr Georgii placed education near the top of his objectives, seeing it as fundamental to the parish's future success. When the Moscow patriarchy transferred Fr Georgii's community from the monastery of the Presentation in 1994, it also closed several parish houses in which his school functioned,

including the kindergarten. His new parish operated a school in a small structure in the neighborhood; it attempted to provide religious education for
people age six through adulthood. In addition, the church had a Sunday
school for children, which was held in the cathedral and had about 150 children who came for instruction.[66]

The religious education received by children in Fr Georgii's school differed
from that in other Orthodox churches in Moscow. Elsewhere, in many church
schools, children were required to be baptized as a precondition for their attendance. Fr Georgii took the opposite position: "We first teach the children
and only after that do we ask them to consider baptism."[67] This approach was
particularly important, he said, in dealing with youth in the fifteen- to twenty-
year-old group. They were the young people who had experienced the greatest
psychological trauma during Russia's transition, and they were among the
most difficult to reach. "We offer them help," Fr Georgii said, "but after that
we let them make their own decisions." His method followed the example set
by Fr Aleksandr Men, whose school exemplified such openness and tried to
serve the needs not only of believers but also of nonbelievers and people struggling, under the most difficult conditions, to make sense of their lives.[68]

A second key feature of the parish's activities concerned its emphasis on
fostering unity while respecting diversity. To Kochetkov, dialogue offered the
most effective and creative method for dealing with many of the difficult issues
that the church presently confronted. The official hierarchy proclaimed the
need for unity as the church attempted to overcome the severe persecutions
of the Soviet period. But Kochetkov claimed that such proclamations were
intended to prevent dissent; he saw the building of unity within the church
much differently than did the official hierarchy. "We do not think that the
Church should withdraw from our society, turn its back on the most difficult
issues of our society, and do nothing," he said, "but should involve itself directly
in these problems and should try to find their solution." The kind of unity
he advocated welcomed diversity. True unity, he maintained, "must be created
by engaging different points of view—the unity of spirit and the diversity of
forms"—and this diversity would embrace the widest possible array of voices.[69]

Kochetkov's earlier experience as a seminary student, his encounters with
members of other religious faiths, and his understanding of Orthodox tradition contributed to this aspect of his parish's activities. The church, he firmly
believed, must "always be in the process of reform and regeneration," and
when it did not evolve, it "ceased to be a living body." In his view, this "living
Church tradition" signified the "ability to be in dialogue with every kind of
people, to discuss every kind of problem, and to be open to everyone." The

Fr Georgii Kochetkov. *Photo courtesy St. Filaret's Orthodox Christian Institute*

parish needed such openness, yet it also needed boundaries, the kind of boundaries that came from a group of people "who support each other and identify with each other." These elements of "openness and brotherhood" characterized his parish, which he contrasted with the official church. The official church, he claimed, lacked any sense of brotherhood and had no boundaries. "Anybody can come to the cathedral and do what he wants, can leave freely, and nobody cares." He viewed such indifference and inability to create a sense of community as a "serious disease."[70]

The third feature concerned the family. Kochetkov believed that parents raising children in "an atmosphere of Christian values" provided the foundation for strengthening the entire society. Since the social network to cope with problems of the family had all but disappeared in Russian society, Kochetkov saw the creation of such a network as a fundamental part of the church's role. Articles published in *Pravoslavnaia obshchina* repeatedly emphasized the importance of building family life on such elements as love, mutual respect, responsibility, and care for children.[71]

Kochetkov's approach to the family had several additional objectives. "We try constantly to raise our voices in defense of women in the Church," Fr Georgii said. His parish community did not speak about women's subordination or, as commonly proclaimed in the church, "women's services." His parish did not believe in defining a woman's family role primarily in terms of her work on the job and her work in the home; rather, she must be encouraged to develop her talents within the total context of the parish. His church had female deacons. Moreover, women fully participated in the parish's theological institutes, where they were among the stronger students. "We must make every effort to support, indeed to challenge, the most capable," he said, and it mattered little to him "whether they were our brothers or our sisters."

His community expressed a great deal of concern with the problems of Russian society—abortion, drug abuse, family violence, and psychological instability, all of which were pervasive issues. Nearly everyone who had become part of parish community had suffered from family stresses on related social problems and had come to his parish seeking help. [72] The church in Fr Georgii's mind must be a "living presence" in the world, drawing on its own theological teachings and traditions to play this role. It must be the "candle in the window," the symbol of crossed destinies, lighting up the darkness, providing hope. These traditional tenets of Orthodoxy lay at the core of his parish's activities and basic convictions. But the methods his community used and the parts of the Orthodox traditions he embraced posed a threat to certain powerful interests that saw him as an outsider to the faith, anathema to the elements of the church that most needed to be recovered and embraced.

In 1997, Fr Georgii's congregation numbered between fifteen hundred and two thousand regular worshippers in the cathedral. These numbers testified to the parish's extraordinary success, and, while he would have denied it, to Kochetkov's energy and personal appeal. The parish represented the largest and one of the most dynamic in Russia. In addition, a much larger number of people came sporadically and for many different reasons. A very high percentage of the people who belonged to it were young. The parish was ethnically diverse; a few members were Jews, whom Kochetkov said, "feel free and comfortable in our community." All the members of his parish were keenly aware that they were trying something new. They believed they stood within the Orthodox tradition and that their only novelty was in applying that tradition to the present. Fr Georgii's enemies would not be long in moving against him and seeking his removal.

"Declaration of War"

The move against Fr Georgii and his parish took place in June 1997. In an incident deliberately prepared by his opponents, Kochetkov and his parishioners suffered a serious reprisal that would threaten not only their existence but also the entire "reformist" element within the Russian Orthodox Church. The incident marked what one newspaper called a "declaration of war" against Kochetkov.[73] Portraying Fr Georgii as an "evildoer," the campaign against him intensified in the early summer, and reached its culmination on June 29, in a scandalous event aimed to discredit everything he represented.

The move was clumsily organized. Because of the rapid growth of Fr Georgii's parish, the parish leadership had for nearly two years asked its bishop to assign them an additional priest. The leadership had requested that the priest be "among the spiritual children of Kochetkov" and be theologically well prepared to conduct his ministry.[74] In late April 1997, a second priest finally was appointed to serve the parish. He was Fr Mikhail Vladimirovich Dubovitskii, a recent graduate of a provincial ecclesiastical seminary, a young priest with little pastoral experience and completely unknown to Kochetkov's parishioners. Not surprisingly, they were dismayed by Dubovitskii's appointment; his reception was exceedingly cool, and the next several months were marked by disappointment both for parish members and for Fr Mikhail. Few parishioners were willing to make confession to him, and the young priest found himself regarded with mistrust and, by some, with disdain. Fr Mikhail did little to earn their trust, even on one occasion charging that the prayers were read from a "noncanonical translation."[75]

On June 29, 1997, the last Sunday of the month, disobeying instructions at the altar during the morning service, Fr Mikhail walked to the church exit still wearing his full priestly vestments. Stopped at the door, he was asked to remove his vestments before leaving. He then moved to the altar, where he was asked again to take off his priestly garments. At that point, an angry exchange ensued between Fr Mikhail and several parishioners, and the incident quickly escalated into a confrontation in which suspicions and passions gathering steam over the last several weeks came to the surface. A policeman was summoned and one of the parishioners, thinking Fr Mikhail to be mentally ill, called a psychiatrist and an ambulance. The doctor decided that Fr Mikhail needed to be hospitalized; the priest was led from the sanctuary, while shouting that he had been physically attacked. His cries, "They are killing me!" rang loudly from the sanctuary into the courtyard as he was taken from the building.

This version of the story, told by Kochetkovites, focused on the young priest's psychological instability resulting in a "severe nervous breakdown." But those who opposed Kochetkov told a different story. They recounted a tale of deliberate falsification and threats of violence. Central to their account was the report signed by the chief of the eighteenth police precinct, A. L.

Rimskii, which stated that "after arriving on the scene, the emergency squad discovered a fight in progress in the sanctuary between two priests, one of whom (later identified as Fr Mikhail Dubovitskii) had signs of a beating and torn clothing."[76] Other opponents pointed out that the order committing the young priest to a mental hospital was given by a psychiatrist who had close ties with Kochetkov's congregation.[77] The leaders of the congregation had concocted a big lie, pronounced the young priest insane, "had taken him to Golgotha" in the most literal sense—a psychiatric hospital—and, just as in Soviet times, had injected him with drugs.[78] Dubovitskii's wife, Tat'iana, a psalmist in a Moscow church, testified that her husband had never been mentally ill and the official charge was a fabrication.[79]

The case quickly built against Fr Georgii. A month after the event in the Dormition Church, on July 29, Patriarch Aleksi II appointed a church commission to investigate the incident. Basing its findings on the police report, the commission found leaders of Kochetkov's congregation guilty of "violence and insult against Father Mikhail Dubovitskii." On October 2, the patriarch placed Georgii Kochetkov under ban, evicting him from the church of the Dormition of the Most Holy Mother of God in Pechatniki, suspending him from the ministry, and excommunicating twelve members of his community, including nearly all his acolytes, members of his parish council, and his seventy-year-old female assistant.[80]

The evidence leading to this verdict was extremely specious, and the testimony supporting the young priest was contradictory. Both the traditionalist and the nationalist press, including *Radonezh,* a nationalist church publication, seized the moment to influence popular sentiment and rally support against Kochetkov and his parishioners. On October 14, however, a second commission appointed to investigate the case of Fr Mikhail's admission to the psychiatric hospital, issued its report. After carefully reviewing the hospital's records and the police report, the commission concluded that, at the time of his hospitalization, Dubovitskii was in an "extreme state of anxiety," indicating an "acute reaction to stress with profound disturbance of behavior in accord with the International Classification of Illnesses."[81] Such findings suggested the forced hospitalization of Fr Mikhail was a reasonable act.

The incident that took place in Kochetkov's church had larger implications, and they went beyond Fr Mikhail's personal circumstances. The forcible removal of a priest, as a leading journalist pointed out, had set an extremely dangerous precedent.[82] It recalled Soviet times, when force against political opponents and incarceration in psychiatric hospitals had often taken place. In his analysis, the journalist also recounted the famous earlier conflict involving the seventeenth-century archpriest Avvakum. Physically removed from his sanctuary by soldiers of the tsar, Avvakum uttered an anguished cry, "Give us back our church," in response to the forces of change and modernization then confronting Russian Orthodoxy both from within and from without. Fr Mikhail bears little personal resemblance to the illustrious Avvakum, but his own cry as he was carried out of the church sounded like a similar protest to changes in the liturgy and other parts of the worship service, changes that he considered heretical.

The assault on Kochetkov targeted a congregation with a diverse composition, whose members came predominantly from the intelligentsia. Ironically, these were people whose support church leaders had considered, during Soviet times, as the most difficult to attract; they were also, because they were the teachers of the young, essential to the church's future.[83] The fresh vision they had sought, the innovations they had promoted, their attempts to relate Orthodox Christianity directly to their society created tensions within the church and ultimately a backlash. In December 1999 and January 2000, "traditionalists" circulated letters in Moscow churches, seeking signatures to "finish off Kochetkov and his followers," accusing him of continuing to teach and spread his harmful innovations.[84] Speaking at a conference on the problems of totalitarian sects and the occult, Fathers Konstantin Bufeev and Mikhail Dubovitskii, Kochetkov's old nemesis, identified Fr Georgii and his followers with the foreign sects then threatening the national security of Russia. The two priests asserted that members of Kochetkov's parish were guilty of "heresy," "schism," and being a "self-endorsed assembly."[85]

In the Dormition Church and its neighboring structures, Kochetkov and his followers had revitalized parish life. Energetic, innovative, internally unified, and evangelical, the parish had grown rapidly from its humble beginnings in 1994 to the summer of 1997.[86] The banning of Kochetkov from the ministry and the excommunication of twelve followers put an end to this successful canonical church parish. In October 1997, Kochetkov asked for the patriarch's forgiveness, but the patriarch and his staff did not respond. [87] Meanwhile, Kochetkov's opponents, the traditionalists within the church, exulted in their triumph, excoriating him and his closest associates and charging them with blasphemy and heresy. Most important, the critical theological issues Kochetkov had raised and with which his name was associated could not, for the present, be easily explored, because such questions invited the charge of being a follower of Kochetkov.[88]

For three years the fate of Georgii Kochetkov and the members of his church remained uncertain. In August 2000, citing Fr Georgii's repentance,

Patriarch Aleksi II absolved him "from the earlier priestly prohibition that had been imposed."[89] Fr Georgii was thus permitted, formally, to engage in priestly work, to baptize, to perform the liturgy, and to minister to a needy population. But he did not regain his former parish in the church of the Dormition of the Most Holy Mother of God in Pechatniki nor was he allowed to continue there what he still called "genuine church regeneration."[90] Meanwhile, in the same decree that lifted the ban on Fr Georgii's ministry, the patriarch ordered the creation of a special commission to investigate Kochetkov's theological views and the innovations he had instituted.[91] Fr Georgii holds services at present at Novodevichy Monastery.

In assessing Kochetkov's significance, it may well be that his importance lies neither in his specific theological views nor in his innovations in the church services. His significance may lie in the relationship he developed between the church leadership and the laity. As Daniel Gorin, a sympathetic observer, maintained, Fr Georgii's Church of the Dormition of God at Pechatniki "was more a community than simply a parish."[92] It was more independent, more decisive, and more coherent; it had among its members a greatly developed sense of collective responsibility that, in the uncertain conditions of present-day Russia, spoke in compelling terms. "From the position of the hierarchy," as a recent writer has said, "it is simple to deal with the crowd that stays put, that is easily pleased 'with the knout and honey' and be made to go in any direction it wishes."[93] By choosing instead to build a flourishing, vigorous community, Kochetkov offered genuine hope and opportunity. Such qualities are essential to the development of civil society. The greatest irony may be that, even in defeat, Kochetkov's community provides a model for the future.

Community was an essential part of Kochetkov's Christianity. He firmly believed that Orthodoxy called for a transformation of the inner self, and it was in the community of the parish that this transformation took place. Ego, selfishness, alienation, and despair would be transformed into a concern for others, compassion, humility, and charity. While his practice of Orthodoxy invited charges of heresy, the core of his convictions, both in theory and practice, drew deeply from Orthodoxy's tradition. He could not separate faith from life, from the poor and destitute of the city, from people searching for meaning and purpose in their lives, from the need to overcome despair, and from the quest for social justice. Above all, his conception of community embraced the doctrine of charity. "If you want to honor Christ," said John Chrysostom, one of Orthodoxy's greatest saints, "do it when you see him naked, in the person of the poor."[94] To Chrysostom, Christ was a "homeless stranger" who "is wandering and begging, and instead of receiving him you make decorations."[95] Like Chrysostom, Fr Georgii did not see Orthodoxy as a conventional religion, a faith of empty forms, but one that called its followers to reach out to strangers, aid the poor, and in meekness and humility embrace suffering humanity.

In his view of community and his articulation of its goals, Fr Georgii contributed in several ways to the development of civil society. His emphasis on grace and charity stood in opposition to the prevalence of violence in Russian society. While ultraconservative groups attempted to inspire hatred against him, Kochetkov repeatedly sought to defuse hatred. He offered a different approach to social relationships, one that stressed humility, inclusiveness, and social obligation. His vision of the church's missionary task called for it to reach out to society, to turn outward to the world, rather than to withdraw from it. Orthodox teachings could provide an ethical foundation for society based on mutual obligation and respect for the dignity of the individual, as made in the image of God. In the words of a recent Russian scholar, "Civil principles of life should spread and take root not as a result of rational plans of eradicating diffuse violence but as a result of the mysterious descent of a deep intense personal faith" in such values in "each human being."[96] Fr Georgii's community embraced these values. By reaching out beyond the physical boundaries of this community, he aspired to nourish them more broadly in Russian society.

Postcommunist Russia has witnessed other attempts to recover stories, redefine identity, and reconstruct community. Kochetkov's efforts took place outside or on the fringes of the official church. The following chapter deals with a much different person, one more typical of religious believers in the former Soviet Union, Mother Serafima, a remarkable woman who was in the mainstream of the Orthodox Church. The story of her struggles with identity and the rebuilding of community produced much different results. Mother Serafima led the recovery of Novodevichy Monastery, one of Moscow's best-known and most beloved religious centers.

4 Novodevichy and the Redefinition of History

Novodevichy Monastery in Moscow stands on the banks of the Moskva River near the junction of the Okruzhenaia Railway embankment. When one approaches the monastery in late afternoon, the sun setting over the river, the blue and gold cupolas of the monastery are spectacular. From the time of my first visit as a student some thirty-five years ago, I have thought of this as a magical, ethereal place. History, the scene suggests, is not preserved only in books; it is an aspect of life, part of the memory. Whether viewed in the twilight of a June evening or on a snowy January night, Novodevichy has a special attraction: here history, beauty, and memory fuse into one.

Novodevichy Monastery provides an excellent perspective from which to view the renewal of the church in Russia. This perspective is, in large part, bound up with the story of a remarkable woman, Varvara Vasil'evna Chichagova, Mother Serafima, and the present chapter focuses on her and her efforts to rebuild Novodevichy. Closed as an active monastery throughout much of the Soviet era and reopened in 1994, its struggles mirror many of those that the church is undergoing in recovering its identity and purpose in Russian society. As a monastery significant in the history of Russia, it was restored after World War II, but it was kept open as a museum, a testimonial to some of the key events marking the growth and national survival of the Russian state.

Novodevichy, therefore, has played a large role in Russia's national memory. But more important, for this book, the monastery provides a viewpoint from which to examine the role of the church in Russian society today. The previous chapter notes the conspicuous presence of women in Fr Georgii Kochetkov's parish community. This chapter explores that theme from another point of view, through the experience of Mother Serafima. She is more typical of Soviet-era Orthodox believers than is Kochetkov. Unlike Kochetkov, she sought to live within the Soviet system and accommodated herself to it, while maintaining a dynamic personal and internal religious life.

The chapter first offers a brief overview of Novodevichy's role in Russian history and its difficult passage during the Soviet era, then focuses on Mother

Serafima. She combined her society's goals with her own fresh perspective, and her journey is, in many ways, a microcosm of the story of Novodevichy—the struggle to regain one's roots, to reestablish identity, and to redefine the church's role in Russian society.

THE MONASTERY IN HISTORY

Novodevichy literally means "convent of maidens," and the name itself suggests the elegance, grace, and sense of women's history that is found here. Built in the shape of an octahedral prism, with columns at the corners, the monastery has a fluid, well-proportioned appearance. It was founded in the first quarter of the sixteenth century by the Moscow Grand Duke Vasilii III, the father of Ivan the Terrible, to commemorate the reunion of Smolensk and the Smolensk territories in 1522 with the principality of Moscow. Vasilii had pledged earlier to build new cloisters to commemorate this military triumph. In Russia it was customary to give expression to an important military victory by a sculptured monument that would celebrate the victory and fix it in the memory; in a list of such monuments, one could include Novodevichy.[1]

Founded on the old road to Smolensk, Novodevichy appeared as the front door to Moscow, the window to the city from the southwest. The monastery served as the main fortress on the southern ring, joining a chain of other fortress-monasteries (Andron'evskii, Danilevskii, Donskoi, Novospasskii, Simonovskii) built to protect Moscow from military attacks or the raids of plundering bands. Just before the construction of the monastery was begun, the Crimean khan Makhmet Girei had crossed the bend in the river and, facing little resistance, had assaulted the city; fear of such Tatar attacks persisted until the end of the sixteenth century, and Novodevichy was built to protect against such raids.[2]

The architectural structure of the monastery is of much historical significance, testimony to the vision and great skill of its founders. The monastery has thick red brick walls, with towers, loopholes, and battlements to protect it from attacks. The walls form an irregular pentagon whose length measures more than three thousand feet. From the beginning, the monastery's main building was the cathedral, a majestic, richly decorated, beautifully proportioned structure that is today one of the country's best preserved monuments of sixteenth- and seventeenth-century architecture. The cathedral holds the icon of the Mother of God of Our Lady of Smolensk, which was presented by the city, following its defeat, to Grand Duke Vasilii III.

Smolenskii Cathedral, Novodevichy Monastery, built in 1524–25, shows the influence of the Kremlin cathedrals and contains frescoes glorifying Prince Vasilii III and other Moscow princes. The cathedral houses the Mother of God icon, brought here after Moscow's capture of Smolensk in 1514, and the icon of Saints Boris and Gleb.

Inside the cathedral, one is presented with a visual feast, simple yet stunning to the eye. The frescoes and murals on the cathedral's interior fit beautifully with the architecture. Painted in the mid-sixteenth century by the Iaroslavl' masters Fedor Karpov and Ivan Elizarov, aided by craftspeople from Kostroma and Ustiug, they are among the best preserved from this period in Russia. Painstakingly restored during the Soviet period, they depict in great and colorful detail the unification of Russia under the Moscow princes, and they emphasize the Moscow rulers as the heirs to the Byzantine emperors. In these murals and frescoes, one sees clearly the idea of "Holy Russia," of "Moscow as the Third Rome," whose glory was intended to last forever.[3]

Prominent also among the many interior features of the monastery is the belfry. Built on the eastern side between 1683–89, the original belfry still stands across from the altar of the cathedral; it is a six-tiered structure some 240 feet in height. Each tier appears to grow out of the previous, and the white stone details of the tiers provide a striking contrast to the red brick walls of the monastery. The top of the belfry offers a splendid view of the historic Sparrow Hills and the city of Moscow.[4]

Soon after its founding, Novodevichy Monastery became a women's

The 240-foot-tall bell tower of Novodevichy Monastery, built in 1690.

monastery of the court. To it were sent the wives and daughters of the great princes—sometimes willingly, sometimes forcibly—and the members of Russia's wealthiest families. Such women included, in 1563, Ul'iana, the sister-in-law of Tsar Ivan IV; in 1581, Elena, the wife of Ivan IV's son Ivan; in 1598, Tsarina Irina, the widow of Tsar Fedor Ivanovich; and, in 1717, Evdokiia Lopukhina, the first wife of Peter the Great. Women entered the monastery for various reasons: some, for true religious reasons, a strong sense of belief and a desire to find sanctuary for meditation and prayer; others, for economic reasons, because their families had fallen on difficult times. In some cases, aristocratic women were forced to take the veil because they were a threat to the prescribed order and challenged the patriarchal values governing this order. Forcing the transgressive females into the monastery became a way to silence them and control their actions.

While women's monasteries may have represented places for control, they fulfilled yet another purpose that, to some women, represented quite the opposite. These women saw the monasteries as places from which they might speak, places where they might find a voice that enabled them to challenge socially prescribed values, either through social action or reflective writing. Such was the case for many Russian women who entered monasteries later, in the nineteenth and early twentieth centuries, women who were seeking alternative communities and ways of providing service to people in need of a helping hand—the unfortunate, dispossessed, disabled, elderly, or impoverished members of society who had nowhere else to go.[5] Aleksandra Filippovna Shmakova, for example, married to a wealthy Baltic Russian nobleman, was discontented with St. Petersburg social life and dreamed of escaping its boredom and sterility and serving a more fulfilling community. In 1865, following the death of a child and then later of her husband, she began construction of a chapel and living quarters that became a holy refuge for a community of women.[6] To the Russian women serving in them, monasteries could be sources of strength, traditional places, but also ones from which women could establish a community at the grassroots level and make small inroads toward personal freedom. These communities, as Brenda Meehan has written, became a "shelter of sorts," a "mirror within a mirror," that provided "services to the sisters which mirror[ed] the services the sisters provide[d] to the population. And such needs and services could not be legislated away by government decrees."[7]

Traditionally in Russia, men and women's monasteries differed in their structure and purposes. Women's monasteries focused more than men's on charitable and pastoral work, serving the poor and destitute and bringing comfort to individuals who had suffered misfortune and had nowhere else to turn. Men's monasteries devoted a great deal of attention to education, especially to older boys and to their preparation for service in the church. Women's monasteries were dedicated to taking care of the most vulnerable and helpless people in the society, orphans, young children, battered women, the elderly, and the homeless. Increasingly during the nineteenth century, these institutions became communal, thereby replacing the old practice of living separately and working independently. In this process, they came to embrace a strong service ethic. Monasteries for women embodied the ideals of compassion, charity, responsibility, and service, ideals that these women believed lay at the core of the church's earthly mission.[8]

At Novodevichy, many times when the taking of vows occurred, the monastery received a large sum of money, land, peasants, precious metals, and expensive clothes, investments aimed at enabling the distinguished person to live comfortably. Novodevichy thus quickly gained great wealth and prestige, a situation that continued throughout the tsarist period of Russian history. At the end of the nineteenth century, it was listed as one of twenty-three monasteries in Moscow, nine women's and fourteen men's. Novodevichy was the only female monastery ranked in the first class (since 1764), joining four other men's monasteries with that classification.[9]

In its historical development, Novodevichy Monastery thus left an ambiguous legacy. On the one hand, its mission was to protect the city of Moscow, as well as to preserve a memory of victory, one achieved by blood. On the other hand, the monastery was a symbol of wealth and power, and its holdings of peasants, land, and precious metals and its connections to the court might easily have separated it from the population and given it a negative meaning in the popular imagination. But Novodevichy was not separated from the people. Like other women's monasteries, its properties included almshouses, where the poor might be fed and destitute women and their children might find solace. The nuns who served at Novodevichy were not isolated from the world and the rest of society but interacted with them in significant ways. In 1724 Tsar Peter I established at Novodevichy a home for abandoned orphans. In the middle of the eighteenth century, approximately 250 girls lived there, where they were instructed in literacy as well as taught crafts of spinning and lace work.[10] Combining home and school, the home flourished until it was closed later in the century upon the creation of a similar orphanage in Moscow. But the memory of that original institution and the service it provided did not end; in 1871 the monastery established another orphanage for girls, called the Filat'evskoe School, that operated until World War I.[11]

In addition to its contribution to the formation of the Russian state, Novodevichy also provided the setting for several key events in Russia's later national memory. In 1610, during the Time of Troubles, the monastery served as the site of bloody combat with Polish armies. In these battles, part of the original monastery was destroyed; the first Romanov tsar, Mikhail Fedorovich, restored the ravaged structures. In 1689, Sophia, the half-sister of Peter the Great, was compelled by him to take the veil here in the power struggle that developed over Peter's taking the throne. Later, when Peter made his historic first trip to Western Europe in 1697, Sophia's family organized the mutinous, old palace guards (*streltsy*) and attempted to seize power. Their uprising led to a bloody confrontation that resulted in the *streltsy*'s and Sophia's family's near-total defeat. Angered by events and determined to smash his opposition, Peter ordered three of the *streltsy* leaders of the uprising to be hanged in the yard, directly beneath Sophia's window in the Naprudnaia tower on the northeast side.[12]

In the nineteenth century, the monastery would also play a key role in Russia's national story. In 1812, as his forces camped on the outside of Moscow, prior to entering the city, Napoleon visited the monastery. Anticipating the arrival of the French, most of the nuns had already left, moving eastward to Vologda and taking with them most of the monastery's treasures for safekeeping. Only a few nuns remained when the French armies closed in on Moscow. After visiting the monastery and inspecting its fortifications, Napoleon on September 25 decided to make Novodevichy the central location for his armies' food provisions. The French forces boarded up the rear gate and sealed it off with earth, built a large earth bastion at the northern gate, and stationed a garrison on the walls. There the French remained during late September and October.

When Napoleon's armies left Moscow and the monastery to begin what would become a disastrous return homeward, his soldiers laid several charges of explosives in an attempt to destroy the cathedral and ignited these charges as they departed. According to Russian sources, the nuns of the monastery, led by Sister Sarra, put out the burning fuses—brave acts performed at great risk to themselves.[13] Their courageous actions preserved Novodevichy from destruction.

In the historical imagination, Novodevichy thus became a place whose relationship to the people was many sided: the monastery played an important part in Russia's early historical development; it was a place of great beauty and serenity; it served as a fortress to which people could go in times of danger; it was a woman's house that protected against invasion and gave refuge in times of misfortune. These multiple elements were part of the national memory, and, while they might be suppressed, they were not obliterated.

The monastery's cemetery, set just below the main grounds on the northern side, contains the graves of some of Russia's greatest cultural figures. They include the writers Nikolai Gogol and Anton Chekhov, the composers Aleksandr Scriabin and Sergei Taneev, the artists Isaac Levitan and Valentin Serov, the actress Maria Ermolova, the theatrical directors Konstantin Stanislavskii and Vladimir-Danchenko, the sculptress Vera Mukhina, the scientists Vladimir Komarov and Otto Schmidt, and the Tretiakov brothers, Pavel and Sergei, founders of the famous art gallery that bears their name. Writers, poets, political leaders, and military figures from the Soviet period are also well represented: Vladimir Maiakovksii, Aleksandr Fadaev, old Bolsheviks, Joseph Stalin's

Novodevichy Monastery, founded by Prince Vasilii III and connected with many significant events in Russian history, including the election of Tsar Boris Godunov in 1598 and the regency of Sophia Alekseevna, Peter the Great's half sister, 1682–89.

second wife, Nadezhda Allilueva who, in 1932, either committed suicide or was killed by Stalin, and Nikita Khrushchev. The graves of many heroes of the war against Nazi Germany may also be found in the cemetery, as well as military leaders from throughout the Soviet period. Several of the larger themes of Russia's history are clearly evidenced in this place: the role of women, the growth and power of the state and church, military triumph and suffering, invasion and endurance, patriotism and artistic creativity and imagination, passion and beauty, the monastery and the world.[14]

Monasticism has played an important part in the religious culture of Russia from the earliest days of the church's foundation. The establishment of the "monastery in the wilderness" and the image of a place set apart from the rest of the world have a powerful presence in the national imagination, and have strongly affected Russian spirituality. As "holy men of God," monks attracted large numbers of people who sought their guidance and often traveled from distant places to see them. Both princes and laypeople sought the advice of these holy men, who became national as well as religious figures. Pilgrimages to the sites where monks lived occurred frequently and have continued into present times. In this tradition, the lives of three monks have held a particularly venerated place in Russia's religious consciousness: St Feodosi (Theodosius), founder of the Monastery of the Caves in Kiev; St Sergius of Radonezh, who established the spiritual community at Sergiev Posad (Zagorsk); and St Serafim of Sarov, the great eighteenth-century hermit in the wilderness. In addition, certain spiritual elders, such as the elder Amvrosii (1812–91) of the Optina hermitage, would give spiritual counseling to two of Russia's greatest nineteenth-century writers, Fedor Dostoevsky and Leo Tolstoy, and would influence both Russian secular and religious culture.[15]

But while the spiritual influence of the monasteries and convents would continue to resonate in the national memory, their physical presence would be severely curtailed. In 1914 the Russian Empire had 1,025 operating convents; by 1929 the government had closed down all of them.[16] Some of them had controlled sizable lands on which they had operated large farm plots, fruit gardens, and beehives, whose operations had sustained the operations of the monasteries and convents, and the Soviet government confiscated these church properties. Equally important, the Bolsheviks wanted to eliminate the monasteries and convents, "islands of spirituality" with their alternative visions of life. Although such "islands" were closed, they would have a brief resurgence in the Second World War. In 1939–40, when the Soviet government annexed Latvia, Lithuania, and Estonia, sixty-four functioning monasteries were absorbed into its territory; during World War II, under the German occupation of these territories, forty additional monasteries were opened.[17] At the end of the war in 1945, 101 convents were in operation. The following year the government permitted the reopening of the Troitse-Sergius Lavra in Zagorsk (Sergiev Posad), the ancient monastery of St Sergius of Radonezh; until 1983, the Troitse-Sergius Lavra was the only monastery the Soviet government allowed to reopen on Soviet territory that the German armies had not occupied during the war.[18]

Monasteries became main targets of antireligious campaigns at the end of Stalin's life and then during Khrushchev's drive against the church, which began at the end of the 1950s. During the latter operation, monks and nuns suffered greatly, as many of the monastic communities were closed overnight, often brutally, by KGB agents and militiamen. During the next two decades, the government did not allow one monastery to open its doors. Only in May 1982, the year of Leonid Brezhnev's death, did the government permit one monastery, the Danilov monastery in Moscow, to reopen and then only in anticipation of the coming celebration of the church millennium in 1988. In the mid-1980s, the Orthodox Church operated only six monasteries and ten convents in the Soviet Union. The convents included: the Convent of St Florus (Florovskii) and the Convent of the Protecting Veil of our Lady

(Pokrovskii) in Kiev; the Holy Trinity Convent at Korets, Kovno oblast, Ukraine; the Convent of the Birth of the Mother of God at Aleksandrovka in the Odessa region; the Krasnogorsk Convent of the Protecting Veil of Our Lady at Zolotonosha in the Cherkassy region; the St Mary Magdalene Convent at Vilnius and the Birth of the Mother of God Convent at Zhirovitsy, both in Belarus; the Convent of the Ascension (Voznesenskii) in Chumalevo and the Convent of St Nikolai at Mukhachevo, both in the Trans-Carpathian region; the Convent of the Ascension at Zhabka, near Kishinev, Moldova; the Holy Trinity–St Sergius Convent at Riga, Latvia; and the Convent of the Dormition at Pyukhtitsa, Estonia.[19] Seven of the ten convents existed in Ukraine, three in the Baltic countries, and one on Moldova; not one convent operated in Russia.

In late 1987, the government returned to the church two famous monasteries: the Tolga Presentation of Mary Convent in Iaroslavl' diocese and the Optina Presentation hermitage in Kostroma diocese.[20] Following the meeting between President Mikhail Gorbachev and Patriarch Pimen in April 1988 and the celebration of the church millennium in Russia, the reopening of monasteries and convents gained momentum. By September 1990, according to the Novosti Press Agency, 25 monasteries and 21 convents were functioning. In late 1993, according to Patriarch Aleksi II, the number of convents had grown to 213, plus 11 convent missions. It is significant that 50 of these convents operated in Russia, scattered all over its vast territory. A decade earlier not one operating convent and only the monastery at Sergiev Posad had existed in the entirety of Russia.[21] Such change, coming so rapidly and with such vitality, is one of the most remarkable aspects of Russia's transformation. Novodevichy Monastery fits into this restoration. In the fall of 1994, the Russian government returned the famous monastery, in the northeastern part of Moscow, to the church; on October 13, Mother Serafima was welcomed into the monastery, given holy orders, and charged with restoring religious life in the monastery. On November 27, 1994, seventy-two years after its closure by the government, Novodevichy Monastery was officially reopened.

A large problem facing the church in the renewal of religion concerns the monks and nuns needed to serve in the newly opened monasteries and convents. The Orthodox Church has lacked the time, resources, and educational base to prepare for the transition, and although the church faced unprecedented opportunities, it was also confronted with difficult problems. Often it had to improvise as best it could under the circumstances, admitting young people to the priesthood without adequate training, compressing instruction into a short period, and hoping new church servitors would be able to learn as they proceeded.[22] In some cases, monasteries and convents were staffed by older people who had a religious upbringing or had made commitments to the church early in their lives.[23] They rejoined their earlier selves, reconnecting to a story they had begun but had not been able to pursue. This process represented an essential part in the recovery of memory, both collectively and individually. It took place in extremely difficult circumstances; although they had great personal gifts, vitality, and experience, such older people had few material resources on which to draw. Mother Serafima and the nuns of Novodevichy Monastery represent one of these stories.

Historically, the church has often tried to accommodate itself to the world and to the established political power and has sustained powerful economic and political groups in society. Marx's devastating critique of religion had focused on this tendency of the church to support the power structure. But the central principles of Christianity hold up a mirror to society and the prevailing power structure; the teachings of Jesus offer a radical critique of the established order. Whether adopted by Leo Tolstoy, Dr. Martin Luther King, Russian dissidents in the 1970s and '80s, or Mother Serafima, they provide an alternative view and a challenge to the dominant political and social structure.

THE MISSING PIECES

When I met Mother Serafima for the first time in the summer of 1995, she had served as the head of Novodevichy for nearly seven months. She was in her early eighties and only about four feet ten inches tall, but neither of these characteristics bears witness to the vitality and strength she obviously possessed. She greeted me with a firm handshake and a warm smile, and one could immediately sense in her a quiet dignity and self-assured demeanor that bespeaks a person who is well educated and deeply spiritual. Her office in a corner of the Smolenskii Cathedral was simply and plainly furnished; when she had finished her duties in the service of the cathedral, she invited me there. With the light of the late afternoon sun streaming in the large window at her back, she recounted the search for her own connections. When I asked her about her background, she immediately pulled from the sideboard a large family album.

Photographs, the historian Michael Ignatieff emphasizes, often become a family's "court of memory," playing a part in preserving a great deal of the twentieth century, providing a sense of connection and rootedness in a time of migration and expatriation. In a secular culture, Ignatieff writes, photographs "are the only household icons, the only objects that perform the religious function of connecting the living to the dead, and of locating the identity of the living in time."[24] The six-penny photograph, he maintains, deserves a key place in the social history of modern individualism because it democratized the family portrait gallery; it enabled poor families to bequeath to their descendants a "new kind of inheritance"—not property, but a sense of belonging to those who lived earlier, to being part of a genetic line. Photographs had a "part in bringing the problem of personal identity to the centre of cultural concern." The belief that the person must create his or her place in time once belonged only to the privileged few; the photograph opened that opportunity to all, made it part of the whole culture. In Russia, where brokenness, expatriation, and the assault on memory have been acute, family photographs occupy a precious place; often, they are one's only connections to the past. Thus they provide the framework for creating one's identity.[25]

The family photograph album that Mother Serafima pulled from the sideboard contained pictures of her relatives, including several uncles who had served the Russian and later Soviet state before disappearing into the labor camps. One of the first photographs in the album shows her father standing with Tsar Nicholas II and his family; in others, her uncle and male relatives are in military uniforms of the prerevolutionary Russian army. She is clearly connected, not only to the Soviet period, but also to the old Russian nobility and to some of the key events in Russia's prerevolutionary history.

Mother Serafima's quest to fill in the missing pieces of her family identity began several years ago, when the policies of *glasnost* encouraged such ventures. The photograph album she showed me contained a black-and-white picture of a handsome, middle-aged officer, sitting in stern repose, decorated with the highest military honors conferred by the Russian government. The picture is of her grandfather Leonid Mikhailovich Chichagov, a commander and hero of the Balkan Wars during the reigns of Tsars Aleksander II (1855–81) and Aleksander III (1881–94). This family line was the most relevant to Mother Serafima; she knew that this part of her family was strongly rooted in the history of Russia in the eighteenth and nineteenth centuries. Admiral Vasilii Iakovlevich Chichagov played a key naval role in the reign of Catherine II; he was the leader of an expedition that tried to find a sea route to North America via the Arctic Ocean. Later descendants served with distinction in the armies of Paul I, Nicholas I, Aleksander II, Aleksander III, and Nicholas II.

Her grandfather Leonid Mikhailovich Chichagov wrote a book about the Russian army in which Mother Serafima took particular interest and considerable pride. This work of more than six hundred pages focuses on Tsar Aleksander II's personal participation in the campaigns along the Dnieper River during the Russo-Turkish wars. Her grandfather's account deals especially with Aleksander II's relations with ordinary soldiers, his warmth, his concern for their individual well-being, his visits to and discussions with his wounded men, and the presentation of awards that he gave with great personal feeling. Written in the form of a diary, the book discusses Leonid Mikhailovich's own ideas about the campaigns and provides a firsthand account of the people around him and events of the war. Fascinated not so much by the military details of the campaign but by her grandfather's portraits of people, Mother Serafima prepared a new edition of the book, whose original version had long since been relegated to rare book collections. Believing that her grandfather's book held much valuable information for students of Russian history, she worked diligently to update the technical features. When she began, she admitted, she understood little about the main ranks in the army and could not distinguish even the chief differences between colonels and generals. She began her project with only a dream and a resolve: "Several historians in Moscow took an interest in my work and some of them wrote commentaries to the book; one historian wrote a new introduction. But it took a lot of time for these scholars to write the commentaries and a few of them never did finish or delayed writing anything at all. So I had to do a great deal of the work myself; I compiled short biographical materials for more than 150 people mentioned in the book. I knew I made mistakes, but I still pressed on. Despite my lack of training and my poor preparation, I was determined to get the book ready for publication."[26]

As Mother Serafima probed more deeply into the background and context of her grandfather's manuscript, she also gained a larger view of him. She discovered that her grandfather's interests ran in several directions and encompassed a larger world than she had originally known; these aspects of his personality she found extremely attractive. Her grandfather wrote a collection of short stories on the relationship between Russian officers and soldiers during the Russo-Turkish wars. In addition to being a talented writer, he also had a considerable interest in music, art, and theology. He painted several icons that the church had preserved. His interest in both the arts and theology were part of a long process in which her grandfather's concerns turned increasingly toward religion and away from the military. At the age of forty, he gave up his position in the army and entered the church, preparing to study for the priesthood. That decision was precipitated by the death of his wife, at the age of thirty-six, leaving him with four children and, it might be supposed, a personal crisis in his own life. Her death might well have brought to a focus trends that were already developing in her grandfather's own personal values, since he turned to the church later in the same year that she died. Thereafter, his career developed in the service of the church; in 1898, he took monastic vows and was given the name Serafim, in honor of the elder of Sarov, whose life and teachings he much admired.[27] Mother Serafima had little detailed knowledge about this service; she knew that he was appointed to the rank of metropolitan in 1917, the ceremony taking place in the Uspenskii sobor in the Moscow Kremlin. One of the photographs of her grandfather shows him standing beside the last Romanov tsar, Nicholas II, and his family.

After his consecration, Leonid Mikhailovich served in a Moscow cathedral located where the Lenin Library now stands. Just behind the library is a small cathedral, the Moscow Church of the Blessed Nicholas, that still remains part of the original church complex where he conducted services for more than twenty years. But the most distinctive feature of his career in the church took place soon after his appointment as metropolitan: his campaign to canonize Saint Serafim of Sarov. For many years the Holy Synod had rejected proposals to canonize Serafim; Leonid Mikhailovich, however, dug more deeply than his predecessors into the service of this remarkable churchman and wrote a book about his activities and contributions that made a convincing case.[28] Mother Serafima had a photograph, taken in January 1917, of Tsar Nicholas II and his family bearing the remains of Saint Serafim. Her grandfather's campaign succeeded when the tsar himself, having read the book about Serafim, became a supporter of the idea of canonization and urged the church's compliance.[29]

Mother Serafima had vivid memories of her grandfather and his dedication to the church, and these memories burned deeply in her mind. But one aspect of his life had remained a mystery to her. She knew little about his last years and especially about his death; that mystery had tormented her and left her without a sense of closure. She knew only that he had been arrested in 1937, at the age of eighty-five, and had disappeared into the labor camps.

The late 1930s were chaotic, mystifying times for many Soviet families, particularly for those whose family members had been arrested. In "Requiem," her famous cycle of poems about the Great Terror, the poet Anna Akhmatova describes the suffering of relatives who had to endure the imprisonment of their loved ones. She portrays an ancient land then struggling under the Soviet police state that locked people away in big, black vans at daybreak:

They led you away at dawn,
I followed you, like a mourner,
In the dark front room the children were crying,
By the icon shelf the candle was dying.
On your lips was the icon's chill.
The deathly sweat on your brow . . . Unforgettable!—
I will be like the wives of the Streltsy,
Howling under the Kremlin towers.[30]

The arrest of her son in March 1938 led Akhmatova first to a desire for
death and then nearly to madness.[31] Like Akhmatova, Mother Serafima experienced a sense of desperation and helplessness after her grandfather's arrest,
and she recalled vividly her despair: "I tried to find him. I went to every prison
in Moscow and its surrounding districts; everywhere I was told he was not
there. At the same time, rumors flew everywhere, because some people did
come back from the prisons. Some of them told me my grandfather had died
in prison. Others said he had been shot. Still others reported that they had
seen him alive." For more than fifty years, Mother Serafima had lived without
any knowledge of the actual circumstances of his death, and during this entire period she had harbored the painful thought that she should have done
more. "Even in the sunset of my life," she said, "I have dreams that I should
have done something more for him. Some people have told me that I should
write about my memories of him. Unfortunately, my grandfather left nothing. Everything, every physical trace of him, was confiscated."

The end of the Soviet state has witnessed the filling in of many blank
spaces in history. For a large number of former Soviet citizens, none has been
as dramatic or as important as the opportunity to discover facts about the fate
of their relatives. In Mother Serafima's case, such a discovery came accidentally, but the effect on her was profound and, ultimately, transforming.

While Mother Serafima had asked the KGB for files on her grandfather,
her requests had repeatedly been met with silence. But in 1994 came an important break. From a friend, she was told about a woman living in Moscow
who had collected information on the labor camps and the people who had
perished there. Mother Serafima was informed that this woman might have
information about her grandfather. The sense of expectation, even of cautious
hope, she said, was nearly overwhelming. She went to the address she was
given, a small one-room apartment in the suburbs of Moscow. She found
there an old woman, living alone in cramped quarters, her apartment filled
with boxes of index cards. This woman, Serafima soon discovered, had worked
for many years collecting the names of people who had been shot and had

transcribed the information, preserving a record and fleshing out the story of those who had disappeared into the death camps. She had learned about these people from various sources, including people who had worked in the archives of the police, and some of the files she had seen herself. "She had the names of twenty thousand people written on the cards," Mother Serafima said; "she had these boxes of cards lining the shelves of her small apartment. She told me that she feared all this work she had committed herself to, had worked on for many years, would be lost from view, because no one heretofore had ever requested from her this information."

The most striking feature of the data was that the woman had managed to work out some system of classifying the materials. She had a special category of priests shot by the NKVD, making them her own particular project and printing the names of each individual priest on a separate card. It was here that Mother Serafima found her grandfather. She learned that he had died and was buried near Butovo, a small village in central Russia that had a special rifle range operated by the NKVD, the state security police. The files of the KGB, according to the woman, who had obviously seen them, had only the names of the priests they prosecuted and then executed; the police files did not reveal very much about the person. But the files had provided a starting point, and this woman had written down the names of the condemned and the date of their execution, and then she tried to find some more detailed information about each person. For many years she had worked on this project, trying to preserve this record, never doubting its value. The boxes that lined the shelves of her small room in Moscow gave vivid testimony to her desire to preserve for history the details of one of the darkest periods in the twentieth century. From these files, Mother Serafima gained the clues that enabled her to complete the missing parts of the puzzle.

After her discovery of this information, Mother Serafima offered to help make it public, knowing that many others might benefit, and she asked the old woman for permission. The woman consented, but also stressed that, while her own name might be used, she did not want to draw much attention to her deed. Her work, she said, had been an act of love and commitment; she did not desire any public recognition for her gift of preserving the memory. Mother Serafima then took some of the materials to Metropolitan Iuvenali, a leading member of the Holy Synod, told him her story, and asked for his assistance. He complied, and together the two of them went in search of Butovo, the former rifle range of the NKVD, and the location of her grandfather's grave. "I shall never forget that excursion," Mother Serafima said. "It was in the middle of winter, and the former rifle range was now part of a large territory, surrounded by some kind of special fence. It had only one entrance gate, which we found and had opened for us, and we located the mass grave, the place where many priests were executed and in 1937 were buried in the field." After the executions, Mother Serafima learned that "the authorities planted fruit trees in the field to provide apples and other fruits for their children who were living nearby. And the police officials took a lot of pride in these fruit orchards."

Following their location of the site, Metropolitan Iuvenali took the lists of the executed church officials to Patriarch Aleksi II, and told him the story of the excursion. The lists, they soon discovered, contained not only the names of priests and bishops of the church, but also many people who had worked closely with them and who had suffered for their beliefs. Additionally, the lists included the names of the last monks of the Troitse-Sergieva Monastery at Sergiev Posad. Over several weeks in 1994, the Orthodox newspaper *Pravoslavnaia Moskva* published the entire list of people, with the accompanying photographs, who were included on the index cards in the old woman's apartment and who had perished in 1937. On Easter 1994, Patriarch Aleksi II consecrated the field where Mother Serafima's grandfather and other leaders of the church were shot. The lists of these formerly missing people gave testimony to the sufferings of many dedicated people of the church in the 1930s. Equally important, the discovery of this story enabled the church to recover an essential part of its memory—its connections to an earlier time and to its own heritage.

"Memory heals the scars of time," writes Michael Ignatieff; "photography documents the wounds."[32] In her family album Mother Serafima had three striking photographs of her grandfather placed side by side, the first of her grandfather as a graduate of the elite Pazhesskii corpus and the Artillery Academy as a young man, his face clearly revealing his confidence in the future and his certainty of his abilities. The other two photographs she obtained recently from the former classified files of the KGB. The security police, she pointed out, took two photographs before the execution of the condemned, one from the front, another from the side. The photographs of her grandfather show a person who had clearly endured a great deal of pain; his beard had been shaved, his gray hair was wildly unkempt, and his once expressive eyes stared blankly into space. These photographs serve as reminders that the past speaks with several different voices. The sense of connection has multiple meanings, and the past must be constructed out of what one chooses to remember and what one elects to forget. Vladimir Nabokov in *Speak, Memory* writes of the stored energies that exile and dispossession release when one tries to reel in the past, when one seeks to reconsider one's own inheritance. "Suddenly," he points out, "just when the colors and outlines settle at last to their various duties—some knob is touched and a torrent of sounds comes to life; voices speaking all together, a walnut cracked, the click of nutcracker carelessly passed, thirty human hearts drowning mine with their regular beats; the sough and sigh of a thousand trees."[33] In Mother Serafima's case, these energies came from her attempt to reclaim the memories of her grandfather. Such energies would lead her to reexamine certain features of her childhood and her career and enable her to reconstruct both her own identity and chart the rebirth of Novodevichy. In order to grasp more fully the sources of this reconstruction and rebirth, it is essential to take a closer look at Mother Serafima's own story.

A Personal Pilgrimage

Mother Serafima's professional career took place entirely within the Soviet period and was greatly shaped by the Soviet scientific establishment, in which she would rise to a prominent position. Her own journey to the top of her profession, however, was one in which fortuitous events, struggles, and remarkable inner resources played a large role. While her background has many features in common with other women of the Soviet period, it also contains some unusual ones.

She was born in St. Petersburg in 1914, but she had no memory of her father, who died on the front lines in the First World War. Both her father and her mother belonged to the Russian nobility; her father had worked in the Finnish legation under Prime Minister Peter Stolypin. In 1917, widowed, afraid of being alone in Petrograd when the Revolution began and German armies pressed near the city, Serafima's mother moved with her two children to Moscow, in order to find protection near their grandfather. Mother Serafima recalled the desperation of their move, her mother's cutting of ties with everything familiar, their house and their lifestyle, now only memories. "We left everything in Petrograd, all that we had known and cherished and we traveled to Moscow, taking only what we could carry in our arms, practically naked."

After their arrival in Moscow in late 1917, her grandfather Leonid Mikhailovich, trying to avoid the turmoil that engulfed the city, sent them outside Moscow to a monastery not far away on the Volga River. Serafima, her mother, and sister had to bide their time, believing that the chaos would soon subside. But the revolutionary fervor did not end quickly, and the family remained in the monastery for eight years, from 1917 to 1925, attempting to adjust to their new circumstances and eke out a meager existence: "Thankfully, my mother had finished the courses in medicine offered in St. Petersburg by Mariia Fedorovna Romanova, and she was able to find work as a doctor's assistant in a nearby regional hospital. My mother was a well-educated woman who spoke several languages, and it was difficult for her—to make the adjustments she was now forced to make, to get over being a Chichagov. But she managed to do it, and somehow, although we had little money, we acquired a cow and a small piece of land." Mother Serafima vividly recalled as a girl of eight, going to the field, planting a small crop, reaping its meager harvest. "We were just trying to survive," she explained, "and we had little else save our own determination."

In 1925 her mother moved to the Moscow region, taking a job in a tuberculosis sanitarium. The two children went to school and often to the church in the monastery in which they lived, and the religious world it offered impressed itself strongly on the mind of the young girl who would become Mother Serafima. "My older sister attended school in the monastery," Mother Serafima said, "and although I was very young, I often went with her to classes. I also regularly attended services in the cathedral. Nobody, as I recall, demanded this from me, I just did it. I awakened at 6 A.M. and went there by myself and, of course, this whole environment, this atmosphere of my childhood, would greatly influence my future development and my internal life."

Mother Serafima recalled the years of her childhood and adolescence as times of study and hard work, of a struggle to survive and to adapt to the rapidly changing circumstances that her family life entailed. At home, inside the family circle, her grandfather was a large presence. He did not seem critical of Soviet power, he simply tried to ignore it, and she does not recall him talking much about it. Neither did he force her to share his religious views: "Perhaps he thought that we lived in such a time that a person had to choose his own way. He knew of course that I attended the church, but I went entirely on my own."

In her later school years, she developed a passionate interest in chemistry, which she intended to pursue. But with her aristocratic and proclerical family background, she knew she had little chance of gaining admission to a university. Moscow State University remained for her a dream, and while she knew she could never realize that dream, she held on to it for many years. Instead, she applied to study in a technical institute in Moscow, choosing to specialize in a subject in which there were then few applicants: higher molecular chemistry. It was a fortuitous choice because it led her into rubber technology, which "few people at that time considered to be very important." During her years of study in the institute, she lived with her grandfather. It was at this time, after she had begun her studies, that he was arrested. "In 1937 we knew that my grandfather would be imprisoned, since he was a well-known leader of the Church. I remember clearly the day when my aunt, who was a nun, came to our apartment to say farewell to my grandfather. That scene has always burned vividly in my mind."

While these tormented feelings continued to plague her memory after her grandfather's arrest, unexpected circumstances would shape her own professional career. The Second World War and the military preparations for it dramatically changed the demand for specialists in her field and the importance of that specialty to the Soviet Union's national survival. During the war, she worked in a plant that produced rubber, and she clearly recalled the enormous effort required both by women and men in her factory to produce the material that the Soviet army required. Many nights "we would sleep only for two hours and sometimes not at all, and we simply went on working almost desperately to produce this material." Memories of her earlier life receded in the difficult efforts and exigencies of the times. But such circumstances did not totally destroy her inner being nor the memories that had earlier defined her world. "During these years," she emphasized, "I tried to keep my faith inside me—in my soul."

In the period immediately after the war, seeing career opportunities for young women in her specialized field, Mother Serafima threw herself into study and research. During the day, she continued to work in the factory, but in the evenings, she began postgraduate study in a Moscow technical institute and concentrated on the production of synthetic rubber. She did not feel any great interest or emotional attachment to the field she chose to study. Her main interests were more theoretical, but practical concerns primarily motivated her action: "I did not have the chance to choose freely the subject I wanted to study. I entered the institute because it had an evening program that allowed me to receive an additional stipend, and I very much needed the money." The plant in which she worked during the day had only five people on its staff, the rest having been evacuated during the war. Mother Serafima recalled the extremely difficult working conditions and the intense heat, a situation that did not attract many people. But when the decision was made shortly afterward to restore and develop this plant, Mother Serafima was in an excellent position to take advantage of this opportunity. Despite the stigma of her aristocratic family background, she had some excellent advantages: she was young; she was willing to work hard; she had already proved herself under intense pressure; she combined the practical with the theoretical in her work—all of which were highly valued in an industry rapidly becoming one of the most prominent in the postwar Soviet Union. She admitted that she became increasingly drawn, intellectually and emotionally, to her subject, and what began as an occupation chosen because of practical necessity became one of deep commitment.

Mother Serafima spent the next forty-five years as a chemist and researcher in the field of rubber technology, charting a highly successful career in Soviet science and technology. She devoted her life to her work, and it shaped who she became, a chemist of considerable professional standing among the technical elite in the Soviet Union. Her accomplishments and the high value in which she was regarded were recognized by the awarding of several prizes in chemistry and her appointment as deputy director of her research institute in Moscow. She was part of a generation that, in the wake of the purges of the 1930s, advanced very rapidly up the career ladder.[34] "I was a typical Soviet high-ranking female administrator of an institute. I worked from very early in the morning until late at night," she said. "As every Soviet woman was told, I was instructed only to work hard. I thought that without my work I would not be able to live."

During these years in which she became increasingly prominent, she did not join the Communist Party. She had no desire to do so, and while this kept her from gaining an even higher appointment, it did not hamper her work. There were conflicts, of course. In the research institute, she said, she faced little political pressure, but in the plant she was urged several times to become a member of the Party. On other occasions, managerial groups in the administration wanted to appoint her director; membership in the Party was a requirement for that position, and she felt strong pressure to join. "I tried to explain to them that I was not yet ready," she said. "I used many such pretexts."

One of the elements that defused some of the political pressure on Mother Serafima, particularly during the intense Party membership drives of the Khrushchev period, related to her mother. In 1953, following the death of Stalin, Serafima's mother returned to the existence she had known as a young woman, spending her last years in a monastery. She entered the Pyukhtitsa Dormition nunnery at Iykhvi-Ukarty in Estonia, one of the three open convents and the largest in the Soviet Union. From the age of seventy until her death at eighty in 1963, she would serve in this well-known convent. While

Mother Serafima did not discuss her own response to her mother's decision, she said that she had mixed feelings about it; her mother, she said, was not always a stable person. Nevertheless, her mother's course of action did remove the political pressure she often faced in the plant. "Once the party administration learned that my mother lived in the convent and went to live there when she was seventy years old, they didn't ask me again to join the Party. They apparently thought that I was a hopeless case," she laughed, and "believed that nothing could be done with me."

Despite the intense personal pressures she sometimes faced, Mother Serafima strove to create for herself a "normal life." She married a man who worked as an art specialist. He was also, she maintained, an extremely religious person, although he kept his beliefs private. Few knew of his deepest commitments, and publicly he kept them separate from his professional activities. But, privately, he explored the religious themes of the art he studied. The couple did not have children; they were committed to their work and to each other, and their work gave both of them a sense of identity and purpose. When they thought about themselves and the future, Mother Serafima said, they did so primarily in terms of their professions.

Mother Serafima's own decision to enter the service of the church, after her long successful career as a chemist, came about for several reasons. The death of her husband in the early 1990s, when she was seventy-seven, left a large void in her life, she admitted, and presented her with a serious personal crisis. The simultaneous political changes in Russia opened up religious opportunities that had been impossible for nearly half a century. Moreover, she was nearing retirement, and as a person who had given herself completely to her work as a chemist, she feared the emptiness she knew lay ahead: "I thought that without my work I would not be able to live. I was afraid to leave the institute and to retire, and the question continued to press hard upon me of 'what to do?'" But the most important element underlying her decision turned out to be the pictures of her grandfather that she had carried all these years deep within her memory and that now spoke to her with more authority. Her struggles recall Susan Sontag's comments in her essay on photography. Sontag has described photographs as figments of identity, shaping the imagination, recalling the past, connecting the individual to the deeper recesses of personality than one may realize in one's own consciousness. "Through family photographs," Sontag writes, "each family constructs a portrait-chronicle of itself—a portable kit of images that bears witness to its connectedness. . . . A family's photograph album is generally about the extended family—and,

often, is all that remains of it."[35] Mother Serafima's experience sought these
connections, both in the photographs she kept and in her grandfather's writings that she treasured; for several years she had thought about working on her
grandfather's materials and trying to recover for others his life and theological
writings. She often saw his face; his eyes seemed to call her, to reach out to her.
But she avoided putting her desires into action, doubting that she had the
intellectual skills to recover her grandfather's ideas. "I could not imagine," she
admitted, "how I, without any theological education or any serious theological knowledge, could describe his internal life and his thought."

After two years of suffering with these doubts, reading intensively in theological literature, and consulting with priests who encouraged her, she decided to proceed with the story of her grandfather. She gathered his sermons,
many of which had remained unpublished, and searched archives for his theological writings. This work moved forward, as she recalled, with great difficulty, and she sifted vigorously—and patiently—through collections that
had been closed for many years. Eventually, she had collected enough materials for two volumes and published them under the title *Da budet voyat Tvoya*
(*Let Thy Will Be*). She issued the volumes under her grandfather's name,
rather than her own, adding a short biography of his life. "I simply could not
accept the fact," she said, "that since 1937 nobody knew about him, and I felt
it my duty to rectify that. Nobody prayed for him in the Church; I simply
could not accept this forgetfulness any longer."

At the same time that she was being pulled in the direction of her grandfather, she was coming closer to her return to the church. She described her
choice as an easy one, but one that left her often feeling unprepared and frus-
trated:

> My decision was quite natural to me. I can't really say how it happened. It
> was not that I was motivated by some special kind of interest or anything like
> that. As a scientist, I had many rewards; my biography, in terms of Soviet life,
> was without any shadow. I understood, of course, that I would have to answer
> for everything. I needed to give up my pride; I needed to discover my humility.
> I decided therefore, to go to work in the cathedral. My job was to sell candles; it
> was the lowest level work in the cathedral, and I did it for more than two years.
>
> And I learned a great deal from the experience because all this time I
> talked with the people. I met the people coming to the cathedral for the first
> time, people who knew nothing about religion, and I had to explain everything
> to them. As a result, many days I only talked; I had no time even to pray. I
> asked the priest what I should do. "I am standing here the whole day," I said,
> "and I couldn't even hear your words."

These recollections are part of Mother Serafima's transformation, since she had to renew her own understanding of the practice and teachings of the church. Her experiences also testify to the attempts to rebuild the church's role in Russian society. She spoke of the popular interest and hunger for greater knowledge of the relationship between religion and Russian culture. In an attempt to respond to this hunger, she organized among the people who came to her in the cathedral a group that met to study religion, art, and architecture and that traveled to many historical sites to examine these connections. Occasionally, her informal group asked priests to meet with them and explain the teachings of great church leaders in the Orthodox tradition. From its extremely modest beginnings as a small discussion circle, her group soon expanded in number and eventually developed, in interests and ideas, into one trying to recover the role of the church in society.

In 1992, Mother Serafima applied to become a nun and, later that year, she was consecrated. In 1994, when the government made the decision to return Novodevichy to the church's possession, she was the person whom the church chose to supervise the monastery's renewal. She combined the new and the old. She was a "modern Russian," a working woman with a career in science, without children, yet with ties to the past, to national history, military successes, the pre-Soviet world, and the old Orthodox Church. Her organizational skills and experience as the former assistant director of a scientific institute and her own personal pilgrimage made her a logical choice to rebuild one of Russia's most historic religious communities, a monastery that, although closed since 1922 and officially called only Novodevichy, was still known popularly to Muscovites as Novodevichy Monastery.

Renewal and the Struggle for Survival

The story of Mother Serafima's attempts to rebuild parish life at Novodevichy illustrates the challenges the church faces as Russia seeks to transform itself from within. The tasks she confronted required her to start nearly at the beginning. While part of the monastery had been restored by the Soviet government, much of it lay in disrepair; most important, the strong traditions attached to the parish—its economic independence, charitable activities, and social services—had to be totally reconstructed. Such challenges and responses bear a closer look because they are indicative of the religious renewal now taking place in Russia.

The first difficulty concerned the relationship between church and state and monastery, which had once functioned as a state museum. This relationship is an extremely delicate one, fraught with many problems. Currently, in Novodevichy Monastery, the church controls only the Smolenskii Cathedral, and it tries to live peacefully with the other parts of the monastery that the state operates as a museum. Several reasons account for the cooperation between these two parts: the museum has more funds than the church and can preserve important art objects in the cathedral, whereas the church has not yet been able to afford specialists to restore the old buildings and the murals. Mother Serafima was fully aware of and appreciated the role of specialists in preserving Russia's religious art, which exists today "only because museum specialists and its workers," since the late 1920s, "did their best to keep from destruction the sacred objects in the Uspenskii and Smolenskii Cathedrals." But she also knew that the whole issue of future control over these buildings and art objects was "filled with potential conflict."[36]

Novodevichy's struggle to reassert itself was also closely related to the problem of finances. The monastery had no regular sources of income; it had to depend almost totally on the donations of the people who worship there and, until it had its own economic services back in operation, it existed in an extremely precarious financial position that threatened to undermine the most energetic efforts. In prerevolutionary Russia, monasteries often had extensive agricultural and craft operations, whose sales sustained religious and social activities. But at monasteries like Novodevichy, these economic traditions have not been preserved.

In addition to these economic challenges, Mother Serafima also had to deal with family problems that confront the nuns in the monastery every day. A large number of women came to the monastery seeking help with the brokenness and social dislocation they had to live with nearly all the time. The problems they brought to Mother Serafima provided clear testimony of the suffering that many Russian women have to bear within their families; the daily visits that many of them made to the monastery speak to the intense demoralization that currently characterizes much of Russian society. "Many women come here asking for help and needing counsel," Mother Serafima said, "because they don't have the means to live or because their husband or son often gets drunk and treats them badly. Sometimes these women simply ask me to bless or pray for them—to give them strength to deal with their hardships." Some of the women who came faced difficult practical decisions in trying to survive in the harsh economic realities of present-day Russia. Many of these women were financially destitute and often were tempted to sell their apartments to gain additional funds. Mother Serafima and her nuns counseled them. "I try to get them to think beyond the moment and consider all the consequences; I always ask them 'What will you do after you sell? Where will you live?' It is often obvious that these women do not have any place to go and will have to live in the railway station, the city gardens, or the metro." Sometimes women came to the monastery searching for food or needing protection from their husbands; a few came to learn about religion. But, according to Mother Serafima, "by far the largest number of women who seek me out do so because of instability in their families," something Mother Serafima had experience with. She emphasized that she tried to treat each case individually, because each of them had a different context. The government-sponsored network of social services had crumbled in the last decade. Despite their extremely limited funds, Novodevichy and other religious institutions were struggling to fill this gap.

Earlier, before the Bolsheviks closed them down, Novodevichy had many craft activities that supported the monastery's social services. These craft activities offered promising sources of economic renewal. But the main problem is that these crafts had to be almost totally re-created, since they too had not been practiced since the monastery's closure in 1922. Rebuilding the crafts of the monastery Mother Serafima saw as one of her greatest challenges. She had made plans to organize several craft shops, and she showed me a small carpet of a covering for the sofa that had already been produced. She would soon establish a sewing center for the monastery to make clerical garments for the nuns that were extremely difficult to buy. She also intended to create a small bakery to produce bread for the services. In these activities, the model she used is based on the Convent of the Dormition in Pyukhtitsa, Estonia, where her mother lived, and the convent at Kolomenskoe, which produced porcelain and embroidered cloth. "We are going to develop such possibilities," she said emphatically. "Right now we are only in the initial stages, but we are going to work hard on these craft activities." At one time, she reminded me, the monastery was economically self-sufficient; it had a very sizable economic base that enabled it to perform its religious functions without fear of collapse. Presently, that economic base existed only in memory.

But her determination and sense of urgency were strong characteristics of Mother Serafima, and her experience working in industry and the organizational skills she developed there were now brought to bear on these tasks. Listening to her talk, one sensed that she is fighting a war, different from the earlier battle with the Germans but no less desperate a struggle for survival, and one that demanded all one's inner resources. "Everything, physical and psychological, was nearly destroyed and needs to be restored," she told me in June

1997; "if I can contribute to this cause, it is primarily because I have fifty-five years of experience in organizational work. Still, it is much easier for me to construct a building than to restore a cathedral with its paintings." Her task involved not the rebuilding of physical structures but the reconstruction of memories, traditions, and spiritual values that nourished a whole way of life.

In dealing with the social challenges the monastery has had to confront, goodwill, vision, and perseverance have played an important role. In 1994 and early 1995, as Novodevichy struggled to reopen many of its former functions, the Russian Cultural Foundation extended to it an extremely helpful hand. In February 1995, the Cultural Foundation organized a concert of Russian religious music performed by the world-famous opera singer Irina Arkhipova in the Bol'shoi Theater. Proceeds from the concert went to Mother Serafima and the nuns at Novodevichy. Following that performance, Arkhipova presented another concert, organized by Mother Serafima, in the spectacular setting of the Smolenskii Cathedral in Novodevichy itself. "This was the first time such a concert had ever been given in our cathedral," Mother Serafima said, "and I worried a great deal about it. I was not sure what kind of reaction I would get from Metropolitan Iuvenali, and while I know that in the West such church concerts are normal activities, in our country it is not in our tradition to have these in the cathedral."

To obtain the metropolitan's permission, Mother Serafima confessed to a little trickery. Chuckling as she talked, she admitted that she waited until the last minute before informing Metropolitan Iuvenali of the concert: "I knew I was taking a great risk in doing this. I went to Metropolitan Iuvenali after all the preparations had been made and told him about the concert that was going to take place," she said. "I felt he could not reject the idea of hosting such a world-famous singer on the eve of the event!" The audience invited to that concert in the cathedral consisted mainly of dignitaries, some of whom made financial contributions to the monastery on that evening. The organizational costs for the concert were minimal, and only the expenses for television coverage had to be paid, with revenues from that evening, like the preceding performance in the Bol'shoi Theater, going to the monastery. The proceeds from these concerts aided greatly in Novodevichy's early recovery.

Novodevichy Monastery has a large piece of land, eleven hectares (twenty-seven acres) in size, located some seventy kilometers (about forty-three miles) from Moscow. In earlier times, the monastery used such land to grow food and to provide funds for its religious activities, but for more than seventy years the monastery has not practiced these agricultural activities. Mother Serafima believed they are fundamental elements in the monastery's revival, and while she desperately needed large sums of money for investment in the land, she nevertheless struggled to do what she could. She remembered some of the agricultural techniques she used in her childhood, and she and the other nuns had planted potatoes and other vegetables. She had organized the nuns to work collectively on the land. "When we go there," she said, "I am always glad to observe the fruits of our labor. The field is green. To see it in such a condition is a wonderful experience."

This plot of land in the Moscow suburbs exists as a subsidiary of Novodevichy, a channel that contributes goods essential to the monastery's survival. On this land stands a small, beautiful church built in the eighteenth century and connected by the nuns to the whole agricultural cycle of the land. Located there is a cattle yard in which the monastery currently maintains the livestock of a small farm—a horse, three cows, several calves, and some goats. The milk, cottage cheese, and potatoes and other vegetables from this operation are brought to Moscow, and they enable the monastery to sustain itself and perform vital functions, including feeding some of the people who come there during the winter. But it is extremely difficult to transport dairy products such a distance, and the monastery cannot rely on their consistent arrival. In restoring its economic operations, the monastery must constantly struggle with uncertainty.

In her attempt to revive the religious life of Novodevichy, Mother Serafima had thus far accepted twelve women for training as nuns. The process of selecting these women revealed, in several ways, the complex social problems that both Russian society and the church face. In her description of the selection process, Mother Serafima emphasized that she had received an enormous number of requests from women of all ages asking to be taken into the service of the church. The letters had come from many parts of Russia, including remote regions in eastern Siberia and from the north. Mother Serafima, however, had hesitated to admit women she did not personally know. She had had to counsel many young women who had come to her, wishing to enter the monastery, telling them that their primary service ought to be the care of their children. Mother Serafima's comments again provided testimony of the intense attraction of religious service to many young women, as well as of the extreme social dislocation and psychological demoralization of Russian society. (See the previous chapter about Fr Georgii Kochetkov's urban community for a similar discussion.)

The monastery is a place of silence, and that silence and communion with both God and the world is its essential meaning. Novodevichy holds the silence; even in the long years when it was closed and had no means of articulating itself verbally, it expressed itself with its silent beauty, its stillness in the midst of the political firestorm outside its stout walls. "So what is silence?" asks the American author Patricia Hampl in a similar context: "Silence speaks, the contemplatives say. But really, I think, silence sorts. An ordinary instinct sets people into the hush where the voice can be heard. This is the intelligence of sorting, marked by the unbroken certainty of rhythm, perfect pitch, the placing of things in right order as in metrical form. Not rigid categories, but the recognition of a shape always there but ordinarily obscured by—what? By noise, which is ourselves trying to do the sorting in an order that may be a heroic effort but is bound to be a fantasy."[37]

Since their quarters were not yet restored, most of the nuns at Novodevichy lived in two worlds, moving between the city and the monastery, between the sounds of the city and the solitude of the monastery. Arriving at the monastery each morning at 6:15 for two hours of prayer, the nuns then helped the priests perform the liturgy, spent the day at various tasks, and concluded with walks through the monastery and another two hours of prayer, before returning late each evening to their apartments in the city. "It is not easy for them to adjust to the monastery," Mother Serafima emphasized, and she dreamed of the day when all her nuns could exercise the discipline and experience the harmony that life in the monastery required.

The selection of women for the monastery was one of Mother Serafima's most important tasks. She tried to take young women "because we have a lot of work to do and we need physically able people." In addition, they had to be women who "live the life of the church." Only five of the twelve women she had accepted into the monastery had so far been consecrated, and Mother Serafima admitted she had a high set of expectations. She examined both the prospective nuns' behavior and demeanor and asked the following questions of those she had admitted: "How do they conduct their work? What are their salient characteristics? Most important, what are their actions in reality? Are they able to give up their personal pride? Do they show proper respect and obey the monastery's rules and orders?" To Mother Serafima, these questions lay at the center of the inner development of monastic life in her parish; as she tried to develop a core of women to serve the church, they were foremost in her mind.

As she thought about this development, Mother Serafima recalled women who served the church, beginning in the 1920s, as the government persecuted religion. Officially, these women were not nuns, since they were not consecrated by the church. But, Mother Serafima said, they were known to us as "secret nuns," and during the years when the church came under severe attack by the government, such women performed unofficially the role of nuns; they were Russia's Sisters of Mercy. Inspired by their faith and courage, they were the people who rendered service to the sick, comforted those who suffered, and embraced ideals that the government berated.

Mother Serafima's ambitious plans to strengthen the physical and economic aspects of Novodevichy Monastery related only to part of the problems she had to face. More difficult even than these was the renewal of the psychological and cultural aspects to which her work related. In the past, the church contributed a great deal to popular attitudes and customs. Such attitudes and customs, especially the sense of compassion, were greatly in need of restoration. In present-day Russian society, the two groups at each end of the age spectrum, the elderly and the young, have experienced the greatest social dislocation, and Mother Serafima's mission related particularly to them. But, in addition, she was concerned with the whole tenor of life and the personal values that were presently shaping it. The renewal of parish life, she believed, required a different set of commitments, including the rebuilding of *miloserdie,* a concept that, to her, was central to those commitments.

THE SENSE OF COMPASSION

Miloserdie literally means "dear-heartedness" or "compassion for others." It is a term close to the Latin word *caritas,* or "charity," but to confine it to that meaning alone or only to the church's charitable activities fails to convey the rich associations that *miloserdie* has in the Russian language. It evokes a whole range of ideas deeply embodied in Christianity: mercy, compassion, kindness, and extension of the self to others. What is especially striking is that *miloserdie* had almost become a forgotten word, exorcised from the Soviet lexicon as "obsolete."[38] The nuclear disaster at Chernobyl' in April 1986, which accelerated the need for social initiative from below, served as a main catalyst for the rebirth of *miloserdie* and, during the administration of Mikhail Gorbachev, it became one of the central terms on which he hoped to build. In response to the nuclear catastrophe, Soviet citizens raised more than 500 million rubles to aid the victims. President Gorbachev's meeting with the patriarch and other church leaders in April 1988 gave back to the church the right to engage in charitable activities, which the government had taken away in 1929. Monasteries, in particular, had conveyed a special image of *miloserdie* in Russia, cultivating such mercy and compassion and projecting them into society. The Soviet government's earlier attacks on the monastery would thus have greater consequences than the destruction of religious institutions. These attacks would also undermine the whole range of ideas and sensibilities that the monastery embodied.

In March 1987, nearly a year after the Chernobyl' nuclear disaster, the prominent newspaper *Literaturnaia gazeta* published an article by the Leningrad writer Daniil Granin, that brought back *miloserdie* to public consciousness. Appearing in a central location in the newspaper, the article made a powerful statement about society and the loss of ideals.[39] Granin sought to restore the concept behind *miloserdie* from the obscure backrooms of Soviet life and to place it squarely at the forefront for discussion and debate. The article was one of those rare pieces that reawakened certain ideas and associations that had long lain dormant in the public mind, and would focus a whole series of concerns then coming together from several different quarters of Soviet life. The issues he discussed would relate directly to the activities that Mother Serafima would later aim to restore at Novodevichy.

Beginning his article with a personal anecdote, Granin described how, walking home early one evening, he slipped on a patch of ice near his apartment and struck his head on the pavement. Bleeding and in severe pain, he walked with great difficulty to his home. No one stopped and offered help or inquired as to his difficulty but, instead, either hurried along or looked away.

This exhibition of public indifference raised in Granin's mind a whole series of larger issues and concerns in his society. He wrote movingly about an event that took place shortly thereafter, when he spent the night in the hospital while being treated for his injury. He described the filth, the overcrowded rooms, the overwhelmed doctors who staffed the hospital, a typical facility in the center of Moscow. During the night, unable to sleep, he wandered along the corridor of the hospital, making his way past the beds that lined the walls, when he heard an old woman crying. Going to her bedside, he saw that she was dying, and he took her hand in his. She told him that she was entirely alone, that her relatives lived at too great a distance to visit her. As she gripped his hand tightly, she softly prayed, and he knew that she was taking her last breath. Granin wrote that he had seen death many times earlier in the war, but the memory of this encounter would not leave him; to be completely alone at such a moment comprised the ultimate torment. The irony of the situation he found extremely troubling: "how did our professed concern with human beings, free medicine, humanity, and collectivity connect with that old woman who, having worked nearly all this century, died in such circumstances? Is this not shameful?" he asked. He found extremely disturbing the loss of connectedness to other people, the indifference to misfortune and suffering that he saw all around him, and the seeming unconcern with the plight of individuals needing help.

Framing his essay with a quotation from Pushkin's poem "Pamiatnik" ("Memorial"), Granin discussed *miloserdie* as one of the key ideals that had inspired Russia's great literature. In that literary tradition, the writer had held a responsibility to the lowly and the downtrodden, which Russia's greatest writers had considered to be a moral demand. This moral demand appeared in many of Pushkin's stories, and would later echo in the works of Gogol and Turgenev, Nekrasov and Dostoevsky, Tolstoy and Korolenko, Chekhov and Leskov. According to Granin, such writers portrayed the unprivileged as a kind of "fourth estate" or as "people with a soul," to whom compassion and respect, on the part of the privileged, had to be extended. In many of Russia's greatest literary works, the main characters were depicted as having a special responsibility to the poverty stricken, the orphaned, and the destitute; that theme was exemplified in such people as Sonia Marmaladov in Dostoevsky's *Crime and Punishment* and Katiusha Maslova in Tolstoy's *Resurrection.* Russia's classical literary works displayed a sense of compassion and responsibility and had cultivated such feelings in Russia's social consciousness.

Granin's article tried to explore the question of why *miloserdie* had diminished in Soviet society: why had our people grown deaf to that old ideal and why did it no longer seem important, had even become superfluous, he asked? Why had the feeling of interdependence been undermined?[40] He sought to explore the reasons underlying the lack of compassion and the loss of trust in Russian society and cultural life in the twentieth century. He attributed much of the problem to the political terror in Russia: Stalin's violent campaign to collectivize agriculture in the late 1920s and 1930s, followed by the great purge, had cultivated a climate of social indifference toward others and a kind of numbness toward suffering. In this setting, self-preservation became the preeminent goal; one simply could not appear sympathetic toward the plight of the victims. The social atmosphere spawned by the terror was one of fear and isolation—indifference toward one's neighbors and estrangement toward anyone accused of criminal activity. Such apathetic attitudes became essential to preserving oneself and one's family. The lies that were propagated, the political sleights of hand that were repeatedly exercised, the deceitful actions that were everywhere manifested in the name of the law combined to coarsen the spiritual health of the Soviet people. They implanted, Granin maintained, a lifelessness, an indifference, and a loss of connectedness to others that undermined and eventually replaced the traditional concept of *miloserdie.* Convinced that human beings have an ingrained need to help those who are less fortunate, Granin claimed that if *miloserdie* is not exercised it will atrophy. Soviet life in the last half century had encouraged such atrophy, and *miloserdie* was now regarded as an archaic concept, no longer relevant or useful in modern life. Granin recalled a street in Leningrad named Miloserdie, whose name had been changed to Tekstilnaia (Textile), symbolic of the hard-nosed goals and technical values that now predominated.

Where in post–World War II literature, Granin asked, could one find compassion for people who were evacuated from their home place? In what works did one discover sympathy for the millions of civilians who suffered from the Fascist occupation in World War II or for the millions of people who felt the pain of captivity? Russian literature, Granin argued, had to listen to the older voice of Pushkin; the writer had to heed the call of *miloserdie,* and for Russia to heal itself, this sense of compassion and responsibility for others had to be regained. It would be a call that Mother Serafima and others like her would hear clearly and that would inspire, in large part, her desire to reconnect to Russia's cultural traditions.

Granin's essay and his discussion of *miloserdie* provoked a lively discussion shortly after the essay appeared. Even in the conservative press, the term received a great deal of attention, especially for its emphasis on moral duty, social cohesion, and the interdependence of members of the community.[41] But to many others like Mother Serafima, *miloserdie* evoked a different kind of response. Nearly a decade after Granin's article appeared, activities at Novodevichy sought to actively apply the characteristics associated with *miloserdie*— characteristics also ingrained in Russian Christianity—particularly the sense of compassion, the responsibility for the destitute, and the holiness of all of God's creation. Mother Serafima's plan for building a hospital, her work with the elderly, and the care of the destitute were related to this concept of *miloserdie;* they represented key parts of her vision for the future. She strongly believed that the monastery, instead of cutting itself off from the world, must be closely connected to it.

The stereotype of the monastery in Russia is of something distant from worldly affairs, removed from society, a refuge from worldly problems and concerns. The image of the monastery in the wilderness, as an escape from the material conflicts of human existence, is a widely prevalent one in writings on the church. Such an image, however, poorly characterizes the monastic life that Mother Serafima sought to restore. As a place of reflection, Novodevichy was not removed from the world, but instead accepted the most difficult social and psychological problems as its own. Rather than seeking to escape,

Mother Serafima wanted it to hold up a mirror to those problems and to take on the search for their solution.

Novodevichy projected a collective responsibility for the sufferings that are everywhere visible; it has meager resources, but those it had were extended to others and, in the summer of 1997, they included helping one of the main children's hospitals in Moscow, caring for the elderly, and feeding the hungry. On August 10, 1997, the day of celebration of the Smolensk Mother of God icon, Mother Serafima was preparing a dining table for 220 people in the refectory of the cathedral. On religious holidays in the village where Novodevichy had a rural parish, she and her nuns often prepared food for all the villagers, approximately 250 people, many of whom were sick and elderly. These were efforts to rebuild the life of the parish, reach out to people in need, and restore the church and the sense of compassion within the whole society.

Her images of the monastery's role in society were also derived from earlier memories and experiences. When she was a younger woman, Mother Serafima had traveled to Italy as part of a Soviet scientific delegation. For many years she carried with her images of that trip abroad; she especially remembered the Catholic nuns and their active involvement in society, particularly in medicine and education. The examples she witnessed in Catholic schools gave her models that she remembered all these years and now, as head of Novodevichy, she aspired to put certain aspects of them into practice. The monastery would soon open its own school near the cathedral. It would prepare children for service in the church and in society, and *miloserdie* will lie at the center of its educational program.

In these concrete ways, Mother Serafima connected Novodevichy to its role in the past and its service to the people. As the photographs of her grandfather recalled her own heritage, Novodevichy represented a kind of photograph of the national past—a place of refuge for people in times of need but also a place that actively reached out to people who were suffering, elderly, destitute, with nowhere else to turn. As Michael Ignatieff suggests, photographs are bittersweet: they remind us of what we have left behind and may not wish to remember, and they recall for us what we have missed and need to recover. At its best, Novodevichy stood as a photo of *miloserdie;* the sense of compassion the monastery exhibited was submerged but not forgotten. In her work Mother Serafima wanted to reinvigorate Novodevichy Monastery with *miloserdie,* which she connected both to its history and to her grandfather. The monastery evoked the large photographs that were forever imprinted on her mind—the memories of her grandfather, pictures of women's

Mother Serafima, director of Novodevichy Monastery from 1994 to her death in December 1999.

work in the world, her remembrances of *miloserdie,* and images of Novodevichy and what it could again become.

It is commonly stated that the strength of Russia's future economy and society will depend on the emergence of a capitalist economy and a consumer culture. Capitalist economic relationships to many people are thus seen as the keys to Russia's transformation. It is assumed that such an economic structure will increasingly draw citizens in to new forms of behavior and interactions with each other.

But a consumer culture does not necessarily lead to altruism; economic relationships need to be bolstered by other factors. As Mother Serafima's life suggests, the most important elements are cultural and religious in nature, which relate to traditions and norms that will structure the market and provide the ultimate context in which it will operate. The irony is that Russia's new globalized economy and the emphasis on a privatized economic structure and heightened sense of competition are also pushing such people as Mother

Serafima back toward an earlier rhythm. Her actions again raise the question of whether or not *miloserdie* is "innate" or culturally acquired and how it might best be nurtured. She was not comfortable with the consumerism and the standard of values that were rapidly developing. "We should not think only about such material wealth as possessing a car, buying furniture, and owning a comfortable apartment," she said. "We must have clearly in our mind other standards." She knew it was not easy to live through these days: "Many people complain about the hardships we have to endure; they do not have enough food and money; social pressures are becoming more intense. Nevertheless, despite the pressures, in my soul I myself feel a certain quietness." This sense of peace, however, did not mean cutting herself off from the world around her. She told me she took an even greater interest than before in the life of her society; she followed closely both world news and the current political and social events in her country. "I want to know what is happening to our people," she said, "but what is happening doesn't depress me or cause me to turn my mind inward. I don't say this because I consider myself unique but because my religion helps me to look at the world through different eyes."

She also knew that the boundaries of her society were changing. *Miloserdie,* the sense of compassion, that she embraced came directly in conflict with the aggressive consumerism that was everywhere evident. In entering the monastery, she had to turn her back on her attachments to possessions, and she had few regrets about her decisions and the radical changes that had resulted from them. She gave away her house in the village and her flat in Moscow: "I had a very good flat with a large library, because in the past I held a high position that helped me acquire these possessions. But such things now mean nothing to me. When my relatives complain that they do not have some item, I talk very tough with them. I try to convince them that all these things lie quite far from what is most important in life."

While Mother Serafima did not dispute the significance of Russia's economic reforms, she did not see them as the forces that will ultimately shape Russia's future identity. She believed that religion was the key to renewal, and the role that the church played would greatly influence Russia's political and social development. Whether the church supported the xenophobic nationalism that its past ideology has so often motivated it to do, or whether the church became a more open, tolerant, compassionate, and socially active institution would play a large part in determining the chances for evolving a democratic structure in Russia.

Civil society is built on a complex web of institutions—voluntary associations, clubs, unions, educational institutions, churches, and charities.[42]

These institutions are in turn built on the family, for it is there that the values supporting the broader culture are nourished and transmitted.[43] Such values depend on the relations between human beings, and it is these relations that Mother Serafima hoped to change and transform. She was involved in social reform, in trying to help women find a better way for themselves and their children, in trying to restore their dignity and resolve. To her, Russian Orthodoxy held the key to rebuilding the family, and the values that are central to its theology—redemption, compassion, kindness, forgiveness, and respect for every individual—provided the basis of her vision.

Her reading of *miloserdie* was a vital part of the reforms she sought. She called, therefore, for a different interpretation of civil society than what is often given, as relating mainly to political and economic reforms. Her view was moral and religious. She believed that women must be given a fair chance and treated as human beings, rather than as objects to be exploited and abused. While she had spent her whole life within patriarchal structures, the scientific establishment, and now the church, she was nonetheless a person who had maintained her integrity and independence, who had sought the highest possible development of her own abilities, and who, through Novodevichy, aspired to help other women develop theirs.

Mother Serafima's odyssey speaks profoundly to the struggle to keep the spirit of compassion and caring alive and to nurture, under the most difficult circumstances, the religious underpinnings of that spirit. Her story presents vivid testimony that outer appearances often conceal deeper aspects of reality. Spending most of her life in the scientific establishment, where she was eminently successful and achieved national prominence, she harbored an inner set of ideals much different from the proclaimed official ones. Sovietologists often refer to this behavior as "internal immigration." But that term, in Mother Serafima's case, does not begin to describe the complexities of her situation. In her public and private life, she tried to develop the scientific and religious elements of her being. While circumstances often led her to conceal the latter, they did not lead to bitterness or betrayal, and she did not recognize any conflict between science and religion: "In my lifetime I easily combined science and religion. I have never felt that science interfered with my internal life. Politics, yes; but science, never!"

Mother Serafima emphasized that in the past it was extremely difficult to identify religious believers in the scientific establishment. Many of her colleagues could not reveal their most deeply held convictions, and her own experience bears witness to the struggle to remain true to them. As evidence, she recalled her trip many years ago to Italy and her visit to the crypt of

St Nicholas of Bari: "As I approached his coffin," she said, "the question that arose in my mind and caused me a great deal of anxiety was 'what should I do to remain true to myself?' So I moved as close as I possibly could to the coffin and did absolutely nothing; I knew that among my colleagues who had traveled with us were several people who would inform on me if I dared to cross myself. I was not afraid; it was not exactly fear that prompted me to act as I did, but I did consider the consequences to my other colleagues and to my institute." Instead, she said, when she went back to her room and was alone, she "immediately began to pray for St Nicholas," and "asked to be forgiven for my behavior." As she recalled her dilemma, she emphasized that she would not act now as she did then: she would not hide her inner feelings and beliefs. "But in those days I felt I had to surrender. I could not be my true self, and that was my weakness."

Like Mother Serafima, the famous monastery whose recovery she directed is testimony to the preservation of Russia's religious spirit. The monastery is connected to the official church, but the ideals of service and compassion that this and other convents hold are much deeper than the official boundaries convey. Many elements have kept the religious spirit alive in Russia in the twentieth century, and some of them are described in this chapter: photographs, social action, passive resistance to state authority, and classical architecture. Mother Serafima and other women of the church belong on this list. After the Russian Revolution, as she reminded me, it was Russian women who continued to uphold and practice religious ideals. In the long period when the church came under severe attack, such women kept religious ideals alive and provided a significant part of the foundation for the renewal of religion in Russia. Silent for much of the twentieth century, they connected the monastery to the world, and brought these two elements together in ways that had profound meaning to Mother Serafima.

The sharp mental pictures of such women and of her grandfather also fused together in Mother Serafima's mind and formed fundamental parts of her identity. She had revisited these memories many times in the last decade. The photographs of her grandfather, one of a young military man, the other two of a broken prisoner, recalled his devotion to parish life; they evoked important guideposts in her efforts to rebuild Novodevichy Monastery. They reminded her of another existence, a set of ideals different from the relentless competition and consumerism around her. As Michael Ignatieff has written, the importance of such photographs does not relate only to preserving the past: "These strangers are dear to me, not because their lives contain the secret of my own, but because they saved their memory for my sake."[44] The photographs enabled her to go forward into the future, and they revealed with great clarity the rich sources on which she had to build.

In the time I spent with her, listening for hours as she recounted her experiences, Mother Serafima impressed me as a person of courage, conviction, and adaptability, who had joined the private and public sides of her life. Her short physical stature belied the intensity with which she spoke, the seriousness with which she conveyed the memories of her family and joined those memories to the present. But everything was not totally serious; her eyes danced as she talked about her struggles with church officials and the methods she had used to gain the resources she needed, and her hands were in constant motion as she described her work in the fields, in the cathedral, and on the memoirs of her grandfather. She related easily to people; she had a natural warmth and a caring demeanor that cut through to the heart.

Kind, unpretentious, full of energy, Mother Serafima had become totally authentic in a way that she could not have realized earlier. And while she had experienced much of Russia's tragic twentieth-century history, it was the inner resources she commanded that stood out most. A person of character, she reminded us that outward appearance often conceals a great deal of what lies within, hidden, powerful resources that have their own way of working themselves out and reappearing, revealing their strength and beauty in unsuspected forms.

POSTSCRIPT

Mother Serafima's attempts to rehabilitate her grandfather, both in name and deed, bore more fruit than restoring her own identity. In February 1997, the bishops' council of the Russian Orthodox Church voted to canonize two major figures in the church in this century, both of whom had perished in Stalin's labor camps: Metropolitans Petr Polianskii and Leonid Mikhailovich Chichagov.[45] Venerated for his courageous actions and humility in the service of the Holy Father, Leonid Mikhailovich represented thousands of church leaders and priests who had suffered greatly before state authorities. But the bishops' decision to canonize him also bore witness to the relentless pursuits of Mother Serafima and her determination to preserve his memory and spirit. Elevated to sainthood in ceremonies in the Cathedral of Christ the Savior on February 23, Leonid Mikhailovich joined the holy martyrs, the "sufferers in Christ," who offer sustenance to the people. "It is as though he stands there and silently looks at me," Mother Serafima said to me; "he has been standing there a long time."

5 Education and a New Society

Following the collapse of the communist state, Patriarch Aleksi II identified religious education of the Russian people as the church's most important challenge. The greatest wrong wrecked on our society by the Soviet government, the patriarch said, was its moral and spiritual assault. This attack on the base of our humanity was the deepest "wound inflicted by the Communist dictatorship." "All other evils," he said, "were the result of the systematic and total eradication from the souls and consciousness of the people of the very notion of spirituality."[1] In attempting to rebuild the spiritual character of the Russian people, particularly of the young, the church faced a daunting challenge. The church had to reconstruct the foundation. It commenced this reconstruction with a leadership that in recent decades had been connected with the former Soviet government and shared many of its characteristics. This leadership now had to seek its own bearings while maneuvering in a turbulent social sea.

How would the church relate its religious vision to the practical social issues it immediately faced? How would it speak to the postcommunist generation in Russia, whose social and spiritual values were so unstable? Could the church provide a vision of hope and of wholeness while it sought to recover its own traditions and memories? These were the questions that Fr Georgii Kochetkov and his parish community had confronted in their own unique way and that others, too, attempted to address.

These issues would receive special attention at three major centers of influence—the university, the press, and the hierarchy of the Orthodox Church—where recovering Russia's religious heritage and seeking to relate parts of that heritage to the present became primary endeavors. Under the Soviets, all three of these institutions had been tightly controlled. As major sources of public opinion, they had contributed to the birth and development of the Soviet propaganda state.[2] After the fall of the Communist state, the academy, specifically Moscow University; the press, especially the newspaper *Nezavisimaia gazeta;* and the church hierarchy would become important agents in restoring Russia's identity and providing religious instruction for its people.

The Patriarch's Challenge to the Church

As a former parish priest with many years of service, Patriarch Aleksi II well knew the educational difficulties his society faced. By the late 1980s, the Soviet Union had one of the most highly educated populations in Western Europe. Its economy had become increasingly productive, and while it had many problems relating to inefficiency, the national economy of the Soviet Union had, in each decade since the mid-1960s, developed a higher standard of living for its citizens. But such measures of prosperity concealed increasingly serious problems. A growing sense of despair, cynicism, and hopelessness also marked the population. Widespread corruption, a loss of purpose, and a sense of national malaise were visible everywhere.

Such problems, beyond their evident moral dimension, were essentially spiritual and religious, the consequences of the many-faceted assault on the religious foundations of the society. In a similar context, Czech political leader and writer Václav Havel expressed eloquently this condition in which spiritual and moral issues had been forced to the margins of society. Asked what lessons his country's experience could offer to the West, Havel warned against "the dictatorship of money, of profit, of constant economic growth, and the necessity, flowing from all that, of plundering the earth without regard for what will be left in a few decades, along with everything related to the materialistic obsessions of this world, from the flourishing of selfishness to the need to evade personal responsibility by becoming part of the herd." Havel argued that "all of these are phenomena that cannot effectively be confronted except through a new moral effort, that is, through a transformation of the spirit and the human relationship to life and the world."[3]

Shortly after his election as Patriarch of Moscow and All Russia on June 7, 1990, and in subsequent addresses, Aleksi II expressed his own vision of education and society. Russians, he emphasized, have a great need to reacquaint themselves with the "huge amount of cultural knowledge which we have lost and neglected."[4] He described the recovery of memory and the rediscovery of cultural and spiritual heritage as the most important issues facing his country. Long neglected, this heritage could not easily be reclaimed. How to organize this immense task and how to approach the education of children, young people, and adults were issues that required immediate and energetic attention. Despite the great difficulties that the church faced as it tried to deal with this task, it must not be afraid, he said; it must be willing to take risks and it must give its best efforts, since "education is the chief concern of the Church."[5] On the success of this educational endeavor, he believed, a large part of the country's future would ride.

The basis for the patriarch's concerns may be found in his concept of education's ultimate purposes. He emphasized that the root meaning of the Russian word "education" (*obrazovanie*) is "image" (*obraz*), and that education's task is to bring out in each person a particular image. In the Christian view, this image is God's (*imago dei*) and it is found in every person. Rather than merely mastering a certain amount of knowledge or passing on a large body of facts, therefore, education means developing in each individual the divine image found within him, an image that often becomes "blurred and obscured." For the patriarch, education is essentially a spiritual transformation, analogous to the work of the "icon restorer, who must clean the deposits off the darkened face and reveal to the world its original beauty, the radiance of its colors and lines, its harmony."[6] The task of the educator requires cleaning off a spiritual face besmudged by a long period of assaults on the spirit, of shallow pursuits and compromises, all of which had covered up the original "image."

Understood in this way, the role of education is not just to uncover the past, this "old tree," as described by a leading Orthodox figure, but also to recover vitality. At the heart of Orthodoxy is a "perpetual resurrection," and education helps uncover and develop this vital sense.[7] Seeing the despair, the rootlessness, and the lack of purpose in present-day Russian society, Aleksi II stressed the fundamental role that religious education had to play. "Today people are desperately gasping for air in the spiritual vacuum in which we find ourselves."[8] He cited various harmful elements that had emerged in this spiritual vacuum—occultism, sectarianism, intolerance, violence, and pornography—all of which had replaced state atheism in waging war against the spirit. It was Orthodoxy's educational role to restore a sense of beauty, to cultivate hope, and to remind human beings of this "perpetual resurrection," to lift them up again, and to develop the "innermost, pure godlike spirit of man" that has been obsessively "blurred by other things."[9] A great deal would depend, he said, on the capability and will of the teachers, whether they continue to draw a line between science and religion, slander Russia's history and cultural heritage, describe Russia as backward and beaten, and treat with disdain its spiritual roots and cultural values, or whether teachers "will seek a different tone of discourse."

What Aleksi II proposed, and what he saw as essential, was to end the sharp distinction between the secular and the sacred. He wanted to see the church actively involved in the world and he believed that new grounds had to be found for cooperation rather than confrontation with the world. Education served as a key to such cooperation. In 1993, the patriarch cited Moscow University as one of the places where the first hopeful steps toward this goal had been taken.

Moscow University—Reclaiming the Tradition

Moscow University is Russia's premier institution of higher learning. Founded in 1755 during the reign of Empress Elizabeth Petrovna, Moscow University rapidly established itself as a citadel of scholarship, teaching, and the collection of research materials. In writing the university's charter, Mikhail Vasil'evich Lomonosov (1711–65), the best-known figure of the Russian Enlightenment, drew a picture of the future in which Russia would be known by the arts and sciences, rather than war, and would produce its own Platos and Newtons.[10] But it was only after the Napoleonic Wars that Moscow University truly began the ascendancy that would bring its long-sought preeminent status. "From [that] time," according to Alexander Herzen, the "university became more and more the centre of Russian culture. All the conditions necessary for its development were combined—historical importance, geographical position, and the absence of the Tsar."[11] Later, in the second half of the nineteenth century, Moscow University was home to a large number of Russia's most distinguished scientists, including the physicists P. N. Lebedev and A. G. Stoletov, the biologists M. A. Mezbir and K. A. Timiriazev, and the founder of geochemistry V. I. Vernadskii. During this same period the university also flourished as a center of research and teaching in the humanities. Many of Russia's greatest historians were trained and began their teaching careers here, among them V. O. Kliuchevskii, A. A. Kizevetter, S. F. Platonov, and P. N. Miliukov.

Not surprisingly, given its rich cultural history, Moscow University served as a focal point for the development of the Russian intelligentsia. It provided a fertile ground for some of Russia's most creative minds and its greatest intellectual debates. The "Slavophiles" associated themselves with Moscow University, and their disputes with the "Westernizers" found expression here. The well-known controversies between the followers of the historian Timofei Granovskii, a representative of Western liberalism, and of his Russian nationalist opponents took place in the lecture halls and student quarters of this university. Moscow's famous graduates included such writers as Mikhail Lermontov, Ivan Turgenev, and Ivan Goncharev, and such leaders of the Russian intelligentsia as Vissarian Belinskii, Alexander Herzen, and Nikolai Ogarev. The university afforded a unique forum in Russian society: in the middle of the nineteenth century, according to Herzen, it was a place where individuals came together irrespective of their rank and status to form an intellectual community. The young men who came from all over the country to the university quickly found that social background had little meaning there. As Herzen described this process, "the youthful strength of Russia streamed to it from all sides, from all classes, as into a common reservoir; in its halls they were purified from the prejudices they had picked up at the domestic hearth, reached a common level, become like brothers and dispersed again to all parts of Russia and among all classes of its people."[12] The university fused such disparate individuals into a "compact mass of comrades," and the discussion of ideas that emanated from it would energize Russia and shape its intellectual future.

In the late nineteenth century, nothing would symbolize better this fusion of disparate individuals at Moscow University than the celebrations held each year on the feast day of Saint Tat'iana, the university's patron saint. St Tat'iana's feast day was January 24, the date also marking the founding of the university in 1755. This occasion served annually as a major holiday in the university. On such a day, religious and cultural elements of the university would come together.

Writing from Prague in 1929, A. A. Kizevetter, the famous Russian social and economic historian who taught for many years at Moscow University, warmly recalled the special events and festivities of Tat'ianin Den.[13] Many hours before the ceremonies started, Kizevetter wrote, professors, students, officials, and alumni gathered in the main auditorium of the university, anticipating the day's events. They began with prayers, a lengthy lecture on some current topic, and comments on the university's traditions. Following these, members of the audience rose together to sing the national anthem and then left for the Moscow restaurants and a full day of joyous pursuits. On this day the police generally ignored the bands of students festively making their way through the streets and milling on the sidewalks and in the central square. Civil servants, lawyers, and other citizens joined the students in small gatherings scattered throughout the city. Later that evening, students and professors reconvened in the Bol'shoi Moskovskii Traktir (inn) downtown for more speeches, then went to one of the city's best-known restaurants, where the crowd, assembled in the inner rooms, would listen to several of the university's greatest professors, including professor of history V. O. Kliuchevskii, recite witty verses, and make impromptu speeches. On this day, social distinctions

were entirely forgotten, as professors and students ate, drank, and danced together. Kizevetter described the occasion: "This was a joyous holiday. It was
very pleasant for everyone to feel, even once a year, that they belonged to a
larger group of cultured individuals bound by common memories and sharing the same mood. All the barriers that separated people—age, politics,
occupation were swept away. . . . What was this, this one-day Moscow carni-
val? Was it just revelry and merrymaking? No, this was a celebration of the
conscious unity of cultured Russia. That cultured Russia was divided by many
disputes . . . but on Tat'ianin Den' the feeling of belonging to the same alma
mater outweighed all the divisions."[14]

As the historian Samuel Kassow has pointed out, Tat'ianin Den' occa-
sioned many ugly incidents as well: merrymaking would occasionally degen-
erate into public drunkenness and rowdy behavior; brawls would sometimes
break out between student groups and city toughs from nearby workers' districts who also crowded city streets on this day. The celebration reflected many
of the ambiguities and paradoxes of prerevolutionary Russia. But the day and
what it represented would be deeply lodged in the historical memory as a time
when religion, culture, learning, and traditions fused into one.

In 1917, most of the educational elite opposed the Bolshevik accession to
power.[15] After that accession, Moscow University along with Russia's other
major universities, lost its autonomy and was forced to serve the needs of the
new government. But the transformation of the university's curriculum and
its teaching and research faculties did not take place immediately or without
significant opposition. In 1924, the university still featured nine courses in religion, and courses in the departments of history and philology continued to
emphasize the church's major contributions to Russian history and culture.[16]

The "great turning point" came in 1928–29, with the "cultural revolution"
associated with Joseph Stalin that radically changed the pedagogical profession, including that in Moscow University. The enthusiasm for ideas deemed
"modern" and "scientific," the eagerness to create a new proletarian class to
serve the five-year plans, and the disdain for anything connected to the "bour-
geois cultural establishment," resulted in a virtual war against remnants of the
past.[17] Until 1917 Red Square had many small churches and structures, consecrated by the church and used mainly for praying. All these places of worship
were closed after the Revolution, and in the late 1920s, were converted into
public toilets. "Such actions," as a professor at Moscow University recently
said to me, "deliberately aimed at trampling on and belittling everything associated with what many of us had considered the sacred forms of our religion
and culture." Since its founding in 1755, Moscow University had included an

Orthodox Church as part of its physical structure and identity. In the late
1920s, that church was closed.

The return of this site to its original purposes in the 1990s, therefore, has
much greater significance than the mere transfer of physical property. It posits
an attempt to recapture the oldest traditions of the university and to recover
what is perceived to be their rightful place. But which parts of these traditions
would be seen as the most important and how would they be embraced and
reconstructed in the present? Early in the twentieth century, the Bolsheviks
saw the relationship between religion and education as one of their main obstacles. At the end of the century, Patriarch Aleksi II had identified restoration
of this relationship as an urgent concern and Moscow University as a focal
point for that restoration.

The exterior features of the university present what seems to be a timeless
appearance. In the courtyard stands the famous statue of M. V. Lomonosov,
Russia's great eighteenth-century scientist and man of letters. The university
was renamed the Lomonosov Moscow State University in 1940. The primary
entrance to the classrooms and offices of the university is located directly behind the statue. Immediately to the right of the courtyard is another building,
connected to the main structure and adjacent to Manezh Square.

Students pass through the courtyard every day, rarely paying attention to
the edifice on the right side. Their primary focus lies directly ahead, past
Lomonosov, to the large yellow stone structure in the center, where the university's main entrance is located. But there, on a simple wooden door, is now
affixed a small inscription, barely noticeable from the central walkway,
Church of the Sacred Martyr Tat'iana. Like much in Russian life, the unre-
markable outer facade conceals the extraordinary story that lies on the other
side of that ordinary door.

Going through the wooden door, one comes upon a bookstore where religious literature is sold and, beside it, a modest-size room that temporarily
serves as a chapel. To the rear is a small area where a student choir sings during the services; nearby, also in the back, is a similar space occupied by several
professional singers from the Moscow Conservatory, whom the church often
engages. The iconostasis is not elaborate; the icons are few in number. The entire effect is extremely simple and modest, bearing little witness that in the
1990s this space was the center of a fierce ideological battle.

Fr Maksim Kozlov is the priest in charge of the university's parish church.
He has been appointed by the patriarch to oversee the parish's regeneration, a
task the patriarch defined as overcoming the "enmity and strife" that had long
characterized "spiritual and secular culture."[18] Fr Maksim began his service in

the parish during the church's struggle to reestablish its prominence at Moscow University. Born and raised in Moscow, he graduated from the philology faculty at Moscow University; he is in his forties, is married, and has three children. His theological training took place at the Spiritual Academy at Sergiev Posad, when the administrative center of the Russian Orthodox Church was located there.

Energetic, resourceful, stern in his demeanor, Fr Maksim is committed to the task to which he has been appointed. He has worked hard to reestablish the university parish, an effort he believes will bear fruitful results. He is not, he said, a reformer. He does not conceive of his purpose in this way, and he is suspicious of attempts to remodel and redefine methods inherited from the past. Like the Spiritual Academy from which he graduated, he has a firmly traditionalist bias.

The past, as historian and geographer David Lowenthal has superbly shown, is never immutable, set in stone, or fixed forever in the imagination.[19] It is always alive, changing, part of the present. Whose version of the Russian past will be most widely accepted is a question that is still evolving, and how it is resolved will contribute greatly to how Russia conceives of itself. Upon entering the church, one walks down a long corridor exhibiting a portrait gallery of such figures as Mikhail Vasil'evich Lomonosov, Tat'iana Shuvalova, and other luminaries important to the history of Moscow University. The portraits shed light on what elements of Russia's past are being recovered and emphasized here.

A founder of Moscow University, scientist, inventor, linguist, poet, and essayist, Lomonosov belongs near the center of the stage in the attempt to reclaim the university's heritage. During the Soviet period, books on the history of science and on the Russian Enlightenment portrayed Lomonosov exclusively as a secular figure, an early leader in the struggle to liberate thought from its social and political restraints who prepared the way later for the radical intelligentsia. Soviet historians generally presented him as a freethinker and a major critic of religion. "As the father of Russian materialistic philosophy, he is one of the greatest philosopher-materialists of the pre-Marxist period," stated a standard Soviet intellectual history.[20] But such an interpretation wrests Lomonosov out of context, failing to note that he was a religious person, a supporter of the church, and a man who strongly believed that thought must draw from secular and sacred sources. In the same portrait gallery hangs a framed statement of Lomonosov's: "Science and Faith are two roads that spring essentially from the same source and ultimately will be joined." The citation and its placement suggest a commitment, in both education and religion, to a worldview that seeks connections between the sacred and secular, rather than promoting their separation.

The portrait of Tat'iana Shuvalova and the name given to the university church, that of her namesake, the Sacred Martyr Tat'iana, present another significant aspect of reclaiming the past. Ivan Ivanovich Shuvalov, member of one of Russia's greatest eighteenth-century aristocratic families and the founder of Moscow University, established the university church in honor of his mother Tat'iana. Her name was associated with the day of celebration at the Moscow University in the nineteenth century, and it was the sense of "cultural unity," the notion of a community of students and professors, expressed on Tat'iana Den', that would be remembered. In the attempt to re-create a parish within the university, this history would again find expression—in the naming of the church, in the day chosen for its consecration, and in the desire to rebuild a community based on religion and service within Moscow University. Concurrent with the reopening of the church, student participants began publication of a newspaper named *Tat'ianin Den'*, issued bimonthly and described as the "Student Orthodox Newspaper of Moscow University."

The long portrait-decorated corridor connects at the other end to a flight of winding stairs. The second floor is the more spacious and, when I first visited the building in 1995, the more mysterious. The top of the stairs opened into an extremely large, dark room covering the entire wing of the building and needing a great deal of restoration. The floor was remarkable: made of rough oak, laid out in squares, it resembled a large chessboard in design and color. At one end of the room was a full-length stage; the windows were painted black and were extremely dirty, although someone had begun to remove the paint and to clean some of them. For many years, this room functioned as a theater. Earlier in the Soviet Union, the student theater had served the state, operating as a training ground for student dramatists who waged a war against religion and belittled the tenets on which it is based. Later, it functioned as one of the main student theaters of Moscow University, where student dramatists learned their craft while performing for student audiences.

In Fr Maksim's mind, the battle to reclaim this theater for the parish signified a definitive moment both in the university's and in the parish's identities. This struggle, which took place in 1994 and early 1995, involved several different issues and groups. Inside the university, throughout 1993 and 1994, discussions were undertaken regarding the curriculum and the university's role in the social transformation of Russia. Such a discussion was part of Moscow University's attempt to redefine itself, recover its autonomy, and deal with important practical matters, including its financial structure and the use of its

physical facilities. In December 1993, the rector of the university signed a decree restoring part of the right wing of the old structure to its original purpose
as the university's church. His decision provoked a furious protest from those
who occupied the building.

According to Fr Maksim, student groups connected to the university had
not been the building's primary occupants in recent years. Instead, a theater
troupe in the city had used this space to stage its own productions, which were
strictly for entertainment and were mostly ribald and coarse in their content.
But they made a lot of money, and the building's prime location in the center
of Moscow insured that the occupants would not accept the rector's decisions
without a struggle.

In protest and to gain support, the theater troupe staged several demonstrations on Red Square. The members tried to enlist people in the artistic and
literary world, arguing that the university administration was launching an
attack on Russian culture and the Russian theater. In their letters to the Moscow city authorities and in public statements, those sympathetic to the theater company claimed that its eviction from the building revived an old
danger: the church's attempt to limit artistic expression and to undermine the
theater. In their rhetoric, the sympathizers claimed that the fundamental issues at stake here were much larger than the use of space.

But to university officials and to Fr Maksim, the basic issue concerned the
autonomy of the university. These officials believed that the university had the
right to define its own purposes and govern its own affairs, regardless of external political and economic pressures. The struggle over the building related to
that concern, and many members of the university community refused to give
in to elements that threatened to limit such autonomy. In May 1994, with students taking the initiative, they and many faculty members engaged in a large
demonstration outside the building. Fr Maksim has posted a photograph of
the event on the wall in the downstairs corridor, which shows a crowd of several thousand supporters engulfing the university's courtyard and filling a large
part of Manezh Square. "The huge crowd of students and professors and the
speeches that day solidified our support," recalled one of the sympathizers; "the
demonstration was one of the turning points in swaying public sentiment."
Soon thereafter, university administrators reaffirmed their earlier decision to
return the building to its original purpose. In January 1995, the building became the church of the university, and later that month, in a special ceremony,
the patriarch consecrated the site, restoring it formally to its earlier function.

The struggle between religious and secular elements is not without complexity. The theater company's argument about preserving Russian culture

Church of the Sacred Martyr Tat'iana at Moscow State University.

and freedom of expression may have been self-serving, but its claim raises serious issues surrounding the present renewal of religious practice. As the church seeks to recover properties lost during the Communist era, the problem of separating Russia's national treasures from objects of religious significance becomes a repeated concern. How should religious institutions relate to society and how should the lines be drawn between them? In reclaiming the physical artifacts of Russia's heritage, both the church and the state struggle with defining this relationship.

In restoring the church's educational mission, Fr Maksim has also faced a challenging assignment. Memories and traditions essential to this mission suffered heavy assault during the Soviet period. Pedagogical methods, both in theory and practice, emphasized the materialist approach to Russian history and often denigrated other aspects of Russia's national heritage. But Fr Maksim's task is not impossible. Inside the university the Soviet attack on cultural memory and on the university's educational mission was not as all-encompassing as it appeared on the surface. In the classrooms, certain "discredited" parts of the past were kept alive and passed on in subtle but crucial ways. Fr Maksim mentioned to me the name of a former professor of classical studies at Moscow University, Andrei Cheslavovich Kozarzhevskii, who provides a primary example of such efforts.

During the last thirty years, until his recent death, Kozarzhevskii taught Latin and the cultural history of the Roman Empire to several thousand students at Moscow University. But in addition to his study of classical history, he also had a great personal interest in architecture, regional studies, and the social and cultural history of Moscow. For many years Kozarzhevskii served on a special Committee on the History of the Streets of Moscow, which met in the Common Hall of the Polytechnic Museum, where he gave many presentations. Kozarzhevskii was a Christian, but during these years he could not express his religious commitments openly. He had to find other, more subtle ways to reveal his own convictions, and he did this through his teaching. He knew the city of Moscow extremely well, including the connection between its religion and culture, and in his Latin classes at Moscow University he often talked about the city's cultural past. As Vladimir Salov, a former student from the 1970s, recalled: "Frequently, in the middle of a lecture on Latin, Professor Kozarzhevskii would interrupt his lecture and talk about the history of the city. He knew many of the stories of Moscow, and would tell them to his classes. He had intimate knowledge of the city's streets, its nooks and crannies, its history in the deepest sense, and this knowledge he communicated to his students. I was aware, for example, from his classes, that part of Moscow University was originally a church, although I did not see that fact written anywhere in Soviet history books."

Kozarzhevskii died in 1995, shortly after the struggle over the university's property ended. He was a charter member of the Church of the Sacred Martyr Tat'iana, and his widow is active in Fr Maksim's parish. His obituary in the student newspaper paid tribute to his teaching gifts and his service to several generations of students, especially his courageous efforts to keep alive parts of the past that were in danger of being forgotten. According to the testimony of his former students, he taught his subject extremely well, but he also taught between the lines of his subject, bringing obscure details to life, seeking to relate his topic to a larger picture and to other fields, and drawing the connections, as few others did, between the history of Russian culture and its spiritual elements.[21] "You remember," according to the writer of Kozarzhevskii's obituary in the student newspaper, "that during the last seventy years in our University there were many religious believers. All of them sat quietly, because whoever dared to reveal religious ideas, Soviet power quickly would permit that person to become a janitor or a charwoman."[22] Under such stressful conditions, Kozarzhevskii demonstrated great courage and creative ability. Fr Maksim and the leaders of the university church saw him as an exceptional example of someone on whom they might rebuild their own institutional identity.

The people who gathered around Fr Maksim and participated in the parish community were extremely committed to restoring this institutional identity. A noteworthy example, drawn from the faculty, is Marina Rumiantseva. A member of the Department of African and Asian Languages and Literature, Rumiantseva is a young professor of Chinese. She has played a large role in establishing the university church. She spends several hours a week volunteering her time to the parish, helping Fr Maksim, and providing orientation for new members. The religious community that is developing here is extremely important to her, and she spoke openly about her own religious pilgrimage: "When I was a student at Moscow University, I did have religious feelings: I felt another connection to the world than the attachments I was being presented with in school, and I sometimes tried to pray. But I had no model and no Bible, and I did not know the proper way. Still, I tried to do what I could, without any real knowledge of what I was doing. It has been only in the last ten years that I have had the opportunity to connect with others, to raise questions as part of a community of believers, and to embrace this experience more fully." Rumiantseva sees bridging the division between secular and sacred as vital to her sense of purpose and hope, and she has placed her twelve-year-old son in the parish's parochial school as testimony of this vision of the future.[23]

When the parish began to function, it had little more than an empty space in which to build. By the summer of 1995, according to Fr Maksim, the parish numbered about sixty-five people who regularly attended the services. The Easter services that spring had attracted a large gathering of university people, crowding into the small chapel and the corridor outside and staying throughout the night. To Fr Maksim this "gradual, steady increase" in the church's constituency was evidence of hope. As the parish became better known, he was convinced, as it rebuilt trust and strengthened its educational program, its constituency would expand.

Marina Rumiantseva, member of the Department of African and Asian Languages and Literature at Moscow State University, and Fr Maksim Kozlov, priest at the Church of the Sacred Martyr Tat'iana.

In 1995, the majority of the church's active participants came from the faculties of philology and history—especially from classical philology, Asian languages and history, Russian language and literature, and Russian history. Kozarzhevskii's legacy in the philology and history faculties might well account for this fact. Several other members belonged to the mathematics faculty. But the church had made little headway among members of the philosophy and science faculties. Fr Maksim expressed confidence that this would change as the church developed greater contact with these faculties. "We have found," he said, "that interest in our parish especially among the students has developed as a kind of chain effect."

The parish publishes a student newspaper titled *Tat'ianin Den'*. Its purpose includes spreading word of the church's existence and activities, but its primary function is the same as the former university holiday of the same name: to unify the disparate members of the university into one community. As the annual celebration in the nineteenth century attempted to bring together the university on an academic occasion, the church newspaper seeks to achieve a similar end. It aims to provide a counterweight to the selfish, status-driven impulses of Russian society. Its articles deal with the church's activities, historical sites, excerpts from recent lectures, and reprints of interesting journal articles on Russian art, literary themes, and world religions. The authors criticize the materialism and personal indulgence that they see as Russia's "current sickness," its "real opium of the people."[24] On these subjects *Tat'ianin Den'* demonstrates a perspective very close to the patriarch's.

As part of its educational mission, the parish has established a parochial school for children, who are accepted for study at the age of ten. Located on the first floor of the church building, this school meets in a small room, equipped, when I first saw it, simply and sparsely. The room contained about a dozen desks and simple wooden benches, neatly arranged and facing a blackboard. The school admits two groups of twelve students. The first-year students spend a year in preparatory classes in which they must demonstrate their facility at learning classical languages. Only the ablest are chosen to continue at the next level. In 1995, two sections of twelve students attended the school, coming six days a week to study with Fr Maksim. The curriculum included Greek, Latin, mathematics, classical art, singing, theology, Russian history, Russian literature, and the English language. Fr Maksim told me the school requires intensive student preparation as it tries to restore a particular tradition of excellence. His parish school aims to provide a solid foundation for educating future leaders of the church, and a classical education is perceived to be fundamental to that training.

As for university students and faculty, the parish seeks to create a religious community within the university. This kind of community is known as a "home parish," and it differs from others that are regional in scope and encompass surrounding neighborhoods. Unlike them, the missionary activity of the home parish operates only within the university itself.[25] As Fr Maksim explained, sermons in the church, as well as all the church's activities—the pilgrimages to historical sites, the special lectures, and studies of religious art—are geared specifically to this community. In an attempt to meet different interests, the parish will soon open a Sunday school with classes in singing, art, and the cultural and religious history of Moscow.

In addition to the creation of a parochial school, the recovery of Russia's national religious heritage, and the attempt to rebuild the university community, the church's educational mission includes another primary objective. Among Fr Maksim's chief concerns is the ethics of work. He gives this subject a great deal of attention in his teaching because he believes that neither the former Communist understanding of labor nor the current free market perspective offers the necessary values on which Russia can build its future. In his view, labor is not an economic commodity, but a sacred gift; as such, it is connected to a person's entire being and purpose. Fr Maksim, like Patriarch

Aleksi II, sees this gift as part of the divine image of the icon within the individual that needs to be uncovered. "It is very important to return to the idea, the understanding, unfortunately lost in the twentieth century, that the workplace is not just where we earn money but also a place where we hear God's voice," he said to me. To Fr Maksim, this understanding of labor is essential to Russia's economic and spiritual renewal, and he sees fostering this understanding as one of the primary purposes of the home parish at Moscow University.

Fr Maksim's ideas derive in part from the writers in *Vekhi* at the beginning of the twentieth century. They too warned of the extreme specialization found in the modern work place. Sergei Bulgakov, one of these writers to whom Fr Maksim refers, developed a "theology of labor" that ran counter both to Marxism and to economic liberalism.[26] Bulgakov tried to refute the view that life was an "economic process"; while he believed in economic planning, he did not believe that economics should control human beings, and he articulated a theology that saw labor essentially as a creative expression, a divine gift. Fr Maksim, likewise, maintains that human labor that fulfills either selfish individual goals or serves only the interests of the state will not lead to the kind of society that Russia most needs.[27] He stresses the importance of personal discipline, control over one's selfish impulses, and a vision of the self as part of a larger whole. These are elements found in the teachings of the Orthodox Church, which he believes Russia needs to recover in order to build a new social order.

Fr Maksim distrusts movements that seek to reform the church to fit Russia's current social and economic circumstances. He is, therefore, extremely suspicious of such reformers as Fr Georgii Kochetkov and Fr Aleksandr Borisov, head of the Russian Bible Society: "We strongly object to the activities of Fr Georgii and Fr Aleksandr Borisov, whose activities aim at creating a church outside the Church. These activities are unacceptable. First, they are not based on Orthodox principles as a whole but on the Protestant inspiration to go back only to a particular period of Church history, while they reject other major parts of the whole of our tradition. The intention of these so-called 'reformers' is the same as Luther's: to modernize the Church. Second, their activities are unacceptable because they violate the Church canon. If the whole Church disagrees with the proposed reforms, their proponents must give them up, in order to preserve harmony and peace within the Church, rather than continue to pursue them."

As a traditionalist, Fr Maksim embraces the liturgy and other religious activities in their original forms. He signed the 1994 letter of church leaders who voiced strong objections to Kochetkov's attempts to modernize the language of the church.[28] Rather than introducing what Fr Maksim calls "heretical innovations," he believes the most important task is to "renew and cleanse the original roots of the Church" that lie "at the core of our religious life." Instead of reshaping these principles to fit present circumstances, Fr Maksim maintains that the Russian people must first be taught the central teachings of Orthodoxy which, he argues, are "poorly understood in our society."

Fr Maksim's views on religious education are similar to those expressed by Patriarch Aleksi II: this education does not come without a great deal of effort and struggle. But in this process of struggle lies much of its strength. As in the case of the icon painter, the attempt to uncover the original image and to understand its beauty requires years of preparation, study, meditation, and prayer. The patriarch had criticized Western missionaries who arrived in Russia armed with easy answers to heal Russia's spiritual malaise—proposing instantaneous solutions and holding out promises of an overnight rebirth. To Fr Maksim, the missionaries resembled the communists in their simplistic approaches. He held a similar view of Fr Georgii Kochetkov and his attempts to express the Orthodox faith in the vernacular. Fr Georgii, he argued, missed the essence of Orthodoxy: the pursuit of beauty and truth is a difficult and complex task.

Fr Maksim Kozlov believes that the renewal of the parish is essential to Russia's future, but he has in mind a different kind of parish than that envisioned by Kochetkov. He sees the parish as a "family of people united around the priest, who served as their spiritual father." The revival of parish life does not require any specific church innovations but rather well-trained, committed priests who can help people understand what the church has been teaching for centuries. The key to the future of Christianity and to Russia's social and moral well being, according to Fr Maksim, lies in recruiting and educating such priests.

In the last four years, the parish at Moscow University has experienced solid, steady growth. In characterizing this period, Fr Maksim cited the maxim "Life takes its own course; life continues to seek its own natural forms." "This expresses," Fr Maksim said, "the development of the parish. Its growth has not taken a geometrical progression. To go from 10 to 50 parishioners is significantly more difficult than to get from 50 to 200." In late May 2001, the parish had between 350 and 400 people, who, according to Fr Maksim, "see themselves as parishioners of our church."[29]

Life has also taken its course in the expansion of the parish's activities. Worship continues to be the main function, but it has taken several new and, for Fr Maksim, "unexpected directions." They include the development of a school of spiritual singing; it began as part of the parish's Sunday school for children from five to seventeen years of age. In the early years, the Sunday school had searched for a clear direction, a distinctive basis on which it could establish itself; singing offered that particular direction and it has been very successful. In late May 2001, the parish school for singing had grown to nearly eighty people, from ages five to twenty-five. The school will soon achieve the status of an institute and in the long term, because of its connection with the university, Fr Maksim plans for it to become a music school.

The parish has also experienced significant expansion in its pilgrimages and excursions to historical sites of religious importance. Several years ago these pilgrimages began with twenty to thirty people, but now they regularly involve some sixty to seventy people, who go on them every two weeks. Moreover, the parish continues to publish its student newspaper *Tat'ianin Den'*. "Not everything that is found in it is of high quality, not everything in it do we like," Fr Maksim admitted, "but all the same the newspaper continues to live." The parish has opened a library. The church remains open longer hours, and it now has not one but three priests as well as a deacon. "In this sense," Fr Maksim noted, "we are growing like a tree. The parish has taken root and is expanding, and that is a characteristic accurately describing our present condition."

Fr Maksim Kozlov's approach to education remains within the church's primary institutional boundaries. He has generally looked inward—rather than outward—at Orthodoxy's own traditions and heritage. He did not attempt to deal directly with Russia's immediate social problems, seeing those problems as symptoms of a moral and spiritual malady that would require a long period of time to heal. His remarks continue to raise the question of how the church might relate more directly and immediately to Russian society in this difficult time. How might the church play a more creative, active role in society, when knowledge of Russia's religious past, among the population, was still very low? The development of a civil society in Russia will greatly depend, as the sociologists of religion Sergei Filatov and Liudmila Vorontsova observed, on Russia's ability to find its own road and its distinctive national identity.[30] How could a larger, more open dialogue about religion and society be created and sustained, a dialogue that would not only examine the church but also hold it to account?

The Moscow newspaper *Nezavisimaia gazeta* has tried to explore these issues. Since the fall of communism, *Nezavisimaia gazeta* has gained a reputation among the Moscow intelligentsia as one of the most respected newspapers for its analysis of important political and cultural topics. Beginning in

1997, the newspaper published a special section on religion, which featured perceptive and often controversial commentary and significantly elevated the level of discussion of religious issues in Russia. Hoping to explore these questions from a different perspective, I sought the views of the creative editor of *Nezavisimaia gazeta*'s special religion section, Maksim Leonidovich Shevchenko.

NEZAVISIMAIA GAZETA—RESTORING THE CONVERSATION

Since its beginnings in December 1990, in the final months of the former Soviet Union, *Nezavisimaia gazeta* has been a newspaper born of the new openness. Early in its existence it distinguished itself for its political reporting of the collapse of the Soviet Union and the dawn of a new era. Its thoughtful, balanced essays on politics and culture quickly earned it a sizable following, especially among the intelligentsia. Founded and edited by Vitalii Tretiakov, it aspired to be an objective, Western-style newspaper, a Russian equivalent of the *New York Times.*

In 1997, *Nezavisimaia gazeta* had a subscription list of fifty thousand readers. This number did not compare to such mass circulation newspapers as *Izvestiia,* which sold 2 million copies, *or Literaturnaia gazeta,* which sold five hundred thousand. But *Nezavisimaia gazeta* had a large readership among political and cultural leaders in Russia, and its influence was much greater than its official circulation numbers would suggest. During the 1990s, its regular readers were among the chief supporters of an open, democratic society.

Early in 1997, Tretiakov created a series of special supplements designed to explore certain important topics in depth. Similar to the *New York Times* daily sections, the newspaper once a week devoted an entire eight- to twelve-page supplement to a major topic: the military, the provinces, new books on politics and culture, or religion. These were topics the editors identified as crucial to Russia's future. The religion supplement appeared during the last week of each month; it quickly became known for its insightful, multisided discussion of issues not normally treated with such critical seriousness. As measured by its readership and the discussion it stimulated, the newspaper had a significant impact on Russia's religious consciousness and the examination of important subjects.

When it began publication, the religion section in *Nezavisimaia gazeta* stated its purpose in a manner much different from other religious publications, such as the church's *Journal of the Moscow Patriarchate,* the mass-circulation *Moskovskii komsomolets,* or the nationalist press. In the first issue on January 30, 1997, the chief editor, Maksim Leonidovich Shevchenko, distinguished it from the advocacy journalism either on the right or the left. "The era of Soviet totalitarianism," he wrote in the lead story, "may have struck a heavy blow on the outer forms of religious life, but it did not destroy its inner foundations." These "ideas and values that lay buried within" needed to be rediscovered, Shevchenko said, in all their multiple forms and expressions; they needed to be brought back to Russian consciousness. Such a task required not just articulating and promoting these ideas and values, but "re-creating them," exploring them, and debating from many points of view their relevance to Russia's present situation.[31]

To Shevchenko and his associate editor, Oleg Mramornov, Russia's religious heritage included not only Orthodoxy but also Islam, Buddhism, Judaism, Catholicism, and other religious faiths. These religions had played major roles in Russia's religious history, and to them the editors gave extensive treatment. In addition, they gave a great deal of attention to a wide diversity of important topics: the Orthodox Church's relationship to the government, the controversial Metropolitan Kirill, the debate on freedom of conscience, the changes in social attitudes toward religion, to name only a few. Such subjects were treated seriously from multiple points of view, and the articles did what the editors intended: they inspired discussion and debate.

The main headquarters of *Nezavisimaia gazeta* are located on Miasnitskaia Street, the former Meatcutter's Row, one of the oldest and busiest streets of the city. Walking up the hill to these offices, one can see clearly the massive gray brown walls of the Lubianka, the infamous prison, standing in the background, a sinister reminder of the totalitarian past and the KGB, whose central offices were housed there. *Nezavisimaia gazeta* and other newspapers had challenged the police state and the concept of a closed society. Such newspapers continued to promote a more open and confident approach to the world, a view the editors have symbolically reinforced by their choice of location.

Nezavisimaia gazeta's central offices are set back from the street in a small courtyard. In late June 1997, the monthly religion supplement had just been issued, and the editorial staff room on the second floor was in chaos: a staff meeting was being organized; the telephone was constantly ringing; reporters and other staff members were scurrying about; excitement and energy were almost tangible.

Maksim Shevchenko seemed the very personification of this sense of purpose and energy. His physical appearance itself is striking: muscular, handsome, his black hair pulled back into a ponytail, he is in his late thirties and clearly a product of the massive changes Russia has experienced in the last decade. His blue eyes are intense, and while he is a careful listener, he is also quick to respond. Sometimes in conversation, when he explored a particular question, he would become so animated that he would get on one knee, sliding off his chair onto the floor, elaborating his point with his hands.

Ukrainian by birth, Russian Orthodox by upbringing, Shevchenko is a person whose life has undergone several decisive changes. Originally, he studied to be a mathematician, graduating from the Institute of Aviation Sciences in Moscow and specializing in systematic analysis. A key military establishment, the Institute of Aviation Sciences prepared its students for a career in the Soviet air force. But like many graduates, Shevchenko never practiced his specialty and never served in the military. After graduation, he began to study history and enrolled in courses at Moscow State University. There, in the late 1980s, while studying Russian history, he met the well-known religious dissident Aleksandr Ogorodnikov. The two men have remained close friends since then, meeting regularly for conversation and sharing their common views of the church's social role.[32]

From 1989 to 1991, Shevchenko wrote for the newspaper of the Russian Christian Democratic Party and taught Russian and Western European history in the Orthodox Classical Gymnasium of the Radonezh Society. After the school closed in 1994, he rejoined his friend Aleksandr Ogorodnikov and worked with him to establish orphanages for street children and soup kitchens for the poor in Moscow. Such experiences have broadened Shevchenko's religious perspective, both theoretical and practical, and they have equipped him with a firsthand knowledge of the social problems facing the church.

Like his associate editor, Oleg Mramornov, Shevchenko is firmly Orthodox and a regular churchgoer. Both men declare their loyalty and commitment to the Russian Orthodox Church and to the Moscow Patriarchate. But while they write from inside their tradition, they do not claim to be publicists for the church. "We believe the Church has a lot of flaws and we do not hesitate to criticize the leadership." Shevchenko told me that his main purpose is to educate and to contribute in depth to a discussion of the importance of religion in Russian history and its current struggles. "Because of the perspective we take," he said, "the effect of our newspaper since its inception in January 1997 has been something new, different, and controversial. Many people have never experienced from inside our country and our tradition the critical, sympathetic, and yet many-sided approach that we have taken. We have had a strong reaction from the public."

Part of this reaction, according to Shevchenko, is a result of the rapid secularization that he sees as a global phenomenon. The public reaction against the secularization of society that has proceeded with such speed and force began, he said to me, in the late 1970s in Iran. The Iranian Revolution witnessed a conflict between two different views of the world, one essentially religious, the other secular, materialistic, and utilitarian. The conflict between these two visions would emerge in different forms later in other contexts—as reactions against attempts to remove religion from the center of life, to separate it from other forces shaping the society, and to relegate it to the ghetto. It was this separation that such Russian religious dissidents as Aleksandr Solzhenitsyn, Boris Pasternak, and Andrei Sinyavsky opposed, claiming that it violated the inherent integrity or wholeness of life. Shevchenko sees the role of his newspaper as rebuilding and reemphasizing the connections between sacred and secular, restoring what he called "Russia's spiritual foundation," which the Bolsheviks had tried unsuccessfully to obliterate.[33]

The Russia that Shevchenko envisions in the future will be built around strong local communities that are self-governed and whose members care for each other. Such a vision contemplates communities with a solid moral foundation shaped by the teachings of the Orthodox Church. They are conciliar communities, only loosely tied to the central church administration, communities based on self-help and mutual aid. They are communities that provide assistance to members who are destitute or suffer from misfortunes. The church will be a central force in these communities, but it will not be a force that constricts freedom and limits creativity. Rather it will stimulate this creativity, nourish the imagination, and rekindle the capacity to hope.

Beneath the surface of Russia's and Ukraine's "official culture," Shevchenko told me, the social structure for these communities has long existed. Independent of the authorities, communities developed their own operating principles, rules of behavior, and social connections. Often in defiance of such authorities, they built their own civil society. Throughout Eastern Europe, the Czech writer and future leader Václav Havel called this phenomenon, this creation of social networks at the grass roots, the "power of the powerless." This independent life, Havel wrote, "sails upon the vast ocean of the manipulated life like little boats, tossed by the waves but always bobbing back as visible messengers of living within the truth, articulating the suppressed aims of life."[34] In Russia and Ukraine, Shevchenko observes similar networks have long governed the life of the community. In his own experiences growing up in Ukraine, he saw them in operation. They were manifested in his community in the resistance to the Soviet government's "strikes against religion."

Born and raised in the Poltava region of Ukraine, Shevchenko knows the region well. "Many times," he said, "a young priest would arrive, heretofore unknown, in our community. He had often just graduated from the seminary, yet within a year he would become a central figure in the lives of the people living there." Through him were conveyed the theological teachings of the church; he filled a vital educational function—unseen on the surface but essential to daily life, to key events, and to a sense of the eternal. "In my youth," he said, "when a priest came to a district in either western or eastern Ukraine, whole villages would come together to listen to him." Then, they would begin to bring food to him. They did this "out of feelings of gratitude," Shevchenko said, "because even among the collective farmers and the Communists, most of them had been baptized when they were infants and they continued to carry within them religious feelings." Despite the official ideology and strictures against the church, Shevchenko observed that many of the Communists in his community "brought their children to be baptized on the side, and they brought the priest food because they could not afford to give him money."

Such commitments and values were deeply ingrained in the society of Shevchenko's youth, and they offered possibilities, he thought, for building the future. But for these possibilities to flourish, the church had to become more decentralized; it needed to rediscover the ancient principles of its tradition and apply these principles—in all their variety, their calls for dialogue, and their openness to the world—to the present. This task he saw as the educational mission of *Nezavisimaia gazeta*'s special supplement on religion. A key part of that tradition, which Shevchenko tried to propagate, was the church's independence, its need to remain true to its own teachings. To him, the church can only become the conscience of the people by breaking its alliance with state power.

In both his writings and his discussions with me, Maksim Shevchenko was extremely critical of present trends within the church. He pointed out that church leaders have not asked forgiveness for their involvement with Soviet authorities and have become increasingly unwilling to seek this forgiveness. He voiced a similar concern about the church's participation in the resurgence of Russian nationalism, particularly its role in the creation of a new Russian national ideology. The development of a national ideology, he maintained, is not the proper function of religion. Moreover, he is anxious about the church's cooperation with the Moscow city authorities in the rebuilding of the massive Cathedral of Christ the Savior, a gigantic project to reconstruct the famous cathedral demolished by Stalin in 1931. The ceremony transferring the cathedral to the church, "presented everything very beautifully," yet "hidden dangers lurked everywhere beneath the surface in that ceremony," especially in what the ceremony conveyed about the "seductive relationship" between the church and the government. It is this seductive attraction to power, to becoming again a close ally of the government, that most troubles Shevchenko. He sees this relationship as potentially undermining the church's independence, subverting its mission, and limiting its social voice.

Shevchenko does not address directly the subject of the Great Church Schism that split the Russian Orthodox Church in the seventeenth century, but it continues to haunt the church. Historians have examined in detail the impact of the schism on Russian society and politics in the years following it. But the psychological consequences were also significant and long lasting. "The official church," B. H. Sumner has written, "which had won the day largely through the backing of the state, became more and more dependent on it, and lost much of what was most living in the religious consciousness of the Russian people just at the time when it most needed cohesion and vigor in meeting the impact of western Europe upon Russia."[35] The task of recovering "what was most living" will require a courageous and fresh encounter with the early teachings of Orthodoxy, and it will also require a careful look at the church's political affiliation with the government. Given the church's present model of leadership, its hierarchical structure, and its psychological allegiance to authority, such a reexamination, Shevchenko maintained, will be extremely difficult.

Another lingering psychological consequence of the church schism is an apprehension concerning any apparent breach with central church authority. After the fall of communism, as Russia again had to confront an economic and spiritual assault from the West, church leaders became increasingly anxious about the potential for schism. In the Kochetkov case, charges of heresy and accusations that they were "schismatics from within" were frequently hurled against Fr Georgii Kochetkov and his followers. Church leaders repeatedly stressed the need for unity and discipline rather than innovation and reform. In this time of social transformation, as the church sought to recover its sense of purpose, these leaders maintained, it had to seek solidarity; it could not afford to be threatened from within its own ranks.

Yet, ironically, as Maksim Shevchenko pointed out, pressure was building from within the church. Such pressure came from individuals and groups unhappy with the leadership's close association with political power, its unwillingness to consider internal reforms, and its theological inflexibility. "A large part of the people who have entered the church since 1988 are dissatisfied; they want the church to move beyond the old concept of patriotic service and association with the Russian government," wrote Shevchenko's associate editor, Oleg Mramornov. The church has other duties, Mramornov said, "than to be transformed into a warrior institution, brandishing its weapons for the amusement of those in power, who long ago ceased to believe either in God or the devil." From this point of view, the main threat of schism comes not from change but from the reluctance to change, not from questioning but from inertia, and not from internal reforms but from an unwillingness to look outward—to develop a more compelling social and educational vision.[36]

Between 1997 and 2000, the leadership of the Orthodox Church struggled with the same issues Shevchenko described. Orthodox leaders were concerned that nearly a hundred years had passed since the church had formulated a new policy dealing with the church's role in society. Yet this had been a tumultuous century, marked by rapid changes in nearly every aspect of life. Church leaders well understood the urgent need for a new social policy.

While *Nezavisimaia gazeta* has no official relationship with the Orthodox Church, the editors of its special religion section brought many pressing issues to the forefront. The fresh examination the editors called for, an examination Shevchenko insisted had to take place, could not long be delayed. Shevchenko's newspaper extended the dialogue about church and society that had begun earlier, nearly a decade before. Now, at the end of the 1990s, the church had to take a stand.

Social Conception of the Orthodox Church

On June 14, 2000, the synodal working group of the Russian Orthodox Church convened a special symposium on church and society in Moscow. The working group had labored for several years to develop a draft conception of the Russian Orthodox Church on church-state relations and problems of today's society as a whole. Present for the symposium were Metropolitan Kirill of Smolensk and Kaliningrad who was chairman of the Department for External Church Relations of the Moscow Patriarchate and of the synodal working group, members of the working group, Metropolitan Iuvenali of Krutitsy and Kolomna, bishops, seminary professors, clergy, leaders of Orthodox and Christian public associations, scholars, members of synodal departments, and foreign guests. They had come to discuss, debate, and eventually to propose what had long been needed, a new social conception for the Russian Orthodox Church.[37]

Metropolitan Kirill of Smolensk and Kaliningrad delivered the keynote address at the symposium. He presented the preliminary report of the working group, outlining the basic principles on which the new conception would be founded. Participants then discussed his report in several plenary sessions and four sections: "Church, Nation, State," "Church and Public Life," "Orthodoxy and the Moral Crisis of Society," and "Orthodoxy and Global Economic and Political Processes." In each of these sections, symposium members tried to relate church traditions and basic teachings to fundamental issues facing Russian society in a national and international setting.[38]

Following the symposium, on June 20, the church held a conference on Christianity at the threshold of the new millennium at the Russian Academy of Sciences in Moscow. The academy and the Ministry of Culture joined the church in hosting the conference. In plenary sessions and special sections, the distinguished participants discussed the themes "Social and Educational Work of the Church," "Church, State, and Civil Society," and "Church Tradition and Historical Science Today." Again, these topics focused on rethinking church-state relations, relating church traditions to new discoveries in science, and reexamining the church's educational role.[39]

The June 20 conference was noteworthy not only because of the presentations made by leading Russian scientists but also by the appearance of Patriarch Aleksi II of Moscow and All Russia. In his keynote speech, Aleksi II defined what he considered to be one of the primary issues of the times: the task of overcoming the sharp division between an "imposed positivistic ideology" and the theology of the church. Such a division, he said, falsely pitted science and religion against each other. The division created two spheres of thinking that had to be better related if Russia was to move forward, and he posited a series of questions that he believed had to be thought out. "All these are not idle or abstract questions," he said, "but problems posed by life itself," and he called on ecclesiastical and secular scholars to work together.[40]

Following these discussions, the Sacred Bishops' Council of the Russian Orthodox Church convened in what proved to be a historic session. Meeting from August 13 to 16 in the Church of Christ the Savior and the Danilov Monastery in Moscow, the bishops' council adopted a new policy expressing the church's social vision. The document the council adopted was titled "Foundations of the Social Conception of the Russian Orthodox Church." It followed more than thirty sessions of lively discussion and debate in which eighty social groups and scientific institutions had participated.[41] Despite this broad participation, the final document bore the strong influence of Patriarch

Aleksi II and Metropolitan Kirill, chairman of the Department of External Church Relations of the Moscow Patriarchate, who had chaired the working sessions.

In adopting the new social conception, the bishops' council asserted its chief purpose as creating a social polity that is in agreement with the "evidence of the Holy Scriptures and Holy Teachings of the Church." According to its preamble, the document "sets forth the basic provisions of her [Russian Orthodox Church's] teaching on church-state relations and a number of problems socially significant today. It also reflects the official position of [the] Moscow Patriarchate on relations with state and secular society. In addition, it gives a number of guidelines to be applied in this field by episcopate, clergy and laity."[42]

The lengthy document covers the subjects discussed in the preliminary working sessions. It is divided into sixteen thematic parts, as follows:

1. basic theological provisions
2. church and nation
3. church and state
4. Christian ethics and secular law
5. church and politics
6. labor and its fruits
7. property
8. war and peace
9. crime, punishment, and reformation
10. personal, family, and public morality
11. personal and national health
12. problems of bioethics
13. the church and ecological problems
14. secular science, culture, and education
15. church and mass media
16. international relations, problems of globalization, and secularism

The bishops' council intended for the "Foundations of the Social Conception" to be used as a perspective and as a guide for the church's various institutions—its synodal bodies, dioceses, monasteries, parishes, and canonical institutions—in dealing with secular organizations and the mass media. More important, the document would serve as a guide for decision-making in the face of the difficult, complex problems of a rapidly changing society. The writers of the document emphasized that it was not a finished product but rather the beginning of a discussion that would be continued and developed in the future. The document would be "included in the curriculum of the theological schools of the Moscow Patriarchate."

The document is written from inside the church and reflects its point of view, taking religious and theological perspectives as the starting point. It is intended for religious believers, but it envisions this audience in the widest sense—all the people who were born into and thus belong to the Orthodox tradition. The document, therefore, is best analyzed from within that tradition—not as a means of convincing secular readers of its correctness but as a guide to those who are already in this faith. It is significant, as the Russian journalist of religious affairs Aleksandr Kyrlezhev has observed, that the document adopted by the *sobor* is titled a "Conception of Society." This title and approach make any attempt to evaluate or to construct a critical analysis of the work extremely difficult. Kyrlezhev likens this attempt to "trying to study the channel of a river while the work over it is still in process."[43]

The "Foundations of the Social Conception" treats a large variety of subjects. The document discusses at length the relationship between the church and the state. It tries to draw a clear line of separation between them, seeing their goals as fundamentally different and their claims on the individual as coming from very different sources. In each sphere, it warns against abuses of power. It proposes the canonization of Tsar Nicholas II and his family, murdered by the Bolsheviks in 1918. It spells out the fields in which the church and the government need to cooperate, including spiritual, cultural, moral, and patriotic education, the restoration of Russia's cultural heritage, concern for the preservation of morality in society, charity and social work, and health care. It speaks of the *symphonia* between the government and the church, the mutual support and respect that marked Russia's earlier tradition and need to be restored.

On specific problems facing the country, the document exhibits a great diversity of viewpoints. Some of these perspectives might be roughly characterized as "liberal," others as "traditional" or "conservative." The *sobor* shows a special concern for ecological issues; mismanagement of such issues, the document says, has "distorted the face of the earth on a global scale." A philosophy of "all permissiveness" has violated this delicate ecological balance, and among society's most urgent needs is the development of ecological ethics. The document calls the pursuit of peace one of the church's main social objectives. It sharply criticizes the unbridled appetite for material goods and emphasizes the fact that "wealth cannot make man happy." The document also devotes a great deal of attention to the family and sexual ethics. It issues a "strong denunciation of drinking," underlining its devastating impact on the family. The document condemns the widespread use of abortion and the practice of euthanasia, and it deplores homosexual relations as a "distor-

tion of God-created human nature." It stresses the political, cultural, and social equality of women, but, within the family, opposes "the tendency to diminish the role of woman as wife and mother." The document recalls the
words of St Paul about the "special responsibility of the husband who is called
to be 'the head of the wife,'" giving that passage a traditionalist, conservative
interpretation.[44]

The church's views on many social issues are presented in great detail and
go beyond the scope of this chapter. But one of the sections in the "Foundations of the Social Conception" directly addresses the chapter's main subject,
namely the part titled "Secular science, culture, and education." This was a
topic given much attention in the meetings of the working group prior to the
sobor. In his June 20 speech at the headquarters of the Russian Academy of
Sciences, the patriarch had also focused on the subject, calling it one of the
primary issues facing the country. "What is the right approach to possible
contradictions between the church tradition and facts found in scientific historical research?" "What should be the new educational doctrine of the Russian Orthodox Church on the threshold of the new millennium?" the patriarch had asked.[45]

In section fourteen, the *sobor* attempts to respond to these questions—in
a preliminary rather than a dogmatic way. The *sobor* connects the problems
Russia faces in this sphere to the issues on ecology discussed in the previous
section of the document. "It is impossible to overcome the ecological crisis in
the situation of a spiritual crisis," the document asserts. This same presump-
tion is carried forward into the discussion of science, culture, and education.

The document explores these three topics by, first, setting them in historical context. The treatment of science begins with a historical overview.
This overview points out Christianity's early contributions to science and describes the way Christianity and science were connected in demythologizing
nature. In time, science emerged as one of the most powerful fields of culture.
By the end of the twentieth century, science and technology were seen as "the
decisive factors in the life of civilization." Despite the early connections between science and Christianity, however, secular ideologies had brought
science under their influence. This had led to tragic consequences, as the history of the twentieth century had clearly shown.

According to the "Foundations of the Social Conception," such tragic
consequences came about because "of the false principle lying at the basis of
the contemporary scientific and technological development." The "false principle" the authors have in mind is the complete separation from science of any
ethical, religious, or philosophical considerations. Science had come to exist

for itself alone; it was neutral toward ethical or philosophical principles. As such, it had fallen under the control of human passions, particularly under the desire for the highest possible level of material comfort. Serving vanity and pride, science rarely expresses its connections with the "spiritual harmony" of the world. "Therefore, to ensure human life," the document emphasizes, "it is necessary today as never before to restore the lost link of scientific knowledge with religious, spiritual, and moral values."[46]

While the document does not address the themes of Soviet science directly, one might speculate that it has these themes and methodologies primarily in mind in voicing its criticisms. Earlier, in the June 20 meeting featuring the patriarch, the famous Soviet scientist Boris Raushenbakh had also delivered a keynote address. A pioneer of the Soviet space age, a nuclear physicist, and for many years the director of the Physics and Technological Institute of the Russian Academy of Sciences, Raushenbakh had been a chief critic of several main pillars of Soviet life: dialectical materialism, scientific atheism, and the "creation of a new morality" based solely on materialism and reason.

In a 1995 interview, Raushenbakh argued that the one-sided emphasis on materialism and rationality in Soviet education over the past seventy years had been misguided, and that religion was an essential ingredient in both human creativity and morality.[47] Earlier, Raushenbakh maintained that Russia not only had to recapture older spiritual voices, such as Dostoevsky and Tolstoy, but also needed to reacquaint itself with the giants of its scientific tradition, especially Mendeleev. In Raushenbakh's view, a key to rebuilding Russia lay in a new "humanizing education"—one that would embrace both the scientific and the spiritual. "We live in a country," he wrote, "that was founded on strong religious principles, on strong religious ideals, but we have gone very far from them, to the other extreme; it is absolutely essential that we recover what we have lost."[48]

The June 20 speech would be academician Raushenbakh's last address; he died shortly thereafter. But the imprint of his views on religion and imagination and religion and science, which he expressed in his writings and public statements in the last years of his life, are unmistakable in section fourteen of the "Foundations of the Social Conception." What the document most opposes is a way of thinking that gives science omnipotence. Such a belief views all other ways of thinking, including religious ways, as inferior. Yet, according to the "Foundations," science and faith cannot contradict each other: they have different goals, use different methodologies, and have different points of departure. The document quotes Mikhail Lomonosov's statement, similar to the one posted on the walls of Fr Maksim Kozlov's church, that science and religion "cannot come into conflict . . . unless someone excites strife in them out of conceit and desire to show off one's ingenuity."[49]

The *sobor* strongly opposed what it called the temptation to view science as a self-sufficient field, "completely independent of moral principles." It refers to science as a "double-edged sword"; recent discoveries in microbiology, chemistry, and physics might bring benefits but, from the church's perspective, might cause great harm. It is thus extremely important, "for the sake of life," to encourage cooperation between science and religion, to nurture dialogue, and to promote their interaction. These actions will foster the kind of "healthy, creative climate" that enables scientific research to flourish.

Throughout the document, there is an emphasis on harmony between the disparate aspects of life. Implicit in this emphasis is a criticism of the previous Soviet model, which had stressed conflict as a basic principle governing society and life. The "Foundations" deliberately seeks connections; it presents a vision of the wholeness of life that goes much beyond the mere criticism of the Soviet past. It criticizes not only conflict and separation but also the extreme specialization, narrowness, and manipulation that have characterized many approaches to education, and it repeatedly calls for the need to "cross boundaries," to discover the hidden bonds, and to build cooperation. These are qualities that Boris Raushenbakh had emphasized. They are also seminal principles found in Russian Orthodoxy that integrates rather than "disintegrates the act of knowing."[50]

As Russia tries to rebuild its educational system, the *sobor* stressed several main points. Schools convey knowledge, but that is not their primary task. Even more important is their role in nurturing and passing on certain principles that are essential to civilization and to Russia's future well-being. The *sobor* identified four of these: morality, love of one's neighbor, the quest for truth, and love for country and its heritage.[51] The *sobor*, therefore, severely criticized educational systems that assail religion, and particularly Christianity, or undervalue its influence on history. Such practices not only distort the past but cut students off from important sources of renewal and hope.[52]

The school serves as a "mediator that hands over to new generations the moral values accumulated" in the past. As a mediator, the school connects the past to the future, providing a sense of purpose and direction. This act of mediation requires a willingness not to look inward, but outward—to the whole world: the *sobor*'s document criticizes the voices inside the church who see the secular schools as untrustworthy. As mediators, religious and secular schools have to work together to develop as fully as possible the life of the mind and the quest for truth. The document quotes St Gregory the Theologian: "Every one of us who has an intellect recognizes scholarship (*paideusin*) as a primary blessing for us. And not only this noble scholarship of our own, which . . . has as its subject only salvation and the beauty of what is contemplated by the mind, but also the external scholarship which many Christians abhor out of ignorance as unreliable, dangerous and diverting from God."[53]

As a whole, the *sobor's* statements on education try to set standards that will guide the church's future. In this effort, the *sobor* looks to the church's own heritage, at Russia's experience in the twentieth century, and toward the future it aspires to build. Critical of utopian attempts to transform the physical world, the document calls for a quieter, simpler vision that emphasizes the inner world. Change should begin there, it maintains, citing St Maksim the Confessor that "man can turn the earth into paradise only if he carried paradise in himself."[54] Education provides the foundation of citizenship. The church and the school, working in concert, offer a base for the development of morality that underlies citizenship. It is that educational mission that the church, in cooperation with secular schools, has the obligation to perform.[55]

The church's attempts to rebuild religious education and re-create its relationship with Russian society have prompted diverse interpretations. Writing in *Nezavisimaia gazeta,* Maksim Shevchenko characterized the church's new social doctrine, on the whole, as a "liberal conception." The document clearly showed, he pointed out, that the church did not speak in only one voice; it evidenced a struggle between "reformist" and "traditionalist" factions in the effort to reconstruct the church's proper role in society. But most important, the document revealed a serious attempt to deal with extremely difficult questions about which the church's leadership had long been silent.[56]

The social critic and writer Aleksandr Kyrlezhev was more critical. Kyrlezhev considered the appearance of the document to be one of the most significant actions in the history of the Russian Orthodox Church in the twentieth century and also an extremely important event in the social life of Russia. The work of the bishops' council promised to fill a deep gap separating the Orthodox Church from the social processes currently changing nearly every aspect of Russian life. But Kyrlezhev admitted a profound sense of disappointment between what the social document had promised and what it delivered. He found most objectionable not the social conceptions treated in the document but its failure to discuss several important topics. To Kyrlezhev such topics lay at the core of the church's task: to fill the spiritual vacuum evident throughout Russian society. Throughout its lengthy, weighty social treatise, the bishops' council made not one mention of the church's need to ask forgiveness for its complicity in the sins of the Soviet government, including its leaders' cooperation with the state security police. Rather, the document avoided any kind of self-criticism, any kind of introspective analysis of the church's own errors. The document revealed a nostalgia for the past, Kyrlezhev said, but until the church first took a "hard look" at itself in the past, it would not be able to deal responsibly with the present.[57]

Kyrlezhev also criticized what he saw as the document's simplistic treatment of secularization. This "complex, ambivalent phenomenon" that "shook the very foundations of the Church" in a social and psychological sense, deserved more careful examination than the document gave it. Such a shortcoming led to the complete omission in the document of any discussion of "postmodernism." There is no historical analysis of what is "modern" and therefore, of what is "postmodern," and yet these issues, Kyrlezhev observed, at the end of the century pose serious challenges to the church.[58] By failing to deal directly with the subject, the church limits its ability to speak to some of the key social and intellectual issues Russia now faces.

For all these legitimate criticisms, it might still be argued that the "Foundations of the Social Conception" represents a significant first step in the attempt to relate Orthodox Christianity to society. Despite its shortcomings and its omissions, the document struggles to take a stand on difficult social issues, to search within the Orthodox tradition and teachings for wisdom in dealing with these complex issues. "I received with great joy the appearance of this document," Fr Maksim Kozlov said; it "provided the basis of a social doctrine; it does not intend to be the last word. It is, as you know, not a statement of dogma, but a working document," in which ideas would be further explored, questions deepened, and analysis elaborated.[59]

In this sense, the document's significance lies not in defining certain prescriptions for action, but in opening the way for dialogue. In Fr Maksim's eyes, it prepares for this dialogue in the "traditional meaning of the term," not as a freewheeling discussion without boundaries, but as a conversation in which the guidelines have been established, a conversation that will seek what he called the "golden mean."

The church's new social conception represents the beginning of a conversation, and its significance may well lie in the process initiated by work on the document itself. Since it is a first step, the document's political direction is difficult to determine. "You know, it is very easy to evaluate a document when there is a previous statement that allows one to distinguish one from the other," the sociologist of religion S. B. Filatov pointed out; "but this is the Church's first document of this kind."[60] In discussing the new social conception, Filatov told me that he could only speak from his own personal experi-

ence, "evaluating the views of those priests and bishops whom I have met."
"Of course," he said, "my views assessing the new social conception lack a firm
scientific foundation":

> Nevertheless, I do have many experiences that underlie my perspective. In my
> view, the convictions of the majority of the most influential members of the
> clergy are more nationalistic, more conservative, and more antidemocratic than
> those to whom this document speaks.
> The document itself is fairly lengthy, but there are several very significant
> moments in it. Among these are: the right and even the responsibility of the
> Church to resist amoralism and to oppose the anti-Christian decisions of the
> government; the principled acknowledgment of the normality of the demo-
> cratic structure of society; and the right of the Church to exist fully within that
> democratic structure. This full acceptance gives the Church several responsibil-
> ities before the society, some of which fall into the sphere of social action. In
> themselves, these decisions, if they become a guide to action, and do not
> become simply declarations, will be an important step forward. But there is
> much doubt whether or not this will happen, because in our Church the situ-
> ation is such that this document could remain only a declaration. If it does not,
> if it becomes the basis for discussion in the Church hierarchy, the parishes, and
> the Orthodox schools, then this social document will become the foundation
> for decisions that will have a very positive social impact.

Currently, it is much too early to tell what the concrete results of the
church's new social conception will be. But perhaps what is most important is
the church's social engagement, both in preparing the document and in projecting its outcome. In discussing the key social issues facing Russia, the leadership of the church recognizes the priority of connecting the church to the
world. In the process of consultation, which lasted for nearly three years, the
church leadership held many discussions, involving a large variety of people,
ranging from national church conferences, the Russian Academy of Sciences,
and the bishops' *sobor.* Civil society requires such engagement. The church's
new social conception points out that the Latin word *cultura* means "cultivation, breeding, educatinn," which in turn "is derived from *cultus,* meaning
veneration, worship, cult. This points to the religious roots of culture."[61] By
continuing to explore the relationship between religion and culture, by seeing
education as a key to citizenship, and by remaining open to engagement in the
world in all its complexity and diversity, the church will have taken a significant step toward developing civil society in Russia.

6 Conclusion

On December 18, 1999, Mother Serafima's funeral was held in the church of the Dormition at Novodevichy Monastery in Moscow. Word of her death two days earlier had spread rapidly throughout the city, and on the day of her funeral, crowds of people overflowed the spacious church that stood near the center of the monastery whose monastic life she had done so much to restore. Spilling out into the courtyard, these people had come to see Mother Serafima off on "the way of all the earth."[1] Standing in the crowd were not only many people whom Mother Serafima had befriended but also such dignitaries as V. I. Kramkov, head of the Narofominsk District of the Moscow region; A. I. Shurko, director of the State Museum of History; A. I. Muzykantskii, prefect of the Central Administrative District of the city of Moscow; and the staff of the Novodevichy museum.

On that cold, snowy December day, mourners walked silently through the pathways of the stunning ancient monastery. The blue and gold cupolas of the monastery shone brilliantly against the sky, bearing witness both to eternal verities and to Mother Serafima herself. Inside the church, a message of consolation was read from His Holiness Patriarch Aleksi II of Moscow and All Russia, expressing gratitude for Mother Serafima's gifts and her faithful service. Metropolitan Iuvenali of Krutitsy and Kolomna, her spiritual father who had worked closely with Mother Serafima in recovering the identity and the fate of priests lost during the great purges, next gave an emotional oration about her life and her humble spirit. The divine liturgy for "the rest of Mother Serafima's soul was celebrated." Metropolitan Iuvenali, assisted by Archbishop Gregory of Mozhaisk and Bishop Tikhon of Vidnoe and clergy of Moscow and the Moscow diocese, then performed the funeral rites. Mother Serafima was buried in the yard of the church of the Dormition of the Novodevichy Monastery, a place she had loved and that she had given herself fully to revive.

The people who convened to honor Mother Serafima were testimony to the large number of people from extremely diverse backgrounds whose lives she touched. "She could inspire people to work for the good of the Church so much that help always came in the right time and sometimes quite unexpectedly," wrote Archbishop Gregory of Mozhaisk in her obituary. "One could not help loving her—so wonderful was her soul."[2] Her sincerity and her ability to reach out to others, from the powerful to the destitute, were among her special gifts.

In recognition of her work restoring monastic life at Novodevichy Monastery, the church had bestowed upon Mother Serafima several major honors in the last years of her life. In 1997, His Holiness Patriarch Aleksi II presented her with the Decorated Cross. In 1999, on her eighty-fifth birthday, the patriarch awarded her the Order of St Princess Olga Equal-to-the-Apostles.

Mother Serafima's life spanned nearly the entirety of the twentieth century. Born in Petrograd on August 12, 1914, at the outset of the First World War in a year that historians often consider the true beginning of this century, she died on nearly the eve of the next one. She lived across an entire age, filled with revolution and war, with industrial and technological transformation, and then returned full circle to many of the images that had characterized the beginning of that period—to the cupolas, bells, and monastic life at Novodevichy. As I read Mother Serafima's obituary on the Orthodox Church's Web site, I was reminded of these ironies and of the distance the church has traveled, from its prerevolutionary times, through the Soviet period, to the post-Communist present. Mother Serafima had traversed the same distance, adapting to the times but also preserving what she believed to be timeless entities.

Reading the announcement of her death, I thought of that small, dynamic, and talented woman standing in the doorway of the church at Novodevichy in the 1990s. Retiring from a brilliant professional career at the age of seventy-three, as the writer of her obituary recounted, she could have chosen a well-deserved life of retirement. She elected another course, beginning work at a candle box in the church of the Prophet Elijah in Moscow. Aiming to learn humility, she entered the service of the church in one of its lowest stations. Her life was the candle, whose light burned in the darkness and illuminated the icons inside the church.

In her last decade, she had led Novodevichy Monastery to a full recovery of its physical beauty, and she had laid the foundation for the regeneration of its physical power. Under her leadership, the monastery reconnected with society, becoming again testimony of the church active in the world. "From the point of view of our monastic educational life, our moral life, and our spiritual life, I unfortunately have not done everything well," she said in her final interview with me, one of the last she gave. "But I have tried to do the very best that I could."[3] In her "very best" and in that of the other individuals studied here lie much of Russia's hope.

From the Ruins of the Cold War
to the Wellsprings of Tomorrow's Russia

When church bells rang again in Moscow and throughout the country, after many years of silence, they brought back more than ancient sacred sounds. They also heralded hope, signaling fresh possibilities for an entire culture. What these possibilities would be and how they would manifest themselves remained open questions. At the end of his great novel *Dead Souls,* Nikolai Gogol had posed the question, "Whither Russia, are you going?" Chichikov's speeding troika, heading off across the steppe, and the ringing of bells, came to symbolize Russia's uncertain future. In 1991, the answer to Gogol's question was still as enigmatic as it had been in his own time.

In relation to the period following the collapse of the Soviet Union, Gogol's question, "Whither Russia," might also apply to its national political and social identity. Has the church supported the rebuilding of an autocratic state or has it provided the impetus for the development of a civil society? Does the evidence suggest movement toward building a new moral and spiritual foundation to support a future civil society, or does it show the opposite trend, a turning inward? These are not easy questions, and they still have not been fully resolved, even though the church has taken many positive steps to connect itself to society.

It has now been more than a decade since the collapse of the Soviet Union. In this decade the eminent sociologist of religion Sergei Filatov has spent much of the time trying to understand the direction of Russian society, particularly the direction of its religious consciousness. A person of great creative energy and clear vision, Filatov has brought many fresh insights to the study of religion and politics, as well as to the changing landscape of religious groups in Russian society. Beginning in the mid-1990s, he embarked on a major study defining these various religious groups, measuring their size, and exploring their beliefs and activities. During this time, he and his associates have traversed the country many times, spending months in provincial outposts, surveying the members of different confessions, interviewing people, living in their midst, and closely observing their behavior. In 2002, he published the results in a work that marks a milestone in religious scholarship; he and his associates produced an encyclopedia of detailed, firsthand information that has not been available on Russia for most of the past century.[4]

In June 2001, as he neared the completion of his project, Filatov discussed Russia's religious experiences in the postcommunist period. Looking back over the entire decade, he reflected on the trends that to him stood out and that defined the period. Some of these trends, he said, he could not have foreseen five years before. He stressed the fluidity, the unpredictability of Russia's situation; he again underscored the importance of studying religious beliefs and their relationship to civil society. In the decade following the collapse of communism, despite the chaos of the period, it is possible, he said, to delineate several fundamental themes or trends.[5]

First, in contrast to what was expected at the beginning of the 1990s—the statements about the high levels of religiosity, the proclamations about faith in God, and the mass attendance at church services—he found little evidence of a widespread revival of religious faith in Russia. The early "religious boom" failed to sustain itself. While various kinds of methodologies are used to define religious beliefs, they all show that, in reality, practicing religious believers in Russia now number less than 10 percent of the total population, a proportion that accords well with countries in Western Europe. One very sharp distinction between Russia and many Western European countries remains: in Russia few people are indifferent or hostile to religion and religious issues. There are now almost no militant atheists. Gone is the time when violent assaults on religious organizations are frequent or condoned, and this change presented a sharp contrast with the Soviet past.

It is the apparent contradiction between these two circumstances that Filatov finds especially fascinating. Seeking an explanation, he cited the outstanding Catholic bishop of Saratov, Klemens Pikkel, and his characterization of Russia's distinctive religiosity. Pikkel said that the greatest victory the Communists had achieved consisted of the near destruction in the Russian people of the capacity to relate to God, to seek beauty, to accept a God who loves, who must be held in awe, a God who is the creator. Such capacities were practically lost. What, then, were the results? For the intelligentsia, as Bishop Pikkel said, religiosity came to mean simply culture; for many of the common people, it suggested superstition. For the pastor or priest of any confession, these perceptions posed a major challenge: "How to overcome the presentation of religion as some kind of verbal exchange, some kind of composed structure, or as a cultural exhibition, when at its core is something altogether different from any of these things?" This is a problem that can only be overcome slowly and with great difficulty.

Second, the decade witnessed a remarkable change in the religious orientation of many Russians. In Moscow, Russian Orthodoxy has not gained many followers and, in fact, the number of practicing Orthodox believers has remained extremely low, amounting to not more than 1 percent of the population. This figure was confirmed, Filatov said, by the low numbers of people who attended services in the city that Easter.

At the beginning of the 1990s in Moscow, there was great anxiety over what seemed then to be a rapid expansion of new religious movements, including violent or totalitarian sects. Looking now at the dynamics of these numbers, Filatov found little evidence of the growth of such sects.[6] The spread of totalitarian religious movements, feared earlier, has not become reality, and the most organized of these groups have changed their character, becoming less aggressive and more open. In the Bogorodichnyi center of the city, for example, an authoritarian sect that flourished nearly a decade ago has transformed itself, abandoning its violent rhetoric and aggressive behavior. The same pattern might be observed among the White Brotherhood and similar groups. Whereas the psychological potential for growth of totalitarian sects had earlier seemed very high in Russia, perhaps higher than anywhere else in Europe, it simply has not happened.

Third, much greater growth, however, could be observed among Protestant organizations. In Moscow a decade ago, Filatov recalled, there existed two Baptist unions—one legal, the other illegal; one Pentecostal congregation; one Adventist congregation; and one Lutheran church, comprised of Germans. In 2001, he observed, one can find in Moscow nearly all Protestant denominations, as well as their various factions—Lutherans of all kinds, Methodists, many evangelical organizations, Pentecostals. "It would be difficult to find any Protestant denomination that is *not* represented here," he pointed out. In Russia, the number of Protestant religious organizations had grown from 900 in 1990 to 4,509 in 2001.[7]

In addition, the decade witnessed a significant change in the social and cultural characteristics of Russian Protestants.[8] Earlier, they were mainly people of little education, workers and peasants. But during the last ten years, a Protestant intelligentsia has emerged, including many humanists and economists. Such people have looked for a more personal form of piety and for a greater sense of community than they have found in Orthodoxy. These Russian Protestants have created their own separate congregations. "Neither our society nor the Protestants themselves," Filatov said, "yet recognize the fact that Protestantism has become a real spiritual and cultural force, capable of becoming a strong political force in the future."[9] Filatov's studies show, for example, that in Siberia and the Russian far east, where the general level of religiosity is low, Protestant organizations are especially active. They have already begun to play an important role in electoral campaigns.

There is a fourth religious trend of the last decade that Filatov also found to be especially significant. This is the strong emergence of regional identities, a phenomenon, he said, that he had not fully expected. He had begun to grasp its importance in the summer of 1997, and he had stressed then the need to appreciate this diversity. In 2001, having completed his study of religion, he was even more convinced of its significance. He pointed out that Russia historically has had a centralized church, whose organizational structure has been rigidly defined. In contrast to the United States or England, where "social leveling came freely and naturally," in Russia it usually "came about as a result of pressure from above." In the 1990s, as this pressure has declined, "I have seen in my study the strong reemergence, in the regions, of historical traditions, distinctive identities in the far east, the northwest, the south with its Cossack military aspirations, and the central region with its noticeable devotion to monarchical ideas." This regional differentiation has created a kind of pluralism that stands out as one of the last decade's most significant social trends.

In defining regional differences, Filatov has found the Russian far east to be more anticlerical and more Protestant than other regions of the country. Novgorod, Arkhangel'sk, and Petrozavodsk display significantly more religious toleration than may be found in such places as Kursk, Voronezh, and Tula. "Still ten years ago," he noted, "it would have been difficult to establish that these sharp regional differences could be so prominent."[10]

In the region near Novgorod, older traditions of civic freedom and the dignity of the individual have reasserted themselves since the collapse of the Soviet state. A certain independence of church life, a vision of parish autonomy, is clearly evident, suggesting that Moscow's autocratic style had not destroyed these self-governing tendencies and democratic aspirations, the respect for law and human rights.[11] Within the Orthodox Church itself, there is tension between the attempts to restore traditional faiths and the creative efforts to speak to present realities and to pressures brought on by non-Orthodox religious organizations. The struggle between all these disparate elements and tendencies are central parts of the present, vital signs of a turbulent and dynamic religious and social order in which much remains to be resolved.

In the mid-1990s, Filatov was optimistic about Russia's chances to develop a civil society. Returning now to the same subject, he acknowledges more pessimism about such a possibility; he admits his disappointment in what he sees as the extremely slow pace in which civil associations, forms of social self-governing organizations, and independent activities have developed. He views this failure as Russia's "greatest misfortune." He refers to Russia's educated citizenry and what he calls "its freedom-loving aspirations," but when confronted only with "power, business, and a sense of defenselessness, its aspirations have little room to develop." Thus in nearly every sphere, civil associations are formulated very slowly and have not yet had the opportunity to become more dominant.

What then are the prospects for civil society in Russia? More than any other institution in Russian society, Filatov insists, the church and other religious organizations contain the potential for developing such a society. "It is one of our greatest calamities," he said, "that the parish life of the Russian Orthodox Church has not had success in transforming our society." Their development has been extremely slow, their impact very gradual. "So much of their story, their success, their progress," he emphasized, "have depended on local circumstances, particularly on the capabilities of local priests and bishops."

In this regard, Filatov has been impressed with the work of Protestants and Roman Catholics in rebuilding parish life in Russia. "They have the potential," in his view, "to become examples for the Orthodox Church," modeling the possibilities of reaching out into the society. Competition with these organizations, Filatov is convinced, may help reenergize Orthodox parish life, and "that effect, on developing civil society, would be remarkable and significant."

From the perspective of the Moscow patriarchy, the story of church-state relations and the development of civil society since the collapse of communism in Russia began with liberal reforms, a new openness in 1990–91, an emphasis on "freedom of conscience," and an attempt to emulate the constitutional models of Western Europe and the United States. Beginning in 1994–95, Russia witnessed a reversal of many of the earlier reforms, a retrenchment that ultimately resulted in attempts to preserve Russia's heritage against cultural assaults from the outside, to establish the Orthodox Church and other "traditional faiths" in privileged positions of power, and to place unity and order at the center of rebuilding efforts.

From the perspectives of the parishes examined in this book, however, the story is different. The central issues concerned how to rediscover Orthodoxy's heritage and theology, how to rebuild parish life, and how to enable the church to speak directly and relate effectively to the parish community. Patriarch Aleksi II, Metropolitan Kirill, and other church voices encouraged these developments, believing that in the parish lay the key to the church's future; from it would come the energy and the direction to rebuild church life at the foundation. Such developments would also bring into focus the social doctrine of the Orthodox Church. It spoke to an old question in the church's history, of whether the church should turn inward, should emphasize its mystical and ascetic qualities, and should cut itself off from the world. Or, conversely, should it turn outward, emphasize its mission in the world, and recapture its social message, as expressed by Father Zosima in Dostoevsky's *Brothers Karamazov*, of whom "the monks used to say," he was "attached in his soul precisely to those who were the most sinful, and that he who was most sinful the elder loved most of all."[12]

In the three parishes examined in this book—at the Church of the Dormition of the Mother of God in Pechatniki, Novodevichy Monastery, and the Church of the Sacred Martyr Tat'iana at Moscow University—attempts were made to look outward, although these parishes did so in diverse forms and ways, reemphasizing different parts of Orthodoxy's tradition. In so doing, they established rich possibilities for dialogue, for rediscovering pluralistic voices within the church's heritage. When faced with these voices, the church unfortunately failed to take advantage of them and limited the discussion. But, it did respond to the pressures developing both within the parishes and the hierarchy to speak more directly to Russian society, and these pressures led to the writing of a new social conception with far-reaching implications. In 2001, Russia had approximately 350,000 registered public organizations; more than 70,000 of them were engaged in charity work, involving between 1 million and 2.5 million citizens who provided charitable assistance to 20 to 30 million people.[13]

In much of Western Europe and the United States, civil society has signified the growth of intermediary associations, standing between the government and society, that nourish independence and individual freedom. Such voluntary groups may spring up from the grass roots of society, and they organize to promote and to carry out many of the functions needed in the society. In his classic *Democracy in America*, Tocqueville viewed the decision-making in these small groups, the consensus-building they cultivated, as preparing the grounds for future leadership and for notions of citizenship in a democracy.

In Russia the conception of civil society has had a different emphasis. Civil society is seen as part of the state, developing alongside it and arising out of its encouragement, not as separate or independent of the state. The state sponsored and protected civil society, by creating a system of laws, by providing political stability and social order. Such notions are deeply rooted in Russia's past. They may be found in Catherine the Great's *Nakaz* (*Instruction*), written in 1766, to her Legislative Commission, where she discussed the importance of the rule of law: "Civil liberty is a Tranquillity of Mind arising from the Opinion that every individual of the whole Society enjoys his personal security. And that People may possess this Liberty, the Laws must be such as that no one Citizen need be in fear of another, but that all alike should fear the Laws only."[14]

Russian scholars have been wary of considering civil society as the social realm dominated by the uncontrolled actions of individuals. Following Hegel and also traditional Russian notions of public order, Russian scholars have viewed civil society as something that did not "exist before the state or outside of it."[15] The state protects civil society; it nourishes the health of its citizens; it establishes law and order. In the words of Oleg Rumiantsev, secretary of the parliamentary Russian Constitutional Commission in 1990–93, "Civil society is not absolutely *autonomous,* because it experiences certain influence from the state, doesn't exist before or outside of the latter, but coexists with its obvious reality which in a way embraces it."[16] In this understanding, civil society, moral responsibility, a feeling of solidarity with one's community, a sense of national pride, social justice, and a law-based state go hand in hand.

In his study of Orthodoxy and civil society, the Russian scholar Oleg Kharkhordin proposed the idea of a Russian civil society founded on Orthodox religious principles. Such a society would differ both from the Anglo-American tradition, based on the writings of John Locke and Adam Ferguson, and the "Mediterranean tradition," based on the Baron de Montesquieu and Antonio Gramsci. In the Atlantic tradition, dominated by Protestantism, the state plays a minimal role; in the Mediterranean tradition, shaped by Catholicism, the state has a strong influence; in the Russian Orthodox case, described by Kharkhordin, the state is absent; it has withered away and has been replaced by an ecclesiastical political order.[17]

In contrast to Kharkhordin and in response to the question about the church's role in the development of civil society, I reach two basic conclusions. First, I do not envision a specifically Orthodox conception of civil society or a uniquely Russian vision, but rather one that is nourished by Orthodox traditions, especially by its principles of freedom and self-determination. It was with these "most precious goods," St Gregory of Nyssa wrote, that God equipped human beings, encouraging them with the means to pursue "all kinds of excellence."[18] The individuals presented here exemplify such endeavors. In striving to achieve social justice, encourage compassion for others, envision an interdependent world, foster reciprocity and tolerance, cultivate truthfulness, and revere honor, these individuals attempted to develop the ethical principles on which civil society is based. The Orthodox concept of *sobornost'* (conciliarity) embraces all these principles, defining civil society, in the philosopher Semen Frank's words, as "a kind of molecular social bonded-ness," connecting the individual parts into a "flexible whole." Such a flexible whole stands apart from the state; it may not be reduced to the "free inter-action of individuals." Rather, to cite Frank again, it is an interdependent community, characterized not by its members' "*self-groundedness*," but by "their *interconnectedness*, their *social unity*."[19]

Second, the initiatives taken by the parishes and the local communities I examine suggest a movement away from the traditional Russian notion of the state and its central institutions as the primary actors in developing civil soci-ety. Such initiatives display great autonomy, individual creativity, and local re-sponsiveness. While the evidence about the progress of civil society over the last decade is mixed, the wellsprings for its development do exist and, with en-couragement, have the potential to shape Russia's future evolution. Such well-springs may be found in the individuals whose lives are portrayed in this book. They may be seen in the desires for a richer dialogue between government and its citizens, as displayed in Vladimir Putin's Civic Forum, held in the Kremlin on November 20–21, 2001.[20] They are located in the attempts to reconstruct parish life and to make it more responsive to the needs of local people. They are present in the reappearance of earlier historical traditions, particularly in the northwest, around Novgorod and its surrounding territories, in which self-government and parish autonomy have strong roots. Fr Aleksandr Ranne's reaction to Sergei Filatov's findings on the religious life of the north-west is instructive. One of the region's most respected and enlightened priests, Fr Aleksandr remarked that Filatov had portrayed the "first green shoots of growth," of religious and social tendencies, that had begun to take shape.[21] After twenty years, Fr Aleksandr said, should everything go well, these "green shoots may portray reality." This comment has relevance much beyond the northwest.

While it is too early to project with confidence the ultimate direction Russia will take, the individuals depicted here have struggled to reconstruct their society, have sought connections to a larger world, have given themselves to service, and in diverse ways, have tried to enrich the dialogue between Or-thodoxy and society. In the long run, these are elements that cultivate social trust, autonomy, and community vitality. Civil society cannot be developed quickly, even within a generation, but as recent scholars have reemphasized, requires many generations to accomplish. Much will depend on the capacity to keep open the dialogue over religion and society, both within and outside the church. The church, Aleksi II has said, "had been separated from the state but not from the society." How loosely the lines are ultimately drawn, both within the church and the state and between the church hierarchy and its own local parish communities will prove extremely important. The evidence of the parishes examined in this book suggests the beginnings of such an evolution, and fits into such trends found elsewhere in society.[22] With some encouragement, they may well lead to a civil society—one that does not resemble either the United States or Western Europe but will be distinctively Russian.[23]

The eventual outcome will greatly depend on Russia's economic condition and its capacity to sustain standards of living at higher levels than in the past decade. It will depend, as well, on how creatively and flexibly the local community is developed. The concept of *sobornost'* underscores the significance of the individual, but it also emphasizes the need for connections to something larger than the self, something beyond the formal, external services and observances of the church, something that is not bound up in structures. Czeslaw Milosz reminded us that "without religious and metaphysical underpinning, the word 'man' is too ambiguous a term," as both communism and Nazism clearly showed.[24] The individuals whose stories are told in this book are all people whose lives bear witness to Milosz's admonition, as they also demonstrate the distance between Russia's Communist past and its uncertain future. All of them, having been shaped by that past, have struggled against parts of it, have sought to reclaim other aspects, and have tried, in very different ways, to build something new. They and others like them will determine the answer to Gogol's question, "Whither Russia." Their various legacies, if honored, will serve to strengthen Russia's moral and religious foundation and aid in the development of social capital. In building civil society in Russia, the Russian Orthodox Church, in its broadest sense, will play a key role.

Notes

Unless otherwise noted, within each chapter, when a citation refers to an interview conducted by the author, subsequent quotations and general information from that source are also based on that interview.

INTRODUCTION

1. The epigraph for this chapter is from Nicholas Zernov, *The Russian Religious Renaissance of the Twentieth Century* (New York and Evanston: Harper and Row, 1963), 36–37.

2. Serge Schmemann, "An Awakened Church Finds Russia Searching for Its Soul," *New York Times*, 26 April 1992, sec. 4, 3.

3. James H. Billington, "The Case for Orthodoxy," *New Republic*, 30 May 1994, 25, and Billington, *Russia Transformed: Breakthrough to Hope* (New York: Free Press, 1992), 168–75.

4. George Fedotov, "The Christian Origins of Freedom," in *Ultimate Questions: An Anthology of Modern Russian Religious Thought,* ed. and with an introd. by Alexander Schmemann (New York and Chicago: Holt, Rinehart and Winston, 1965), 285. This definition and conception of civil society are elaborated in Christopher Marsh and Paul Froese, "The State of Freedom in Russia: A Regional Analysis of Freedom of Religion, Media, and Markets," *Religion, State, and Society* 32, no. 2 (June 2004): 138–39.

5. Robert D. Putnam, *Making Democracy Work: Civic Tradition in Modern Italy* (Princeton, N.J.: Princeton University Press, 1993), 182–83, and Putnam, *Bowling Alone: The Collapse and Revival of American Community* (New York and London: Simon and Schuster, Touchstone, 2000), 338–39. Recent literature on the study of civil society is much too large to be cited adequately here, but see especially the collection of essays in Don E. Eberly, ed., *The Essential Civil Society Reader* (Boulder, Colo.: Rowman and Littlefield, 2000); Adam B. Seligman, *The Idea of Civil Society* (Princeton, N. J.: Princeton University Press, 1995, c1992); Ernest Gellner, *Conditions of Liberty: Civil Society and its Rivals* (London and New York: Penguin, 1996); John Ehrenberg, *Civil Society: The Critical History of an Idea* (New York and London: New York University Press, 1999); Jude Howell and Jenny Pearce, *Civil Society and Development: A Critical Exploration* (Boulder and London: Lynne Rienner, 2001); Lawrence Chickering, *Beyond Left and Right: Breaking the Political Stalemate* (San Francisco: ICS Press, 1993); Stephen L. Carter, *Civility: Manners, Morals, and the Etiquette of Democracy* (New York: Basic Books, 1998); Michael Walzer, "The Idea of Civil Society," *Dissent* (Spring 1991): 293–304; Michael Walzer, ed., *Toward a Global Civil Society* (Providence, R.I.: Berghahn Books, 1995); Nicolai N. Petro, *The Rebirth of Russian Democracy: An Interpretation of Political Culture* (Cambridge, Mass.: Harvard University Press, 1995); and Christopher Marsh, ed., *Burden or Blessing? Russian Orthodoxy and the Construction of Civil Society and Democracy* (Boston: Institute on Culture, Religion, and World Affairs, 2004).

6. Charles Taylor, "Modes of Civil Society," *Public Culture* 3, no. 1 (Fall 1990): 95–118; Seligman, *Idea of Civil Society,* 10, 18–25.

7. Alexis de Tocqueville, *Democracy in America,* trans. George L. Lawrence, ed. J. P. Mayer (Garden City, N.Y.: Doubleday, Anchor Books, 1969), 294–95, 444–49.

8. Cited in Petro, *Rebirth of Russian Democracy,* 24. See also Václav Havel, "Letter to Dr. Gustáv Husák, General Secretary of the Czechoslovak Communist Party," and "The Power of the Powerless," in *Living in Truth: Twenty-two Essays Published on the Occasion of the Award of the Erasmus Prize to Václav Havel,* ed. Jan Vladislav (London and Boston: Faber and Faber, 1987), 29–30, 36, 59–63.

9. Civil society may not be visible until it comes to the surface in times of crisis, when it emerges to confront the actions of the state. Among its chief characteristics is the ability to mobilize quickly, to organize in support of a particular cause, whether in the form of a strike, a demonstration, a campaign, or a citizens' patrol to combat crime. In the late 1980s and 1990s, voluntary associations and networks engaging in civic activity flourished in Russia (Christopher Marsh and Nikolas K. Gvosdev, eds*., Civil Society and the Search for Justice in Russia* [Lanham, Md.: Lexington Books, 2002], 4–5).

10. Vacláv Havel, "Politics, Morality, and Civility," in *The Essential Civil Society Reader,* 394.

11. Ibid., 395. See also Adam Michnik, *The Church and the Left,* ed., trans., and with an introd. by David Ost (Chicago and London: University of Chicago Press, 1993), esp. 159–70, and Niels C. Nielsen Jr., *Revolutions in Eastern Europe: The Religious Roots* (Maryknoll, N.Y.: Orbis, 1991).

12. Boris Viktorovich Raushenbakh, "Religiia i nravstvennost'," *Znamia* no. 1 (January 1991): 211–16; Dmitrii Sergeevich Likhachev, "Kul'turnoe odichanie," *Izvestiia,* 29 May 1991, 3; Billington, *Russia Transformed,* 172; "Kul'tura, nravstvennost', religiia: materialy 'kruglogo stola'," *Voprosy filosofii* no. 11 (1989): 30–63.

13. Raushenbakh, "Religiia i nravstvennost'," 214–15; Likhachev, "Kul'turnoe odichanie," 3.

14. Billington, *Russia Transformed,* 173; Vladimir A. Zviglyanich, *The Morphology of Russian Mentality: A Philosophical Inquiry into Conservatism and Pragmatism* (Lewiston, N.Y.: Edwin Mellen Press, 1993), 65.

15. D. S. Likhachev, "Russkaia kul'tura: nasledie proshloe i real'naia sila segodnia," *Sem'ia* no. 24 (15 June 1988): 14–15.

16. Quoted in Sergei Pushkarev, "The Role of the Orthodox Church in Russian History," in Sergei Pushkarev, Vladimir Rusak, and Gleb Yakunin, *Christianity and Government in Russia and the Soviet Union: Reflections on the Millennium,* trans. Anne Mortensen (Boulder, San Francisco, and London: Westview Press, 1989), 4.

17. Sergei Pushkarev, *Self-Government and Freedom in Russia,* trans. Paul Bannes, with an introd. by Nicholas V. Riasanovsky (Boulder and London: Westview Press, 1988), 3.

18. In 1096, for example, as Prince Vladimir Monomakh and his allies prepared to go to war against Prince Sviatopolk of Kiev, the people of Kiev, fearing this conflict, asked Metropolitan Nikolai to intercede. According to the *Primary Chronicle,* the chronicle kept by the Kievan monks, Nikolai passionately appealed to Vladimir Monomakh and his allies, beseeching them to desist: "Prince, we pray that you and your brothers will not destroy the Russian lands. For if you begin fighting among yourselves, the pagans (the Polovtsians) will rejoice and conquer our land, which your fathers and grandfathers earned with much labor and valor." When he heard the words of Metropolitan Nikolai, Vladimir Monomakh "did not refuse his request, because he loved the metropolitan, his bishops, his abbots, and especially the monks" (quoted in Pushkarev, "Role of the Orthodox Church in Russian History," 5).

19. Pushkarev, "Role of the Orthodox Church in Russian History," 3.

20. Vasilii Osipovich Kliuchevskii, *O nravstvennosti i russkoi kul'ture* (Moscow: Institut rossiiskoi istorii RAN, 1998), 71, and Kliuchevskii, *Tri lektsii* (Paris: YMCA Press, 1969), 18–19, 38.

21. Kliuchevskii, *O nravstvennosti i russkoi kul'ture*, 70–71.

22. Pushkarev, "Role of the Orthodox Church in Russian History," 3–4.

23. Quoted in ibid., 7 n. 1.

24. Russia did not become autocephalous until the late sixteenth century, and the head of the church, the patriarch, lived in Constantinople, one of the constraints that limited the Kievan prince's political authority over the church.

25. John Meyendorff, *Byzantine Theology: Historical Trends and Doctrinal Themes,* 2nd ed. (New York: Fordham University Press, 1979), 214.

26. Ibid., 215.

27. Petro, *Rebirth of Russian Democracy,* 61–62.

28. Pushkarev, *Self-Government and Freedom in Russia,* 2.

29. Petro, *Rebirth of Russian Democracy,* 61.; Kliuchevskii, *Tri lektsii,* 13–14.

30. Pushkarev, "Role of the Orthodox Church in Russian History," 9–10.

31. Petro, *Rebirth of Russian Democracy,* 63–64.

32. Dmitrii Sergeevich Likhachev, *Natsional'noe samosoznanie drevnei Rusi: ocherki iz oblasti russkoi literatury, XI–XVII vv.* (Moscow: Izd-vo Akademii nauk, 1945), 68–76; and Likhachev, "Further Remarks on the Problem of Old Russian Culture," in *The Development of the USSR: An Exchange of Views,* ed. Donald W. Treadgold (Seattle: University of Washington Press, 1964), 167–72.

33. Adam Ferguson, quoting Simon de St Quintin, in *An Essay on the History of Civil Society,* ed. Fania Oz-Salzberger, Cambridge Texts in the History of Political Thought (Cambridge: Cambridge University Press, 1995), 100.

34. R. A. Kireeva, "Luchshii obrazets russkoi istoricheskoi literatury," introd. to Vasilii Osipovich Kliuchevskii, *O nravstvennosti i russkoi kul'ture* (Moscow: Institut rossiiskoi istorii RAN, 1998), 11.

35. Kliuchevskii presented a special public lecture concerning this topic in 1892, on the five hundredth anniversary of St Sergius's death, "Znachenie prep. Sergiia dlia russkogo naroda i gosudarstva," in *O nravstvennosti i russkoi kul'ture,* 92–108.

36. Kireeva, "Luchshii obrazets russkoi istoricheskoi literatury," 11.

37. Kliuchevskii, *O nravstvennosti i russkoi kul'ture,* 108.

38. Quoted in Pushkarev, "Role of the Orthodox Church in Russian History," 22.

39. Pushkarev, "Role of the Orthodox Church in Russian History," 22.

40. Ruslan Grigor'evich Skrynnikov, *Tsarstvo terrora* (St. Petersburg: "Nauka," St. Peterburgskoe otdelenie, 1992), 324–28, 334–41, and Skrynnikov, *Ivan the Terrible,* ed. and trans. Hugh H. Graham (Gulf Breeze, Fla.: Academic International Press, 1981), 112–16.

41. Pushkarev, "Role of the Orthodox Church in Russian History," 38 n. 2.

42. Ibid., 30.

43. Gregory L. Freeze, "Handmaiden of the State? The Church in Imperial Russia Reconsidered," *Journal of Ecclesiastical History* 36, no. 1 (January 1985): 86.

44. Alexander V. Muller, ed. and trans., *The Spiritual Regulation of Peter the Great* (Seattle and London: University of Washington Press, 1972), xi.

45. Ibid., 10–11.

46. Robin R. Milner-Gulland, *The Russians* (Oxford: Blackwell, 1997), 128.

47. Freeze, "Handmaiden of the State?" 86.

48. Muller, *Spiritual Regulation of Peter the Great,* 3.

49. See Evgenii Viktorovich Anisimov's valuable revisionist study, *The Reforms of Peter the*

Great: Progress through Coercion in Russia, trans. and with an introd. by John T. Alexander (Armonk, N.Y., and London: M. E. Sharpe, 1993).

50. Evgenii Viktorovich Anisimov, "Progress through Violence from Peter the Great to Lenin and Stalin," *Russian History/Histoire Russe* 17, no. 4 (Winter 1990): 413–14.

51. Anisimov, *Reforms of Peter the Great,* 208.

52. Ibid., 203–16.

53. The general descriptions and stereotypes about the Orthodox Church are well summarized by Nikolas K. Gvosdev, in *Emperors and Elections: Reconciling the Orthodox Tradition with Modern Politics* (Huntington, N.Y.: Troitsa Books, 2000), 15–38.

54. Richard Pipes, *Russia under the Old Regime* (New York: Charles Scribner's Sons, 1974), 243.

55. Petro, *Rebirth of Russian Democracy,* 66.

56. Dimitry V. Pospielovsky, *The Orthodox Church in the History of Russia* (Crestwood, N.Y.: St. Vladimir's Seminary Press, 1998), 178. The encouragement of seminary students to enter the secular universities also resulted in a decline of the educated seminarians who entered the priesthood.

57. Arthur E. Adams, "Pobedonostsev's Religious Politics," *Church History* 22, no. 4 (December 1953): 314.

58. Ibid., 323–24.

59. Konstantin P. Pobedonostsev, *Reflections of a Russian Statesman,* trans. Robert Crozier Long (Ann Arbor: University of Michigan Press, 1965), 2, 26, 30, 32–44.

60. James Cracraft, *The Petrine Revolution in Russian Culture* (Cambridge, Mass., and London: Belknap Press of Harvard University, 2004), 179–80; Gvosdev, *Emperors and Elections,* 37.

61. Robert L. Nichols, "Orthodoxy and Russia's Enlightenment," in *Russian Orthodoxy under the Old Regime,* ed. Robert L. Nichols and Theofanis George Stavrou (Minneapolis: University of Minnesota Press, 1978), 70.

62. Freeze, "Handmaiden of the State?" 82, and Freeze, "Subversive Piety: Religion and the Political Crisis in Late Imperial Russia," *Journal of Modern History* 68, no. 2 (June 1996): 310.

63. Donald W. Treadgold, "Russian Orthodoxy and Society," in *Russian Orthodoxy under the Old Regime,* 36.

64. Nichols, "Orthodoxy and Russia's Enlightenment," 79–84; Treadgold, "Russian Orthodoxy and Society," 37–39; Brenda Meehan, *Holy Women of Russia: The Lives of Five Orthodox Women Offer Spiritual Guidance for Today* (New York: HarperCollins, 1993), 17–40, 95–141; Zernov, *Russian Religious Renaissance,* 57–59, 288.

65. D. S. Likhachev, "Pamiat' preodolevaet vremia," *Nashe nasledie* no. 1 (1988): 1–4.

66. D. S. Likhachev, "Russkaia kul'tura: nasledie proshloe i real'naia sila segodnia," 14–15. Despite their scholarly nature, Likhachev's writings have had broad appeal; in 1992 the popular journal *Ogonek* referred to him and A. S. Sakharov as the two most respected public figures in present-day Russia (Dmitrii Gubin, "Simvol very," *Ogonek* no. 47 [18–23 November 1991]: 1–2).

67. Likhachev, *Natsional'noe samosoznanie drevnei Rus,* 55–57, and Likhachev "Russkaia kul'tura: nasledie proshloe i real'naia sila segodnia," 14–15. These ideals of self-sacrifice, independence, and creativity can be found repeatedly. Likhachev cites the case of the nun Ul'ianiia Osor'ina, who worked with such heart and diligence that she had little time to attend church, approached her work as a sacred task, and carried it out totally in the service of others. Her self-sacrificial labor and organizational skills enabled members of her community to survive famine.

68. D. S. Likhachev, "Russkaia kul'tura: nasledie proshloe i real'naia sila segodnia," 14–15.

69. See Gregory L. Freeze, *The Russian Levites: Parish Clergy in the Eighteenth Century* (Cambridge, Mass.: Harvard University Press, 1977), and Freeze, *The Parish Clergy in Nineteenth-Century Russia: Crisis, Reform, Counter-Reform* (Princeton, N.J.: Princeton University Press, 1983).

70. Pierre Pascal, *The Religion of the Russian People,* trans. Rowan Williams (Crestwood, N.Y.: St. Vladimir's Seminary Press, 1976), 119.

71. Likhachev, "Russkaia kul'tura: nasledie proshloe i real'naia sila segodnia," 15.

72. Several recent studies also provide much additional useful information. See, in particular, Pospielovsky, *The Orthodox Church in the History of Russia,* which offers a survey of Church history, focusing on church-state relations; and Valerie A. Kivelson and Robert H. Greene, eds., *Orthodox Russia: Belief and Practice under the Tsars* (University Park: Pennsylvania State University Press, 2003). The latter work explores many facets of the church's influence on daily life and practice; essays in the volume show emphatically the significant role of ritual and church observances in everyday activities.

CHAPTER 1

1. V. Itkin, "Kto podnial ruki na sviashchennika?" in Sergei Bychkov, *Khronika neraskrytogo ubiistva* (Moscow: Russkoe reklamnoe izd-vo, 1996), 3. In the English text of this book, I have anglicized references to Fr Aleksandr Men, but in the notes and bibliography references are written in the transliterated form Aleksandr Men.'

2. Men sharply criticized the government's relationship with the church: "The government has always aspired that the Church would not develop independent thoughts, nor take an independent position whatsoever on any kind of concrete real-life problem" ("Mozhno li reformirovat' pravoslavnuiu tserkov': Neizvestnoe interv'iu Aleksandra Menia," *Nezavisimaia gazeta,* 2 January 1992, 6; Men's interview was also published as "Problemy tserkvi iznutri," in *Kyl'tura i dukhovnoe voskhozhdenie,* ed. R. I. Al'bertkova and M. T. Rabotiaga [Moscow: "Iskusstvo," 1992], 440–45). To urban intellectuals especially, Men provided a link to early twentieth-century philosophers, such as Solov'ev and Berdiaev who, for them, "stood apart from this tragic tradition of subservience and obscurantism" (David Remnick, *Lenin's Tomb: The Last Days of the Soviet Empire* [New York: Random House, 1993], 363).

3. Boris Raushenbakh, interview with author, Moscow, 3 November 1994.

4. Aleksandr Malkin, quoted in Remnick, *Lenin's Tomb,* 364.

5. Aleksandr Borisov, "Nekotorye zamechaniia o sovremennom sostoianii Russkoi Pravoslavnoi Tserkvi," *Biulleten' Khristianskoi obshchestvennosti* no. 8 (May 1988), 110.

6. V. Levi, "Prikhodilo zhivoe schastie," *Stolitsa,* nos. 31–32, 1991, quoted in Elizabeth Roberts and Ann Shukman, eds., *Christianity for the Twenty-first Century: The Life and Work of Alexander Men* (London: SCM Press, 1996), 18–19.

7. William B. Husband, *"Godless Communists": Atheism and Society in Soviet Russia, 1917–1932* (DeKalb: Northern Illinois University Press, 2000), 71–72.

8. Kallistos [née Timothy] Ware, *The Orthodox Church* (New York: Penguin, 1963), 46; M. M. Persits, "Zakonodatel'stvo oktiabr'skoi revoliutsii o svobode sovesti," *Voprosy istorii religii i ateizma: sbornik statei,* vol. 5 (Moscow: Akademiia nauk SSSR, 1958): 54.

9. Husband, *"Godless Communists,"* 46–47.

10. See especially, Gregory L. Freeze, "Counter-reformation in Russian Orthodoxy: Popular Response to Religious Innovation, 1922–1925," *Slavic Review* 54, no. 2 (Summer 1995): 305–39; Edward E. Roslof, "The Heresy of 'Bolshevik' Christianity: Orthodox Rejection of Reli-

gious Reform during NEP," *Slavic Review* 55, no. 3 (Fall 1996): 614–35; Daniel Peris, "Commissars in Red Cassocks: Former Priests in the League of the Militant Godless," *Slavic Review* 54, no. 2 (Summer 1995): 340–64, and Peris, *Storming the Heavens: The Soviet League of the Militant Godless* (Ithaca, N.Y.: Cornell University Press, 1998).

11. Roslof, "The Heresy of 'Bolshevik' Christianity," 616–20, 624–25, and Roslof, *Red Priests: Renovationism, Russian Orthodoxy, and Revolution, 1905–1946* (Bloomington: Indiana University Press, 2002).

12. Both in its formulation and implementation, government policy on religion throughout the Soviet era was inconsistent and complex, especially in the years after 1943. "In the years of Soviet power not one book was written on Church and state relations using primary sources, if we exclude the works designed to promote agitation," lamented the Russian scholar M. V. Shkarovskii; see Nadezhda Iur'evna Cherepnina and Mikhail Vital'evich Shkarovskii, eds., *Sankt-Peterburgskaia eparkhiia v dvadtsatom veke v svete arkhivnykh materialov, 1917–1941: sbornik dokumentov* (St. Petersburg: "Liki Rossii," 2000), 4. See also especially Mikhail Vital'evich Shkarovskii, *Russkaia Pravoslavnaia Tserkov' i sovetskoe gosudarstvo v 1943–1964 godakh: ot "peremiriia" k novoi voine* (St. Petersburg: DEAN+ADIA-M, 1995), and *Obnovlencheskoe dvizhenie v Russkoi Pravoslavnoi Tserkvi XX veka* (St. Petersburg: "Nestor," 1999); Tat'iana Aleksandrovna Chumachenko, *Church and State in Soviet Russia: Russian Orthodoxy from World War II to the Khrushchev Years,* ed. and trans. Edward E. Roslof (Armonk, N.Y.: M. E. Sharpe, 2002); Mikhail Ivanovich Odintsev, *Gosudarstvo i tserkov' v Rossii: XX vek* (Moscow: Izd-vo "Luch," 1994), and *Russkie patriarkhi XX veka: sud'by Otechestva i Tserkvi na stranitsakh arhivnykh dokumentov* (Moscow: RAGS, 1999); Valerii Arkad'evich Alekseev, *Illiuzii i dogmy* (Moscow: Politizdat, 1991); Nathaniel Davis, *A Long Walk to Church: A Contemporary History of Russian Orthodoxy,* 2nd ed. (Boulder, Colo.: Westview Press, 2003).

13. Stephen F. Cohen, "The Friends and Foes of Change: Soviet Reformism and Conservatism," in *Rethinking the Soviet Experience: Politics and History since 1917* (Oxford and New York: Oxford University Press, 1985): 128–57.

14. Ibid., 130.

15. Wallace Daniel, "Religion and the Struggle for Russia's Future," *Religion, State, and Society* 24, no. 4 (December 1996): 375–77; Viktor Vladimirovich Aksiuchits, interview with author, Moscow, 29 May 1991; A. Salmin, "Natsional'nyi vopros i religiia v kontekste gosudarstvennogo stroitel'stva v postkommunisticheskom mire," in *Liberalizm v Rossii: sbornik statei,* ed. Iu. Krasheninnikov (Moscow: "Znak," 1993), 23–40; John B. Dunlop, "The Russian Orthodox Church and Nationalism after 1988," *Religion in Communist Lands* 18, no. 4 (Winter 1990): 292–305.

16. Aleksandr Men', "The Russian Orthodox Church Today," in Roberts and Shukman, *Christianity for the Twenty-first Century,* 167.

17. Aleksandr Men', "Vozvrashchenie k istokam," in *Kyl'tura i dukhovnoe voskhozhdenie,* 259–78, and Men', "Russia in Crisis," *Christianity for the Twenty-first Century,* 138–50.

18. Such parallels were first suggested to me by Dmitrii Shusharin, then religion journalist for *Segodnia,* interview with author, Moscow, 22 May 1992.

19. Gellner, *Conditions of Liberty,* 10, 41.

20. Billington, *Russia Transformed,* 173, and Billington, *Russia in Search of Itself* (Washington, D.C.: Woodrow Wilson Center Press, 2004), 106–107.

21. Fr Andrei Il'ia Osipov, interview with author, Sergiev Posad, 11 June 1994.

22. The large number of printed copies issued attest to the heavy demand for Men's publications; see, for example, Aleksandr Men', *Byt' khristianinom* (Moscow: "Protestant," 1994), 3 million copies; *Syn chelovecheskii* (Moscow: "Protestant," 1994), 200,000 copies; *Istoriia re-*

ligii: v poiskakh puti, istiny i zhizni (Moscow: Izd-vo Sovetsko-Britanskogo sovremestnogo predpriiatiia "Slovo," 1991), 100,000 copies; *Tainstvo, slovo i obraz: bogosluzhdenie Vostochnoi Tserkvi* (Leningrad: Ferro-Logos, 1991), 200,000 copies; and *Svet vo tme svetit: propovedi* (Moscow: AO "Vita-Tsentr," 1991), 100,000 copies.

23. Igor' Ivanovich Vinogradov, interview with author, Moscow, 14 June 1994; Sergei Borisovich Filatov, interview with author, Moscow, 29 June 1995.

24. Fr Andrei Il'ia Osipov, interview with author, Sergiev Posad, 11 June 1994; Metropolitan Kirill (Gundiaev) of Smolensk and Kaliningrad, "Called to One Hope—The Gospel in Diverse Cultures," Address to Conference on World Missions and Evangelism, World Council of Churches, Salvador, Bahia, Brazil, 24 November–3 December 1996 (mimeograph copy), Keston Institute; Sergei Borisovich Filatov, interview with author, Moscow, 8 June 1997; Fr Vsevolod Chaplin and Andrei Borisovich Zubov, roundtable discussion on "Orthodoxy, Civil Society, and Democracy," Danilov Monastery, Moscow, 9 July 2003; Metropolitan Kirill (Gundiaev), "Tserkov' v otnoshenii k obshchestvu v usloviiakh perestroiki," *Zhurnal Moskovskoi Patriarkii* no. 2 (February 1990): 36–37.; Andrei Lorgus, "'Kruglyi stol' po aktual'nym problemam tserkovnoi zhizni: vozrodit' zhizn' prikhoda," *Zhurnal Moskovskoi Patriarkhii* no. 6 (June 1990): 21–22; see also Edward E. Roslof, "The Myth of Resurrection: Orthodox Church in Postcommunist Russia," *Christian Century* 110, no. 9 (17 March 1993): 290–93.

25. Aleksandr Men', "The Russian Orthodox Church Today," 169.

26. *New York Times,* 26 April 1992, sec. 4, 3.

27. Sanford Kessler, "Tocqueville on Civil Religion and Liberal Democracy," *Journal of Politics* 39, no. 1 (February 1977): 120; Nikolas K. Gvosdev, "'Managed Pluralism' and Civil Religion in Post-Soviet Russia," in Marsh and Gvosdev, *Civil Society and the Search for Justice in Russia,* 81.

28. Nikolas K. Gvosdev, "The New Party Card? Orthodoxy and the Search for Post-Soviet Russian Identity," *Problems of Post-Communism* 47, no. 6 (November–December 2000): 29.

29. Sergei Borisovich Filatov, "Russkaia pravoslavnaia tserkov' i politicheskaia elita," in *Religiia i politika v postkommunisticheskoi Rossii,* ed. L. N. Mitrokhin (Moscow: Institut filosofii RAN, 1994): 99–100.

30. Sabrina Petra Ramet, "Religious Policy in the Era of Gorbachev," in *Religious Policy in the Soviet Union,* ed. Sabrina Petra Ramet (London: Cambridge University Press, 1993), 33.

31. Loren R. Graham, *Science, Philosophy, and Human Behavior in the Soviet Union* (New York: Columbia University Press, 1987), ix–x.

32. Filatov, "Russkaia pravoslavnaia tserkov," 100.

33. Ibid.

34. Yuri Bondarenko, "The Church Regains the Optina Monastery," *Religion in USSR* no. 2 (February 1988): 23.

35. Quoted in Michael Bourdeaux, *Gorbachev, Glasnost, and the Gospel* (London: Hodder and Stoughton, 1990), 44.

36. N. Davis, *Long Walk to Church,* 66–67; Aleksandr Nezhnii, "Zakon i sovest'," in *Ogonek-88: luchshie publikatsii goda,* ed. L. Gushkin, S. Kliakin, and V. Iumashev, 318–23. Moscow: Ogonek, 1989.

37. Valentin Nikitin and Fr Mark (Smirnov), "The New Saints Come Marching In," *Moscow News,* June 1988, 1–2.

38. Filatov, "Russkaia pravoslavnaia tserkov'," 101.

39. Ibid., 100.

40. Fr Vladimir, "Ne khlebom edinym," *Nash sovremennik* no. 6 (1990): 55–56.

41. Stanislav Korolev, "Pravoslavie i Velikaia Otechestvennaia Voina 1941–1945 godov," *Molodaia gvardiia* no. 5 (1990): 204–208; Eduard Volodin, "Vozvrashchenie k istokam," *Nash sovremennik* no. 4 (1991): 191–92; Mikhail Antonov, "Etika zhivogo khristianstva: problemy filosofii khoziaistva v trudakh S. N. Bulgakova," *Nash sovremennik* no. 12 (1990): 154–59.

42. See Wallace Daniel, "The Vanished Past: Russia's Search for an Identity," *Christian Century* 110, no. 9 (17 March 1993): 293–96.

43. Cohen, "The Friends and Foes of Change," 128–57.

44. Clyde Haberman, "Gorbachev Lauds Religion on Eve of Meeting Pope," *New York Times*, 1 December 1989, 1, 22A.

45. Vladimir Viktorovich Sogrin, "Novaia ideologiia dlia Rossii: drama iz sovremennoi istorii," *Obshchestvennye nauki i sovremennost'* (1993): 9–11.

46. Ibid., 7–11.

47. Elena Petrenko, "Kul'turnyi sdvug ili relig'nyi bum?" *Moskovskie novosti,* 11 August 1991, 9.

48. Dmitrii Efimovich Furman, "Veruiushchie, ateisty i prochie: novoe issledovanie rossiiskoi religioznosti," *Svobodnaia mysl'* no. 1 (January 1997): 83.

49. N. Davis, *Long Walk to Church,* 65, 77, 136.

50. Igumen Innokentii, "Deklaratsiia mitropolita Sergiia i sovremennaia tserkov'," *Nezavisimaia gazeta,* 29 July 1992, 5; an English translation may be found in *Russian Studies in History* 32, no. 2 (Fall 1993): 82–88.

51. Sergei Filatov and Aleksandr Shchipkov, "Ural: prel'shchenie monetarizmom," *Druzhba narodov* no. 12 (1996): 133.

52. Sergei Lezov, "Est' li u russkogo pravoslaviia budushchee? (ocherki sovremennogo pravoslavnogo liberalizma)," *Znamia* no. 3 (March 1994): 174–75. See also Lezov's comments on the influence of Aleksandr Solzhenitsyn and his *Gulag Archipelago* on the minds of a generation of young people in the 1970s and early 1980s: "In essence, this text was addressed primarily to the young, to those who did not experience Stalinism, but who all the same lived under the 'burden of communism.' The writer took by the hand the beloved komsomolets and led him into the circle of hell, constantly opening up for him the truth." Lezov emphasizes also the influence of Solzhenitsyn's "Letter to the All-Russian Parliament," in the collection *From under the Rubble,* in which the latter draws the connection between Orthodoxy and anticommunism ([Boston: Little, Brown, 1975], 174–75).

53. Viktor Popkov, "Tserkov' segodnia," *Russkaia mysl'* (24 November 1989): 9.

54. Boris Raushenbakh, interview with author, Moscow, 3 November 1994.

55. Popkov, "Tserkov' segodnia," *Russkaia mysl'* (15 December 1989): 11. Other issues: (22 December 1989): 9; (5 January 1990): 13; (19 January 1990): 9; (26 January 1990): 9.

56. Popkov, "Tserkov' segodnia," *Russkaia mysl'* no. 22 (December 1989): 9.

57. Metropoplitan Kirill (Gundiaev), "Tserkov' v otnoshenii k obshchestvu v usloviaikh perestroiki," 38.

58. N. Davis, *Long Walk to Church,* 84–85.

59. *Zhurnal Moskovskoi Patriarkhii* no. 10 (October 1990): 16; see also the statement of Archbishop Chrysostom, (Martyshkin) of Vilnius, quoted in N. Davis, *Long Walk to Church,* 284 n. 67.

60. Aleksandr Nezhnii, "The Fifteenth Patriarch," *Moscow News* no. 24 (1990), reprinted in *Religion in Communist Areas* 29 (Winter 1990): 37.

61. "The KGB, the Moscow Patriarch, and the State of the Russian Orthodox Church," *Glasnost No. 13* no. 5 (October 1988): 2–15.

62. Georgi Edelshtein, "The Election of a Patriarch—Crossroads or Dead-End?" *Religion in Communist Lands* 18, no. 3 (Autumn 1990): 270.

63. Ibid., 269.

64. Valentin Nikitin, "New Patriarch, New Problems," *Religion in Communist Lands* 18, no. 3 (Autumn 1990): 271–72.

65. Ibid., 272.

66. Quoted in Schmemann, "An Awakened Church," 3.

67. Quoted in Serge Schmemann, "Patriarch's Church Revives, but Will Spirituality?" *New York Times,* 9 November 1991, sec. 1, 2; see also N. Davis, *Long Walk to Church,* 94–95.

68. Mikhail Pozdniaev, "Ego partiia," *Stolitsa* no. 36 (1992): 1–7.

69. N. Davis, *Long Walk to Church,* 92–93. This number in the Soviet Union was approximately ten thousand.

70. G. Alimov and G. Charodeev, "Faith without Deeds Is Dead—An Interview with Patriarch Aleksi II," trans. Suzanne Oliver, *Religion in Communist Lands* 18, no. 3 (Autumn 1990): 266.

71. See especially Vasilii Osipovich Kliuchevskii, "Monastyri v russkoi istorii," in *Russkie monastyri: tsentral'naia chast' Rossii,* ed. Anatolii A. Feoktistov (Moscow: Izd-vo "Ocherovannyi strannik," 1995), 18–26; Tamara Vasil'evna Barsegian, "Tipologiia pravoslavnykh monastyrei Rossii," in *Monastyri v zhizni Rossii: materialy Nauchnoi Konferentsii posviashchennoi 600-letiiu prepodobnogo Pafnutiia Borovskogo i 550-letiiu osnovaniia im Rozhdestva Bogoroditsy Pafnut'ev-Borovskogo monastyria (19–20 aprelia 1994 goda),* comp. V. I. Osipov (Kaluga: Borovskii muzei, Filial Kaluzhskogo kraevedcheskogo muzeia: Russkoe geograficheskoe obshchestvo, Obninskii otdel, 1997), 6–10; and Leonid Ivanovich Denisov, *Pravoslavnye monastyri Rossiiskoi imperii: polnyi spisok vsiekh 1105 nynie sushchestvuiushchikh v 75 guberniiakh i oblastiakh Rossii (i 2 inostrannykh gosudarstvakh) muzhskikh i zhenskikh monastyrei arkhiereiskikh domov i zhenskikh obshchin* (Moscow: Izdanie A. D. Stupina, 1908).

72. Billington, "The Case for Orthodoxy," 27.

73. Aleksi II, "Education and the Christian View of Man," *Russian Social Science Review* 35, no. 6 (November–December 1994): 45.

74. Ibid.

75. "Text of the Law of the USSR on Freedom of Conscience and Religious Organizations," printed in *Pravda,* 9 October 1990, articles 121, 139, English language text and commentary by Giovanni Codevilla, in *Religion in Communist Lands* 19, nos. 1–2 (Summer 1991): 119–45.

76. Ibid., 121.

77. Ibid., 125. The law did not, however, specify what would happen to the property of a local church should that organization cease to exist; its property would not automatically revert to the ownership of the Orthodox Church. The Orthodox Church had also wanted full ownership of church buildings that had been repaired at the expense of their congregations. The law was ambiguous on both of these circumstances (N. Davis, *Long Walk to Church,* 89).

78. Filatov, "Russkaia pravoslavnaia tserkov'," 103.

79. Information in the two preceding paragraphs relies heavily on Filatov, "Russkaia pravoslavnaia tserkov'," 103–104.

CHAPTER 2

1. A. Karpov, "Personality and the Church: The Problem of Personality in the Light of Christian Teaching," in *The Church of God: An Anglo-Russian Symposium,* ed. E. L. Mascall, with a preface by the Right Rev. W. H. Frere (London: Society for Promoting Christian Knowledge, 1934), 135.

2. James H. Billington, "Russia's Fever Break," *Wilson Quarterly* 15, no. 4 (Autumn 1991): 60.

3. Aleksi II, "Zaiavleniia Patriarkha Moskovskogo i Vseia Rusi," *Izvestiia*, 20 August 1991, 3.

4. Billington, *Russia Transformed*, 127–28; and Billington, "The True Heroes of the Soviet Union," *New York Times*, 30 August 1991, A23.

5. Sogrin, "Novaia ideologiia dlia Rossii," 16.

6. "Yeltsin Attends Sunday Church Services," *Summary of World Broadcasts*, 1408 B/1, 16 June 1992.

7. Jane Ellis, *The Russian Orthodox Church: Triumphalism and Defensiveness* (New York: St. Martin's Press, 1996), 146.

8. Igor' Ivanovich Vinogradov, interview with author, Moscow, 14 June 1994; Sergei Borisovich Filatov, interview with author, Moscow, 29 June 1995; Fr Vsevolod Chaplin, secretary for relations between church and society of the Department of External Church Relations of the Moscow Patriarchate, discussion at international conference "Orthodoxy, Civil Society, and Democracy in Russia," Woodrow Wilson International Center for Scholars, Washington, D.C., 24–26 March 2004.

9. Evgeniia Viktorovna Ivanova, interview with author, Moscow, 3 July 1995.

10. Ibid. See also S. B. Filatov's excellent short article "The Prospects for Catholicism in Russia," *Religion, State, and Society* 22, no. 1 (1994): 69–72, and especially his conclusion: "Catholicism is present in Russia with organizational forms and intellectual ballast which could provide examples for Orthodoxy to work through creatively. The very existence could soften the blow of a new anticlerical wave. In many cities where there are no Catholic parishes, surveys reveal that 1–2 per cent of the people consider themselves Catholics. These are spontaneous, self-styled Catholics, who have no connections with a church."

11. Filatov, "Russkaia pravoslavnaia tserkov'," 106. Such issues relating to the transfer of church property are elaborated by Filatov.

12. Ibid., 107.

13. Ibid., 107–108.

14. Ibid., 108.

15. Ibid., 108–109.

16. Aleksandr Men', "Mozhno li reformirovat' pravoslavnuiu tserkov'? Neizvestnoe inter-v'iu Aleksandra Menia," *Nezavisimaia gazeta*, 2 January 1992, 6.

17. Filatov, "Russkaia pravoslavnaia tserkov'," 110.

18. Pavel Semenovich Gurevich, "Vse religii ravny, no est' bolee ravnye?" *Literaturnaia gazeta*, 22 September 1993, 10; Filatov, "Russkaia pravoslavnaia tserkov'," 111.

19. Elena Kopylova, "Kamen'—v sobstvennuiu svobodu," *Moskovskie novosti*, 19 September 1993, 9; Filatov, "Russkaia pravoslavnaia tserkov'," 111.

20. Giovanni Codevilla, "Commentary on the New Soviet Law on Freedom of Conscience and Religious Organizations," *Religion in Communist Lands* 19, nos. 1–2 (Summer 1991): 142. In June 1994, Fr Andrei Il'ia Osipov, director of graduate education at the Spiritual Academy of the Moscow Patriarchy, said, "We have not had time to train our priests properly. Monasteries are reopened, but we lack sufficient numbers of well-trained priests to serve in them. We are making priests of people who are poorly prepared and this shortcoming seriously affects the internal life of the Orthodox Church" (interview with author, Sergiev Posad, 11 June 1994).

The kind of education that Fr Andrei envisioned included in-depth study of the Scriptures, the history and texts of the church, the lives of saints, and Orthodox theology—in other words, a thorough and traditional education. Such preparation could not be done overnight, and yet the demand for priests to fill the new positions, Fr Andrei emphasized, is nearly overwhelming (see Daniel, "Religion and the Struggle for Russia's Future," 375).

21. Filatov, "Russkaia pravoslavnaia tserkov'," 109.

22. The reasons, other than military, are developed by D. E. Furman, "Religiia, ateizm i perestroika," in *Na puti k svobode sovesti. Perestroika: Glasnost', Demokratiia, Sotsializm,* ed. D. E. Furman and Fr Mark (Smirnov) (Moscow: Progress, 1989), 11–12, and Lev Nikolaevich Mitrokhin, *Filosofiia religii (opyt istolkovaniia Marksova naslediia)* (Moscow: "Respublika," 1993), 375–77.

23. Furman, "Religiia, ateizm i perestroika," 11–12.

24. As Furman points out, this situation was distinct from early periods of Russian history, when the church served an absolutist government that identified with Orthodoxy.

25. Furman, "Religiia, ateizm i perestroika," 11–12.

26. Filatov, "Russkaia pravoslavnaia tserkov'," 117.

27. Gleb Iakunin, "V sluzhenii kul'tu (Moskovskaia Patriarkhiia i kul't lichnosti Stalina)," in Iakunin, *Na puti k svobode sovest. Perestroika: Glasnost', Demokratiia, Sotsializm,* 172–207, and "The Moscow Patriarchate and Stalin's Cult of Personality," *Glasnost No. 13,* nos. 21–23 (March–May 1989): 8–15.

28. Filatov, "Russkaia pravoslavnaia tserkov'," 115.

29. See the description and analysis of the autumn crisis in Jonathan Steele, *Eternal Russia: Yeltsin, Gorbachev, and the Mirage of Democracy* (Cambridge, Mass.: Harvard University Press, 1994), 371–87; David Remnick, *Resurrection: The Struggle for a New Russia* (New York: Random House, 1997), 37–83.

30. Aleksandr Kyrlezhev and Konstantin Troitskii, "Rannekhristianskaia tserkov' i transformatsiia khristianskogo soznaniia," pt. 2 of "Sovremennoe rossiiskoe Pravoslavie," *Kontinent* no. 76 (April–June 1993): 281–303.

31. Aleksi II, "Appeal of the Patriarch of Moscow and All Russia," San Francisco, 22 September 1993, in *Information Bulletin,* Department for External Church Relations, Moscow Patriarchate, no. 19 (18 October 1993): 8.

32. Ibid., 1, 8, and "Participation of the Russian Orthodox Church in the Mediation Mission to Overcome the Political Crisis in Russia," Moscow, 29 September 1993, in *Information Bulletin,* Department for External Church Relations, Moscow Patriarchate, no. 19 (18 October 1993): 1.

33. "Participation of the Russian Orthodox Church in the Mediation Mission," 1.

34. Ibid.

35. Aleksi II, "Appeal of the Patriarch Aleksi II of Moscow and All Russia to the Holy Synod of the Russian Orthodox Church and Hierarchs Who Came to the Trinity–St Sergius Lavra for the Commemoration Day of St Sergius of Radonezh," Trinity–St Sergius Lavra, 8 October 1993, in *Information Bulletin,* Department for External Church Relations, Moscow Patriarchate, no. 19 (18 October 1993): 12.

36. Ibid.

37. Iuvenali, Metropolitan of Krutitsy and Kolomna, "Address to His Holiness Aleksi II of Moscow and All Russia Before the Prayer Service at the Vladimir Icon of the Mother of God," Cathedral of the Epiphany, Moscow, 3 October 1993, in *Information Bulletin,* Department for External Church Relations, Moscow Patriarchate, no. 19 (18 October 1993): 20.

38. See Ellis, *Russian Orthodox Church,* 154.

39. Aleksandr Kyrlezhev and Konstantin Troitskii, "Tserkov' v oktiabre 1993 goda," *Nezavisimaia gazeta,* 2 November 1993, 2; Filatov, "Russkaia pravoslavnaia tserkov'," 116–17.

40. Fr Vsevolod Chaplin, quoted in Gvosdev, "The New Party Card?" 32.

41. Cited in Vera Tolz, "The Moscow Crisis and the Future of Democracy in Russia," *RFE/RL Research Report* 2, no. 42 (22 October 1993): 9. In evaluating the church's role in the crisis, one might ask whether the church contributed to the idea of compromise. In its attempt to

play the role of arbiter, the church faced an extremely complex and difficult situation. The efforts at mediation began after the positions of both sides had hardened: by October 1 the government had issued an ultimatum to the deputies, and the parliamentary forces had barricaded themselves in the White House. On both sides, groups sent to negotiate with Patriarch Aleksi II, Metropolitan Kirill, and Metropolitan Iuvenali comprised several hard-line figures, who were not given to political accommodation. Metropolitan Kirill described the negotiations that took place as "difficult." Nevertheless, by 2 October some agreements had been reached: on reducing the scale of force on both sides, on television coverage, and on the power supply to the White House. In the stenographic reports of the mediation, church representatives repeatedly spoke of the need for compromise and the need to see other points of view. The record shows that the church tried to move both opponents away from resolving their differences by the use of violence. Thus it would seem that the church made a positive contribution through political compromise and in that sense supported the democratic process (see Wendy Slater, "The Church's Attempts to Mediate in the Russian Crisis," *RFE/RL Research Report* 2, no. 42 (29 October 1993): 8–9; A. Iakovlev, M. Khromchenko, and V. Povoliaev, eds., *Tishaishie peregovory: 1–3 oktiabria 1993 g.: zapis' fonogrammy peregovorov v Sviato-Danilovom monastyre* (Moscow: "Magisterium," 1993), 88–90, 214, 218, 338).

42. Iurii Buida, "Tserkov', slava bogu, vne politiki," *Nezavisimaia gazeta,* 9 October 1993, 1, cited in Slater, "The Church's Attempts to Mediate," 10.

43. Aleksi II, "Appeal of Patriarch Aleksi II of Moscow and All Russia to the Holy Synod," 12.

44. Kimmo Kääriänen and D. E. Furman, "Veruiushchie, ateisty i prochie [evoliutsiia rossiiskoi religioznosti]," *Voprosy filosofii* no. 6 (1997): 41–42. Many Russians described themselves as neither believers nor atheists but as "seekers" or as "nonbelievers." They had an "undefinable worldview," which may not have signified a lack of religious belief but rather an unwillingness to embrace institutional religion or the "official religion" of the Russian Orthodox Church (D. E. Furman, interview with author, Moscow, 6 June 1994, and Kimmo Kääriänen, *Religion in Russia after the Collapse of Communism: Religious Renaissance or Secular State?* [Lewiston, N.Y.: Edwin Mellen Press, 1998], 96). Furman is the author of a brilliant study on Stalinism and religion and an editor, with Filatov, of *Religiia i demokratiia,* a collection of penetrating, provocative, and valuable articles about religion in Russia in the early 1990s (D. E. Furman, "Stalinizm i my s religiovedcheskoi tochki zreniia," in *Osmyslit' kul't Stalina,* ed. Kh. Kovo [Moscow: Progress, 1989], 402–26; Sergei Borisovich Filatov and Dmitrii Efimovich Furman, eds., *Religiia i demokratiia: na puti k svobode sovesti* [Moscow: Progress-Kul'tura, 1993]).

45. These characteristics continue to describe Russian youth early in the twenty-first century. See Miran Petrovich Mchedlov, "Vliiani religioznogo faktora na mirovozzrencheskie ustanovki rossiiskoi molodiozhi," in *Obnovlenie Rossii: trudnyi poisk reshenii: godichnye nauchnye chteniia "Rossiia segodnia,"* ed. M. K. Gorshkov and M. P. Mchedlov (Moscow: RNISiNP, 2001), 106–17.

46. Liudmila Mikhailovna Vorontsova and Sergei Borisovich Filatov, "Russkii put' i grazhdanskoe obshchestvo," *Svobodnaia mysl'* no. 1 (1995): 62–63. Like his mentor, Filatov focused his earlier research on the sociology of religion in America; he is the author of a well-regarded monograph titled *Catholicism in the United States* (*Katolitsizm v SShA: 60–80e gody* (Moscow: Nauka, 1993). But now his work deals entirely with the study of religion and society in his own country; he and Furman have brought to their subject the passion, research skills, and hard-minded pragmatism that it has lacked for most of the twentieth century.

47. Vorontsova and Filatov, "Russkii put' i grazhdanskoe obshchestvo," 66–67.

48. Iurii Leonidovich Vasilevskii, "Veriat, ishchut, ostaiutsia ateistami," *Nezavisimaia gazeta—religii,* 26 April 1997, 2.

49. Boris Vladimirovich Dubin, "Religiia, tserkov', obshchestvennoe mnenie," *Svobod-*

naia mysl' no. 11 (1997): 94–103, and available in an English translation by Michael Vale, "Religion, the Church, and Public Opinion," *Russian Social Science Review* 39, no. 6 (November–December 1998): 51–66.

50. Igor' Volgin, "'V tocke samoubiistva . . . ,'" *Nedelia,* 4 January 1995, 2.

51. Metropolitan Kirill of Smolensk and Kaliningrad, "Called to One Hope—The Gospel in Diverse Cultures," presented at World Council of Churches Conference on World Missions and Evangelism, November 1996, Salvador, Bahia, and Brazil, reprinted in John Witte Jr. and Michael Bourdeaux, eds., *Proselytism and Orthodoxy in Russia: The New War for Souls* (Maryknoll, N.Y.: Orbis, 1999), 73.

52. John Witte Jr., introd. to *Proselytism and Orthodoxy,* 1.

53. Mark Elliott and Anita Deyneka, "Protestant Missionaries in the Former Soviet Union," in Witte and Bourdeaux, *Proselytism and Orthodoxy,* 200, 220–21.

54. Witte, introd. to *Proselytism and Orthodoxy,* 1, 7.

55. "Yeltsin Comments on Cooperation with Orthodox Church," *Interfax,* 6 August 1997, reprinted in *FBIS Report,* Eurasia, FBIS-Sov-97–218, 8 August 1997.

56. Boris Yeltsin, 4 August 1993, quoted in W. Cole Durham Jr., Lauren B. Homer, Pieter van Dijk, and John Witte Jr., "The Future of Religious Liberty in Russia: Report of the De Burght Conference on Pending Russian Legislation Restricting Religious Liberty," *Emory International Review* 8, no. 1 (Spring 1994): 10.

57. Anatolii Vasil'evich Pchelintsev, interview with author, Moscow, 3 June 1997; Ekaterina Aleksandrovna Smyslova, interview with author, Moscow, 8 July 1997. Pchelintsev is director of the Institute of Religion and Law in Moscow and a member of the working group that reviewed the draft legislation, and Smyslova, in 1997, served as editor of the institute's journal, *Religiia i zakon.*

58. Marsh and Froese, "The State of Freedom in Russia," 139–40. Interpreting the 1997 law as part of the collaboration between the state and the Moscow Patriarchate, Zoe Knox offers an extremely useful analysis of the law's passage and aims in "The Symphonic Ideal: The Moscow Patriarchate's Post-Soviet Leadership," *Europe-Asia Studies* 55, no. 4 (2003): 575–96.

59. Witte, introd. to *Proselytism and Orthodoxy,* 26.

60. Ibid., 12. The 1997 law has been extensively discussed and analyzed in many publications; see W. Cole Durham Jr. and Lauren B. Homer, "Russia's 1997 Law on Freedom of Conscience and Religious Associations: An Analytical Appraisal," *Emory International Law Review* 12, no. 1 (Winter 1998): 101–246; Witte, introd. to *Proselytism and Orthodoxy,* 1–27, and the essays by T. Jeremy Gunn, "The Law of the Russian Federation on the Freedom of Conscience and Religious Association from a Human Rights Perspective," 239–64; Harold J. Berman, "Freedom of Religion in Russia: An Amicus for the Defendant," 265–83; Lauren B. Homer and Lawrence A. Uzzell, "Federal and Provincial Religious Freedom in Russia: A Struggle for and against Federalism and the Rule of Law," 284–320, all in Witte and Bourdeaux, *Proselytism and Orthodoxy in Russia.* See also Lee Trepanier, "Nationalism and Religion in Russian Civil Society: An Inquiry into the 1997 Law 'On Freedom of Conscience,'" in Marsh and Gvosdev, *Civil Society and the Search for Justice in Russia,* 57–73; Derek H. Davis, "Editorial: Russia's New Law on Religion: Progress or Regress?" *Journal of Church and State* 39, no. 4 (Autumn 1997): 645–55.

61. In his press release, the president cited his own difficulty in reaching a decision and he stressed the "need to protect the moral and spiritual health of Russians." Yet he also emphasized that the provisions of the new law "encroached upon the rights and freedoms of the individual and the citizen, established inequality between confessions, and contradicted Russia's international obligations" ("Obrashchenie k grazhdanam Rossii Prezidenta Rossiiskoi Federatsii B. N. El'tsina v sviazi s otkloneniem federal'nogo zakona 'O svobode sovesti i o religioznykh ob'edineniiakh,'" mimeographed copy, Moscow, 22 July 1997).

62. The dangers of these restrictions are explored in Anatolii Pchelintsev, "Religiia i prava cheloveka," in *Religiia i prava cheloveka,* vol. 3 of *Na puti k svobode sovesti,* ed. L. M. Vorontsova, A. V. Pchelintsev, and S. B. Filatov (Moscow: "Nauka," 1996), 7–11.

63. These themes are explored in Pchelintsev, *Religiia i prava cheloveka;* Anatolii Vasil'evich Pchelintsev, interview with author, Moscow, 3 June 1997.

64. The election is discussed by Christopher Marsh in *Russia at the Polls: Voters, Elections, and Democratization* (Washington, D.C.: CQ Press, 2002).

65. Vladimir Putin, quoted in Michael Wines, "Putin Describes an Ill Russia and Prescribes Strong Democracy," *New York Times,* 9 July 2000, 3A.

66. This subject is explored by Christopher Marsh in "The Challenge of Civil Society," in *Russia's Policy Challenges: Security, Stability, and Development,* ed. Stephen K. Wegren (Armonk, N.Y.: M. E. Sharpe, 2000), 141–58, and Gleb Pavlovsky, "The Prospects of a Civil Society in Russia," *Izvestiia,* 3 July 2002, WPS Monitoring Agency, archived at www.wps.ru/e_index .html; accessed on 21 June 2003.

67. "Russian Patriarch Wants Union with Belarus, Slams Pope," *Interfax,* 4 December 1999, reprinted in *FBIS Report,* Central Eurasia, FBIS-SOV-1999–1205, 6 December 1999.

68. Cited in Gvosdev, "The New Party Card?" 32.

69. "Aleksi II: Putin's Vertical of Power to Promote Stronger Statehood," ITAR-TASS, 9 June 2000, reprinted in WNC-SOV, 9 June 2000.

70. "Putin Praises Orthodox Church," Reuters, 9 June 2000, reprinted in WNC: SOV (9 June 2000).

71. Quoted in Gvosdev, "The New Party Card?" 32.

72. "Putin Hopes Orthodox Christianity Will Strengthen Russia," *Interfax,* 6 January 2000, archived at http:www.stetson.edu/~psteeves/relnews/0001a.html; accessed 14 August 2003; also quoted in Gvosdev, "The New Party Card?" 33.

73. According to a survey conducted by the Public Opinion Foundation in 1997, the Orthodox Church enjoyed the highest rating of public trust of any institution in the society. In the survey, more that 54 percent of Russians expressed trust in the church, compared to 42 percent in the army, 35 percent in city mayors and local officials, 32 percent in the media, and 19 percent in law enforcement agencies. Similar levels of trust in the church could be found across all social groups, while trust in the army came mainly from elderly people; confidence in the media depended on educational background; respondents with the most education had the most critical views ("Russia: Russian Poll Measures Trust in Institutions," *Interfax,* 26 June 1997, reprinted in *FBIS Report,* Central Eurasia; Russia, FBIS-SOV-97–177, 27 June 1997).

74. Dmitrii Efimovich Furman, in *Rodina,* cited by Andrei Zolotov, "Ten Years after Coup, Putin Seeks Inspiration from Russia's Christian Roots," *Christianity Today,* 27 August 2001, archived at http://www.christianity today.com/ct/2001/135/23.0.html; accessed 13 August 2003.

CHAPTER 3

1. Aleksei Stepanovich Khomiakov, "On Humboldt," in *Russian Intellectual History: An Anthology,* ed. Marc Raeff, with an introd. by Isaiah Berlin (New York: Harcourt, Brace and World, 1966), 212; emphasis in original.

2. Ibid., 208.

3. See Alexander Zinoviev, *Homo Sovieticus,* trans. Charles Janson (Boston and New York: Atlantic Monthly Press, 1982), 84–85, Zinoviev, *Kommunizm kak real'nost': krizis kommunizma*

(Moscow: Tsentrpoligraf, 1994), 188–89, and Zinoviev, *My i zapad: stat'i, interv'iu, vystupleniia, 1979–1980* (Lausanne: L'Age d'Homme, 1981), 52–53; Vorontsova and Filatov, "Russkii put' i grazhdanskoe obshchestvo," 67.

4. Vladimir Poresh, "Secret Police Harass Poresh," *Religion in Communist Lands* 8, no. 2 (Summer 1980): 103; this appeared originally in Russian in *Obshchina* no. 2 (1978): 149–58. Philip Walters, "The Ideas of the Christian Seminar," *Religion in Communist Lands* 9, nos. 3–4 (Autumn 1981): 111; Aleksandr Ioilovich Ogorodnikov, "Ot sostovitelei," *Obshchina* no. 2 (1978): 1; Jane Ellis, "USSR: The Christian Seminar," *Religion in Communist Lands* 8, no. 2 (Summer 1980): 92–112.

5. Andrei Lorgus, "Prikhodskaia zhizn': tol'ko v ograde khrama," *Zhurnal Moskovskoi Patriarkii* no. 6 (June 1990): 20. Fr Vladimir was leader of the Moscow church at Nikolo-Kuznetskii.

6. Ibid., 20; Lorgus, "'Kruglyi stol' po aktual'nym problemam tserkovnoi zhizni," 21–22.

7. Lorgus, "Prikhodskaia zhizn'," 20.

8. V. Zelinskii, quoted in Geoffrey Hosking, *The Awakening of the Soviet Union* (Cambridge, Mass.: Harvard University Press, 1990), 115.

9. Hosking, *Awakening of the Soviet Union*, 115.

10. Kirill (Gundiaev), "Tserkov' v otnoshenii k obshchestvu v usloviiakh perestroiki," 36–37.

11. Ibid., 37.

12. Serge Schmemann, *Echoes of a Native Land: Two Centuries of a Russian Village* (New York: Alfred A. Knopf, 1997), 257. Schmemann is quoting from a letter of a relative, Georgii Osorgin, who was writing in March or April 1928, from Sergeevskoe.

13. Fr Vladimir Paissy, interview with author, Oxford, England, 6 July 2000.

14. Evgeniia Viktorovna Ivanova, interview with author, Moscow, 8 June 1994. Ivanova is a scientific worker in the World Literature Institute of the Russian Academy of Sciences, secretary of the commission on Fr Pavel Florinskii, and author of many studies of Russian religious philosophy at the end of the nineteenth and early twentieth centuries.

15. This topic is examined in more detail later in this chapter.

16. Aleksandr Kyrlezhev, "Ponimaet li bog po-russki? Spor o iazyke bogosluzheniia," *Nezavisimaia gazeta*, 21 April 1994, 5.

17. Fr Andrei Il'ia Osipov, interview with author, Sergiev Posad, 11 June 1994.

18. See Paul Miliukov, *Outlines of Russian Culture*, vol. 1, *Religion and the Church*, ed. Michael Karpovich, trans. Valentine Ughet and Eleanor Davis (New York: A. S. Barnes, 1960), 27–76.

19. James H. Billington, *The Icon and the Axe: An Interpretive History of Russian Culture* (New York: Random House, 1966), 121–23.

20. Fr Georgii Kochetkov, interview with author, Moscow, 1 July 1995.

21. Ibid.

22. Evgeniia Viktorovna Ivanova, interview with author, Moscow, 15 June 1997.

23. Fr Georgii Kochetkov, interview with author, Moscow, 1 July 1995.

24. Kyrlezhev, "Ponimaet li bog po-russki? Spor o iazyke bogosluzheniia," 5.

25. *Pravoslavnaia obshchina*, published bimonthly, ranged in length from 75 to 140 pages per issue. Among the journal's stated goals was the purpose of "reawakening after the century-long slumber and of establishing the base for those lay people in authentically Orthodox communities, despite the fact that at the present these communities had not yet reached maturity." The main sections of *Pravoslavnaia obshchina* varied, but usually they included such divisions as sermons, church life, the liturgy and sacraments, culture and art, excerpts from diaries, letters, and memoirs of Orthodox spiritual leaders, mostly in the twentieth century. In several

issues a special section was devoted to "community and conciliarity" (*Obshchina i sobornost'*), specifically discussing this topic in the writings of contemporary Russian authors. An additional section appearing in most of the issues was titled "Theology and Philosophy"; that section often contained an examination of Russia's great philosophical-religious school of thought at the beginning of the twentieth century. *Pravoslavnaia obshchina* offered a means of relating religion to the rebuilding of community in Fr Georgii's parish.

26. The *sobor* of the Russian Orthodox Church, meeting 6–9 June 1988, issued the charter. It formally recognized the parish as the fundamental self-governing unit of the church. The parish could protest the appointment of priests by the bishop, but did not require bishops to adhere to this decision. The charter made several important structural changes in church administration: it called for the election of a diocesan council for each bishop; it limited the authority of the patriarch; it gave church *sobors* judicial power over the patriarch. The charter, however, as Dimitry Pospielovsky points out, retained the synod's authoritarian structure, making it extremely difficult to convene a *sobor* without the synod's consent. See Dimitry V. Pospielovsky, *The Orthodox Church in the History of Russia*, 356–57.

27. Georgii Kochetkov, "Prikhodskie obshchiny v pravoslavnoi tserkvi i problemy sovremennogo obshchestva v SSSR," *Pravoslavnaia obshchina* no. 1 (1991): 22.

28. The failure to do so, Kochetkov claimed, and the tendency to look only inward would have dire consequences; it would open the church offices to many "people on the make," to charlatans, and would also lead to the revival of an old ideology.

29. Kochetkov, "Prikhodskie obshchiny v pravoslavnoi tserkvi," 25.

30. Details of the Kochetkov incident are discussed in an interview with Fr Georgii Kochetkov, Aleksandr Kopirovskii, and Aleksandr Kyrlezhev, conducted by Igor' Ivanovich Vinogradov and Sergei Iurov, in July 1994; see Igor' Vinogradov and Sergei Iurov, "Vstrecha v redaktsii 'Kontinenta,'" *Kontinent* no. 3 (1994): 207–19; further details were provided to me by Igor' Ivanovich Vinogradov, chief editor of *Kontinent,* interview with author, Moscow, 14 June 1994. See also Philip Walters, "Current Developments in Russia and the Response of the Russian Orthodox Church," in *Christianity after Communism: Social, Political, and Cultural Struggle in Russia,* ed. Niels C. Nielsen Jr. (Boulder, Colo., and Oxford: Westview Press, 1994), 99.

31. "Antikhrist v Moskve" *Russkii vestnik* no. 2 (21 February 1994): 24–25, and "Tserkov' protiv modernizma," *Russkii vestnik* nos. 3–6 (28 February 1994): 8.

32. "Vstrecha v redaktsii 'Kontinenta,'" 208.

33. Igor' Ivanovich Vinogradov, interview with author, Moscow, 14 June 1994.

34. Fr Georgii Kochetkov, interview with author, Moscow, 1 July 1995.

35. Ibid., 25 March 1995.

36. These remarks harken back to a warning issued by Russian philosophers and theologians at the beginning of the twentieth century. These philosophers and theologians, writing in a collection of essays called *Vekhi* (*Signposts*), had attacked the "cult of the people" that had prominently featured in the revolutionaries' political program. Such tendencies to place everything in the "interest of the people" fostered violence and destruction, because it simplified everything and made dissent disagreeable: "This is the way we are: not only can we not dream about fusing with the people but we must fear them worse than any punishment by the government, and we must bless that authority which alone with its bayonets and prisons manages to protect us from the popular fury." In the 1990s such warnings were again extremely relevant. Faced with an internal crisis, certain groups were again calling for this dangerous phenomenon of "fusing with the people" (Orlando Figes, *Natasha's Dance: A Cultural History of Russia* [New York: Henry Holt, 2002], 264).

37. Fr Georgii Kochetkov, interview with author, Moscow, 25 March 1995.

38. Ibid.

39. *Tserkovnie Vedomosti* no. 3 (1906), 100, quoted in Gvosdev, *Emperors and Elections,* 3; Zernov, *Russian Religious Renaissance,* 70.

40. Danièle Hervieu-Léger, *Religion as a Chain of Memory,* trans. Simon Lee (Cambridge, England: Polity Press, 2000), 168.

41. Ibid.

42. Zernov, *Russian Religious Renaissance,* 64; James W. Cunningham, *A Vanquished Hope: The Movement for Church Renewal in Russia, 1905–06* (Crestwood, N.Y.: St. Vladimir's Seminary Press, 1981), 98–99.

43. Zernov, *Russian Religious Renaissance,* 71.

44. Sergei Witte, quoted in Zernov, *Russian Religious Renaissance,* 71–72.

45. Zernov, *Russian Religious Renaissance,* 73–74.

46. Simon Dixon, "The Church's Social Role in St. Petersburg, 1880–1914," in *Church, Nation, and State in Russia and Ukraine,* ed. Geoffrey A. Hosking (London: Macmillan Academic and Professional, 1991), 186.

47. Anton Vladimirovich Kartashev, "Vremennoe pravitel'stvo i russkaia tserkov'," in *Iz istorii khristianskoi tserkvi na rodine i za rubezhom v XX stoletii: sbornik,* ed. A. V. Kartashev, I. A. Stratonov, and Metropolitan Elerferii (Bogoiavlenskii) (Moscow: Krutitskoe patriarshee podvor'e, 1995), 13–21.

48. See especially Dimitry V. Pospielovsky, *The Russian Church under the Soviet Regime, 1917–1982,* vol. 1 (Crestwood, N.Y.: St. Vladimir's Seminary Press, 1984), 31–32; John Shelton Curtiss, *The Russian Church and the Soviet State, 1917–1950* (Boston: Little, Brown, 1953), 45–48; Nikita A. Struve, *Christians in Contemporary Russia,* trans. Lancelot Sheppard and A. Manson, 2nd rev. ed. (New York: Charles Scribner's Sons, 1967), 27–29; Matthew Spinka, *The Church in Soviet Russia* (New York: Oxford University Press, 1956), 13–15. From the end of the seventeenth century until 1918, Russians used the Julian calendar, which, in the twentieth century, was thirteen days behind the Gregorian calendar used in the West.

49. "Message from Patriarch Tikhon, dated 19 January 1918," in Struve, *Christians in Contemporary Russia,* 343–45; see also Matthew Spinka, *The Church and the Russian Revolution* (New York: Macmillan, 1927), 118–22.

50. Struve, *Christians in Contemporary Russia,* 31. During this period, the future church leader S. N. Bulgakov resigned his academic position at Moscow University to prepare for the priesthood. An excellent account of his inner searchings and personal perspectives on these events, as well as a firsthand account of the turmoil in the streets, may be found in Sergei Nikolaevich Bulgakov, *Avtobiograficheskie zametki,* Posmertnoe izdanie (Paris: YMCA Press, 1946), 34–43.

51. Zernov, *Russian Religious Renaissance,* 196–97; Struve, *Christians in Contemporary Russia,* 30; Aleksandr Aleksandrovich Bogolepov, *Church Reforms in Russia, 1905–1918,* in commemoration of the fiftieth anniversary of the All-Russian Church Council of 1917–18, trans. A. E. Moorhouse (Bridgeport, Conn.: Publications Committee of the Metropolitan Council of the Russian Orthodox Church of America, 1966), 47–54. The synod was to be comprised of bishops; the high commission of the church would be composed of three bishops, five priests, one monk, and six laymen.

52. Struve, *Christians in Contemporary Russia,* 30.

53. Georgii Kochetkov, "Pravoslavnoe bogoslovskoe obrazovanie i sovremennost'," *Pravoslavnaia obshchina* no. 6 (24) (1994): 95, 99, "Preodolenie raskola mezhdu svetskim i dukhovnym v cheloveke i obshchestve," *Pravoslavnaia obshchina* no. 3 (21) (1994) : 57, and "Russkaia kul'tura i Pravoslavie segodnia," *Pravoslavnaia obshchina* no. 3 (33) (1996): 70. See also "Iz materialov Sviashchennogo Sobora Rossiiskoi Pravoslavnoi Tserkvi, 1917–1918 gg.," *Khristianskii vestnik* no. 3–4 (65–66) (1994): 12–13, and Pospielovsky, *Russian Church under the So-*

viet Regime, vol. 1, 34–35; Struve, *Christians in Contemporary Russia,* 31; Zernov, *Russian Religious Renaissance,* 199.

54. Leonid Stolovich, "Religioznoe vozrozhdenie ili nravstvennye iskaniia?" *Nauka i religiia* no. 7 (July 1989): 15–17. Cox wrote the *Secular City* after spending a year in Berlin, while teaching in an adult education program, whose branches extended on both sides of the Berlin Wall. Berlin is the home of Dietrich Bonhoeffer, and during that year Cox read a great deal of his work. Several elements of Bonhoeffer's thought had a large impact on Harvey Cox: Bonhoeffer's emphasis on the "hiddenness of God" in the world, and his writings about secularization, which he did not consider an evil and did not oppose to religion, and which, he said, may actually have positive benefits for religion. Secularization "frees religious groups from their own theocratic pretensions and allows people to choose among a wide range of ethical and spiritual options." See Harvey Cox, "The 'Secular City' Twenty-five Years Later," introd. to *The Secular City: Secularization and Urbanization in Theological Perspective* (New York: Macmillan, 1990), xi–xxiii.

55. Quoted by Cox in "The 'Secular City,'" xix.

56. Stolovich, "Religioznoe vozrozhdenie," 16.

57. Clement of Alexandria, quoted in Kallistos [née Timothy] Ware, *The Orthodox Church* (New York: Penguin, 1963), 229.

58. "Vstrecha v redaktsii 'Kontinenta,'" 211.

59. *Khram uspeniia presviatoi Bogoroditsy v pechatnikakh na Sretinke, 1695–1995* (Moscow: Prosvetitel'sko blagovoritel'noe bratsvo "Sretenie," 1995), 4, 20. At the end of the sixteenth century, the wall surrounding the interior "white city" of Moscow had twenty-eight towers and nine main gates, including the Sretinskie gates, which received their name from the nearby Sretinskii monastery.

60. Roman Sokolinskii, "Khram Uspeniia Presviatoi Bogoroditsy v Pechatnikakh," *Pravoslavnoe bratstvo Sretenie* no. 2 (1995): 27–28.

61. Zhirinovskii began his well-financed campaign to become president of Russia in February 1996 by identifying himself with the Orthodox Church. He chose simultaneously to celebrate the twentieth anniversary of his marriage and to open his political campaign by holding a ceremony in the Church of St Michael the Archangel in the Moscow Kremlin. Outside the sixteenth-century, gold-domed church, Zhirinovskii professed his commitment to the Russian family, proclaimed his intention to restore Russia's military greatness, and emphasized his support for a union of church and state in recovering Russia's faded glory. Having made these pronouncements, the nationalist leader retired inside the church, where he and his wife, Galina, renewed their wedding vows. The church gave him a hearty welcome. (See Michael R. Gordon, "Russian Nationalist Woos Voters with Vows and Vodka and Gifts," *New York Times,* international ed., 12 February 1996, 1A, 6.)

62. In the summer of 1995 and the spring of 1997, I visited Kochetkov's parish repeatedly, observing the congregation, standing shoulder to shoulder with the worshippers, and taking part in a liturgy that I always found beautiful and meaningful and that Bishop Kallistos has described as a "living experience" (Kallistos [née Timothy] Ware, *The Orthodox Way,* new rev. ed. [Crestwood, N.Y.: St. Vladimir's Press, 1999], 8). This particular experience was taken from a service in July 1995.

63. Georges Florovsky, "The Lost Scriptural Mind," in *Bible, Church, Tradition: An Eastern Orthodox View,* vol. 1 of the *Collected Works of Georges Florovsky* (Belmont, Mass.: Nordland Publishing, 1972), 9.

64. Florovsky, "St. Gregory Palamas and the Tradition of the Fathers," in ibid., 105.

65. Georgii Kochetkov, "Prikhod, obshchina, bratstvo, tserkov' (Ob opyte zhizni missionersko-obshchinnykh prikhodov)," *Pravoslavnaia obshchina* no. 3 (9) (1992): 29–30, 32; S. Smirnov, "Storozh! Skol'ko nochi? . . . (Iz interv'iu s o. Georgiem Kochetkovym)," *Khris-*

tianskii vestnik (1997): 57–59; I. B. Eshenbakh, "Teoriia i opyt obshchinnoi zhizni," *Pravoslav-naia obshchina* no. 1 (1992): 49, 54.

66. The commune did not have additional space and money, and these activities were supported entirely by donations. The educational program was divided into a Sunday school for children age six to fifteen, a youth group from fifteen to twenty years old, and special courses for people twenty-one and older. The adult group included some people born in 1914 to 1916, before the Revolution, who were studying religious subjects for the first time. After one year of such study, they were eligible for baptism.

67. Fr Georgii Kochetkov, interview with author, Moscow, 25 March 1995.

68. In addition to these educational activities, the parish operated a gymnasium and a small religious institute at a higher graduate level. The gymnasium had a six-year program, including two years of in-depth study in theology. The institute had a similar six-year curriculum that concluded with the writing of a thesis. Although the institute did not yet have a graduate, its first-year class, according to Kochetkov, had thirty-five students, nearly all of whom had formerly graduated from the university or an institute; several of the students had written doctoral theses in other fields. Most of these students, Kochetkov pointed out, "are not preparing for service as priests; they are seeking only a good theological understanding," filling in a large gap in their education.

The institute was staffed by teachers and professors who performed their work almost as a charitable service. Such teachers included Vitalii Borovoi, a theologian; Andrei Zubov, a religion journalist for *Kontinent* and the newspaper *Segodnia;* Christopher Zlutner, a professor from Vienna and author of many books on East-West relations; and Sergei Averintsev, the well-known philologist and academician, who lived in Vienna but returned often to Moscow.

69. In addition, to those in agreement with Fr Georgii, his array would include extremely conservative views. He is critical of the intolerant aspects of religion that aspire to drive out dissenters, and he uses as his primary example the seventeenth-century Old Believers, who suffered great persecution and were forced to withdraw to the periphery of the state. Fr Georgii believes that the Orthodox Church must draw on many different traditions and expressions within its own faith and with the Old Eastern religions, which "have historical connections with Orthodoxy." Most important, the church needs more diversity in its own religious life: "We have for so long tried to put everything on the same level; it has not only been the state and our society that has tried to level everything, but also the Church has engaged in this same destructive process."

70. Fr Georgii Kochetkov, interview with author, Moscow, 1 July 1995.

71. See, for example, Kochetkov, "Prikhodskie obshchiny v pravoslavnoi tserkvi," 26–27, and "Iz propovedei (aprel' 1991 g.)," *Pravoslavnaia obshchina* (1993), nos. 4–6 (16–18): 29–30; Ieromonakh Mikhail (Gribanovskii), "V chem sostoit tserkovnost'?" *Pravoslavnaia obshchina* no. 1 (1991) : 12–13; A. Platonov, comp., "E. E. Golubinskii o reforme v Russkoi tserkvi," *Pravoslavnaia obshchina* no. 5 (1991): 40–41.

72. While I have little means of substantiating his claim, Kochetkov said that his community had experienced a great deal of success in dealing with such problems. After some period of time attending classes and becoming part of the community, a member's alcohol, drug dependency, or psychological instability, he said, had "all but disappeared" (Fr Georgii Kochetkov, interview with author, Moscow, 1 July 1995).

73. Maksim Shevchenko and Oleg Mramornov, "The Largest Moscow Parish Remains without Its Beloved Rector," *Nezavisimaia gazeta—religii,* 24 July 1997, archived at http://www.stetson.edu/~psteeves/relnews/kochetkov2407.htlm; accessed on 20 July 1997.

74. Shevchenko and Mramornov, "Largest Moscow Parish Remains without Its Beloved Rector."

75. The young priest thereby charged Fr Georgii with an act of heresy, a charge that he, as a private individual, had no right to make. This act incensed some members of the congregation not only for its lack of decorum but also for what these members regarded as its deliberately provocative character.

76. "Police Report by Sr. Lt. A. L. Rimsky (addressed to Patriarch Aleksi II)," *Radonezh,* 1 July 1997, archived at http://www.stetson.edu/~psteeves/rel news/dormitiondocuments; accessed on 20 July 1997.

77. Tikhon Shevkunov, "This Carthaginian Lie Must Be Destroyed," *Radonezh,* 1 July 1997, archived at http:www.stetson.edu/~psteeves/relnews/radonezh1197.html.; Olesia Aleksandrovna Nikolaeva, "The Story of Joseph and His Brethren in a New Key," *Nezavisimaia gazeta—religii,* 4 October 1997, archived at http:www.stetson.edu/~psteeves/relnews/nikolaeva0410.html; accessed on 10 October 1997.

78. Shevkunov, "This Carthaginian Lie Must Be Destroyed," 1 July 1997.

79. See the testimony of Tat'iana Dubovitskaia in the nationalist publication *Radonezh,* "Renovationists Have Resorted to Criminal Methods," 1 July 1997, archived at http://www.stetson.edu/~psteeves/relnews/radonezh1107.htlm; accessed on 20 July 1997.

80. Boris Kalymagin, "Father Kochetkov's Congregation Expelled Despite Official Exoneration," Brotherhood of St Filaret, 1 November 1997, *Russian Religion News,* October 1997, archived at http:www.stetson.edu/~psteeves/relnews/9710a.html; accessed on 15 November 1997. Andrei Platonov, "We Are Regarded as Deceivers, Yet We Are Genuine, as Dying, Yet We Live," *Nezavisimaia gazeta—religii,* 27 February 1998, archived at http.www.stetson.edu/~psteeves/relnews/platonov9802b.html; accessed on 10 March 1998.

81. Quoted by Platonov in "We Are Regarded as Deceivers."

82. Shevchenko and Mramornov, "Largest Moscow Parish Remains without Its Beloved Rector."

83. Dmitrii Gorin, "Silence of the Pastors," *Nezavisimaia gazeta—religii,* 3 November 1999, archived at http.www.stetson.edu/~psteeves/relnews/gorin9910a.html; accessed on 1 November 1999.

84. Maksim Shevchenko, "Denunciation at Beginning of Century," *Nevavisimaia gazeta—religii,* 26 January 2000, archived at http://www.stetson.edu/~psteeves/relnews/0001d.html; accessed on 29 July 2003.

85. Maria Kozlova, "Some More 'Witnesses' Have Burst into Moscow," *Nezavisimaia gazeta—religii,* 8 December 1999, archived at http://www.stetson.edu/~psteeves/relnews/9912a.html; accessed on 16 December 1999.

86. Shevchenko and Mramornov, "Largest Moscow Parish Remains without Its Beloved Rector."

87. Gorin, "Silence of the Pastors."

88. Shevchenko and Mramornov, "Largest Moscow Parish Remains without Its Beloved Rector."

89. Metropolitan Kirill (Gundiaev), "Test Everything: Hold Fast That Which Is Good," *Anthology, St. Filaret's Christian Institute,* August 2000, archived at http:www.stetson.edu/~psteeves/relnews/0008e.htlm; accessed on 25 August 2000.

90. Georgii Kochetkov, "Indeed, I Can Affirm and Sign All of This," *Nezavisimaia gazeta—religii,* 28 June 2000, archived at http//www.stetson.edu/~psteeves/relnews/0007a.html; accessed on 3 July 2000.

91. Metropolitan Kirill (Gundiaev), "Test Everything: Hold Fast That Which Is Good."

92. Gorin, "Silence of the Pastors."

93. Ibid.

94. Quoted in Georges Florovsky, "St John Chrysostom: The Prophet of Charity," in

Aspects of Church History, vol. 4 of *The Collected Works of Georges Florovsky* (Belmont, Mass.: Nordland Publishing, 1975), 83.

95. Ibid.

96. Oleg Kharkhordin, "Civil Society and Orthodox Christianity," *Europe-Asia Studies* 50, no. 6 (September 1998): 965.

CHAPTER 4

1. Lev Vladimirovich Tsiurik, *Novodevichii monastyr': al'bom putevoditel'* (Moscow: "Sovetskaia Rossiia," 1970), 4.

2. Ibid., 4–8.

3. Ibid., 12–14; Vasilii Vasil'evich Zverinskii, *Material dlia istoriko-topograficheskogo issledovaniia o pravoslavnykh monastyriakh v rossiiskoi imperii, s bibliograficheskim ukazatelem,* vol. 2 (St. Petersburg: Tip. V. Bezobrazova i komp., 1892): 244.

4. Ivan Pavlovich Mashkov, *Arkhitektura novo-devich'ego monastyria v Moskve* (Moscow: Izd-vo Akademii Arkhitektury SSSR, 1949), 48.

5. Claire Louise Claus, "Die Russischen Frauenkloster um die Wende des 18. Jahrhunderts Ihre Karitatative Tatigkeit und Religiose Bedentang," *Kirche im Osten: Studien zur osteuropaischen Kirchengeschichte und Kirchenkunde,* vol. 4 (1961): 147; Brenda Meehan-Waters, "Russian Convents and the Secularization of Monastic Property," in *Russia and the World of the Eighteenth Century,* Proceedings of the Third International Conference Organized by the Study Group on Eighteenth-Century Russia, Bloomington, Indiana, September 1984, ed. R. P. Bartlett, A. G. Cross, and Karen Rasmussen (Columbus, Ohio: Slavica, 1988), 115.

6. Her story is eloquently recounted by Meehan in *Holy Women of Russia,* 79–94. The community was officially recognized in 1865 as the Holy Trinity Tvorozhkovo women's community (Sviato-Troitskaia Tvorozhkovskaia zhenskaia obshchina).

7. Ibid., 121.

8. Ibid., 78, and Meehan, "Metropolitan Filaret (Drozdov) and the Reform of Russian Women's Monastic Communities," *Russian Review* 50, no. 3 (July 1991): 319, 321–22.

9. Mashkov, *Arkhitektura,* 5–9; Vasilii Vasil'evich Zverinskii, comp., *Statisticheskii vremennik rossiiskoi imperii* ser. 3, no. 18: *Monastyri v rossiiskoi imperii* (St. Petersburg: Izdanie Tsentral'nogo statisticheskogo komiteta ministerstva vnutrennikh del, 1887), 42–43. Men's monasteries listed in the first class included Donskoi, Novospasskii, Simonov, and Chudnov (in the Kremlin).

10. Petr Georgievich Palamarchuk, *Sorok sorokov: al'bom-ukazatel' vsekh moskovskikh tserkvei v chetyrekh tomakh,* ed. S. Zvonarev, vol. 1 (Paris: YMCA Presss, 1988–90), 205; Denisov, *Pravoslavnye monastyri Rossiiskoi imperii,* 499–500.

11. Palamarchuk, *Sorok sorokov,* I: 208; Denisov, *Pravoslavnye monastyri Rossiiskoi Imperii,* 503.

12. In addition, the Smolenskii Cathedral bears the graves of several important women in Peter's life, whom he associated with Moscow: Sophie (d. 1704); his unwanted first wife, Eudokhiia Lopukhina (d. 1731); and his half-sister Catherine (d. ?).

13. Ivan Alekseevich Snegirev, *Moskva: podrobnoe istoricheskoe i arkheologicheskoe opisanie goroda,* vol. 1, 2nd. ed. (Moscow: Izdanie A. Martynova, 1875): 8; Tsiurik, *Novodevichii monastyr',* 9. Karl Baedeker, *Russia, with Teheran, Port Arthur, and Peking: Handbook for Travelers* (Leipzig: Karl Baedeker, 1914), 307; Ivan Myachin and Vladimir Chernov, *Moscow* (Moscow: Novosti Press Agency Publishing House, 1967), 202–203.

14. G. G. Antipin, *Khudozhestvennye nadgrobiia, 1914–1969* (Moscow: "Reklama," 1970), 9–11.

15. Ellis, *Russian Orthodox Church,* 124.

16. N. Davis, *A Long Walk to Church,* 164.

17. Ibid.

18. Ibid., 164–65.

19. Ellis, *Russian Orthodox Church,* 124–25. In reality, two communities of nuns were attached to monasteries, bringing the total to twelve. These two were located at the Monastery of the Dormition in Zhirovitsy, Belorussia, and the Monastery of the Holy Spirit (Sviatodukhovskii) in Vilnius, Lithuania.

20. N. Davis, *Long Walk to Church,* 62–63.

21. The figures in this paragraph are drawn from N. Davis, *Long Walk to Church,* 172–73.

22. Fr Andrei Il'ia Osipov, interview with author, Sergiev Posad, 11 July 1995.

23. N. Davis, *Long Walk to Church,* 175.

24. Michael Ignatieff, *The Russian Album* (New York and London: Penguin, 1988), 2.

25. Ibid., 3.

26. Published as Mitropolit Serafim (Chichagov), *Doblesti russkikh voinov: rasskazy o podvigakh soldat i ofitserov v russko-turetskoi voine 1877–1878 gg.* (Moscow: "Palomnik," 1996).

27. While Leonid Mikhailovich is obviously an important figure, little published information exists on him; see the brief account in *Polnyi pravoslavnyi bogoslovskii entsiklopedicheskii slovar'* (London: Variorum Reprints, 1971), vol. 1, cols. 1322 and 2041. For more recent biographical sketches, see V. V. Chernaia, "Mitropolit Serafim (Chichagov)," *Zhurnal Moskovskoi Patriarkhii* no. 2 (1989): 13–18; A. E. Krasnov-Levitan, "Mitropolit-geroi Plevnoi," *Moskovskii Tserkovnyi vestnik* no. 17 (October 1991): 10–11, and the biographical sketches by Metropolitan Pitrim of Volokolamsk and Iur'ev and Arkhimandrat Georgii (Tertiushnikov) of the Sviato-Troitse-Sergieva Lavra, in the introductory materials to Mitropolit Serafim (Chichagov), *Da budet volia Tvoia,* pt. 1: *Ishchite Tsarstviia Bozhiia,* comp. Varvara Vasil'evna Chernaia-Chichagova (Moscow and St. Petersburg: "Palomnik," 1993), 5–17.

28. Leonid Mikhailovich Chichagov, *Letopis' serafimo-diveevskogo monastyria,* 2nd ed. (St. Petersburg: Tip. M. M. Stasiulevicha, 1903). The first edition was published in Moscow in 1896. Throughout his entire life, Leonid Mikhailovich engaged in literary activity, writing not only stories about soldiers but also works on medical science, parish life, and theology. He saw these subjects as part of his duties as a priest. In 1891, he wrote a small book on the history of medicine, in which he connected its emergence to religion and healing; parish priests, he believed, had to be concerned with such healing and with the health and care of the people (Leonid Mikhailovich Chichagov, *Kratkoe izlozhenie meditsinskikh besed* [Moscow: Tipo-lit. T-va "I. N. Kushnerev," 1891]). He also wrote a major work on parish life, *Obrashchenie Preosviashchennogo Serafima, Episkopa Kininevskogo k dukhovenstvu eparkhii po voprosy o vozrozhdenii prikhodskoi zhizni* (Kishinev: Eparkhial'naia tipografiia, 1909). In this work, Leonid Mikhailovich provided a detailed critique of parish life, including the struggle with drunkenness and the need for self-discipline, strictness, and temperance. He described parish life in the Orel region, in which he emphasized the importance of a higher level of education for local priests. He was responding to the Holy Synod's resolution of 18 November 1905 that called for strengthening and reconstituting parish life and the importance of these tasks for the future of the church.

29. Robert L. Nichols points out Leonid's important role in this process, but he also sees the efforts to gain canonization as having much wider support than Mother Serafima outlines; see "The Friends of God: Nicholas II and Alexandra at the Canonization of Serafim of Sarov, July 1903," in *Religious and Secular Forces in Late Tsarist Russia: Essays in Honor of Donald W.*

Treadgold, ed. Charles E. Timberlake (Seattle and London: University of Washington Press, 1992), 214–15.

30. Anna Akhmatova, *The Complete Poems,* trans. Judith Hemschemeyer, ed. and with an introd. by Roberta Reeder (Boston: Zephyr, 1997), 386. See also Roberta Reeder, *Anna Akhmatova: Poet and Prophet* (New York: St. Martin's Press, 1994), 216.

31. Reeder, *Anna Akhmatova,* 218.

32. Ignatieff, *Russian Album,* 7.

33. Vladimir Nabokov, *Speak, Memory: An Autobiography Revisited* (New York: Random House, Vintage Books, 1989), 171–72.

34. See Sheila Fitzpatrick, "Stalin and the Making of a New Elite, 1928–1939," *Slavic Review* 38, no. 3 (September 1979): 377–402.

35. Susan Sontag, *On Photography* (New York: Farrar, Straus and Giroux, 1973), 8–9.

36. Mother Serafima mentioned the church's present need for small prayer rooms in the monastery where nuns might go for contemplation and prayer. The Smolenskii Cathedral, she said, has no such places, and the nuns find it extremely difficult to perform these functions in the present circumstances in the monastery.

37. Patricia Hampl, *Virgin Time* (New York: Farrar, Straus and Giroux, 1992), 218.

38. Bourdeaux, *Gorbachev, Glasnost, and the Gospel,* 189.

39. Daniil Granin, "O miloserdii," *Literaturnaia gazeta* no. 12 (18 March 1987): 13.

40. Granin recalled walks with his father in his childhood and other memories of his father, who would never pass a destitute person on the street, begging for money, without stopping, reaching for a copper coin, and telling the boy to place it in the hand of the unfortunate. The father always responded to such human suffering, despite the family's own meager circumstances and the boy's wish to spend the coin for his own purposes.

41. See, for example, Larisa Kozhatkina, "Lechit'sia nado vsem," *Tverskaia* 13, no. 23 (5–11 June 1997): 4; Episkop Bronitskii Tikhon, "Milost' serdtsa," *Rus' pravoslavnaia,* in *Sovetskaia rossiia* no. 37 (30 March 1997): 4.

42. Francis Fukuyama, *Trust: The Social Virtues and the Creation of Prosperity* (New York: Free Press, 1995), 4.

43. Ibid., 4–5.

44. *Russian Album,* 185.

45. Maksim Shevchenko, "Kanonizatsiia Nikolaia Romanova ne sostoialas'," *Nezavisimaia gazeta,* 20 February 1997, 3.

Chapter 5

1. Aleksi II, quoted in Schmemann, "An Awakened Church," 3E.

2. See Peter Kenez, *The Birth of the Propaganda State: Soviet Methods of Mass Mobilization, 1917–1929* (Cambridge and London: Cambridge University Press, 1985).

3. Václav Havel, "Paying Back the West," *New York Review of Books,* 23 September 1999, 54.

4. Alimov and Charodeev, "Faith without Deeds Is Dead," 265.

5. Aleksi II, "Education and the Christian View of Man," 45.

6. Ibid., 47.

7. See Kallistos [née Timothy] Ware, *The Orthodox Way,* new rev. ed. (Crestwood, N.Y.: St. Vladimir's Press, 1999), 9.

8. Aleksi II, "Education and the Christian View of Man," 47.

9. Ibid., 46–47.

10. Hans Rogger, *National Consciousness in Eighteenth-Century Russia* (Cambridge: Harvard University Press, 1960), 259.

11. Alexander Herzen, *My Past and Thoughts: The Memoirs of Alexander Herzen,* trans. Constance Garnett, revised by Humphrey Higgens, with an introd. by Isaiah Berlin, vol. 1, (New York: Alfred A. Knopf, 1986), 94.

12. Ibid., 95.

13. Aleksandr Aleksandrovich Kizevetter, *Moskovskii universitet i ego traditsii: rol' Moskovskogo universiteta v kul'turnoi zhizni Rossii* (Prague: Tip. "Politika," 1927), 12–18.

14. A. A. Kizevetter, quoted in Samuel D. Kassow, *Students, Professors, and the State in Tsarist Russia* (Berkeley, Calif.: University of California Press, 1989), 13–14.

15. Sheila Fitzpatrick, *Education and Social Mobility in the Soviet Union, 1921–1934* (Cambridge, Eng., and New York: Cambridge University Press, 1979), 64.

16. Ibid., 69–70.

17. Ibid., 126–37, 156–57, and Fitzpatrick, "Cultural Revolution as Class War," in *Cultural Revolution in Russia, 1928–1939,* ed. Sheila Fitzpatrick (Bloomington and London: Indiana University Press, 1977), 8–40; Gail Warshovsky Lapidus, "Educational Strategies and Cultural Revolution: The Politics of Soviet Development," in Fitzpatrick, *Cultural Revolution in Russia,* 78–104.

18. Aleksi II, "Education and the Christian View of Man," 47.

19. David Lowenthal, *The Past Is a Foreign Country* (Cambridge: Cambridge University Press, 1985), 362, 396. As Lowenthal maintains, "History continually tailored to our conceptions is more and more a joint enterprise; your past resembles mine not only because we share a common heritage but also because we have changed it in concert. But this fabricated consensus is highly evanescent. We outdate history with increasing speed, so that even quite recent views of the past, available in voluminous detail on tape and film, now seem quite strange" (362).

20. A. I. Pashkov, ed., *Istoriia russkoi ekonomicheskoi mysli,* vol. 1, *Epokhi feodalizma,* pt. 1, 9–18 v.v. (Moscow: Gos. izd-vo politicheskoi literatury, 1955), 371.

21. Elena Lebedova, "Tretii Rim," *Tat'ianin Den'* no. 3 (June 1995): 10, and Sergei Pravdoliubov, "Nashi vypuskniki: pamiati uchitelia," *Tat'ianin Den'* no. 3 (June 1995): 10–13.

22. V. L. Makhnach, "Prosvetitel'," *Tat'ianin Den'* no. 3 (June 1995): 4.

23. Mariia Rumiantseva, interview with author, Moscow, 6 July 1995.

24. Dmitrii Smirnov, "Bibleiskie 'skazki,'" *Tat'ianin Den'* no. 2 (March 1995): 12–13.

25. "Domovaia tserkov'," *Tat'ianin Den'* no. 3 (June 1995): 2.

26. Bernice Glatzer Rosenthal, "The Search for an Orthodox Work Ethic," in *Between Tsar and People: Educated Society and the Quest for Public Identity in Late Imperial Russia,* ed. Edith W. Clowes, Samuel D. Kassow, and James L. West (Princeton: Princeton University Press, 1991), 66–67.

27. An early issue of *Tat'ianin Den'* published an article by the archpriest Dmitrii Smirnov titled "Bibleiskie 'skazki'" under the caption "Opium of the People," which dealt with the story of Adam and Eve, self-love, and egoism, and related these topics to the present time; the author portrayed such personal indulgence as the current "sickness," the real narcotic of society.

28. "Tserkov' protiv modernizma," *Russkii vestnik,* 28 February 1994, 9.

29. Fr Maksim Kozlov, interview with author, 25 May 2001, Moscow. The interview was conducted with the assistance of Vladimir Salov.

30. Vorontsova and Filatov, "Russkii put' i grazhdanskoe obshchestvo," 58–68.

31. Maksim Shevchenko, "Tseli," *Nezavisimaia gazeta—religii,* 30 January 1997, 1.

32. Maksim Shevchenko, interview with author, Moscow, 2 July 1997.

33. Shevchenko, "Tseli," 1.

34. Václav Havel, "The Power of the Powerless," 85.

35. B. H. Sumner, *A Short History of Russia* (New York: Reynal and Hitchcock, 1943), 183.

36. Oleg Mramornov, "Prokliatye voprosy i suzhenie religioznogo prostranstva," *Nezavisimaia gazeta—religii,* 29 May 1997, 1.

37. "Symposium on Church and Society—2000," archived at http://www.russian-orthodox-church.org.ru/ne006143.htm; accessed on 23 July 2003.

38. Ibid.

39. "An International Conference on Christianity on the Threshold of a New Millennium Opens in Moscow," archived at http://www.russian-orthodox church.org.ru/ne006204.htm; accessed on 23 July 2003.

40. Ibid.

41. Aleksandr Kyrlezhev, "Religiia i obshchestvo," *Russkaia mysl'* (31 August–6 September 2000): 21.

42. Jubilee Bishops' Council of the Russian Orthodox Church, "Foundations of the Social Conception of the Russian Orthodox Church," archived at http://www.russian-orthodox-church.org.ru/sd00e.htm; accessed on 23 July 2003. Unless otherwise noted, the following information about the church's new social doctrine is from this document.

43. Aleksandr Kyrlezhev, "Tserkov' i mir v sotsial'noi kontseptsii Russkoi Pravoslavnoi Tserkvi," *Russkaia mysl'* (21–27 September 2000): 20.

44. Jubilee Bishops' Council, "Foundations of the Social Conception of the Russian Orthodox Church," 52.

45. "An International Conference on Christianity on the Threshold of a New Millennium Opens in Moscow," 1.

46. Ibid., 73.

47. See Wallace Daniel, "Religion, Science, Russia: An Interview with Boris Raushenbakh," *Christian Century* 113, no. 7 (28 February 1996): 232–35. Raushenbakh expressed similar ideas on the need for a new worldview in his seminal 1989 article, "K ratsional'no-obraznoi kartine mira," *Kommunist* no. 8 (May 1989): 89–97, and again in "Religiia i nravstvennost'," *Znamia* no. 1 (January 1991): 204–16. This viewpoint was strongly expressed in the document "Foundations of the Social Conception of the Russian Orthodox Church" (see Miran Petrovich Mchedlov, gen. ed., *O sotsial'noi kontseptsii russkogo pravoslaviia* [Moscow: Respublika, 2002], 118).

48. Raushenbakh, "Religiia i nravstvennost'," 215.

49. Jubilee Bishops' Council, "Foundations of the Social Conception of the Russian Orthodox Church," 73. The document also cited the similar words of St Filaret of Moscow: "The faith in Christ is not in conflict with the true knowledge, because it is not in union with ignorance."

50. James H. Billington, "Orthodox Christianity and the Russian Transformation," in Witte and Bourdeaux, *Proselytism and Orthodoxy,* 61. See also Mchedlov, *O sotsial'noi kontseptsii russkogo pravoslaviia,* 127–28.

51. Jubilee Bishops' Council, "Foundations of the Social Conception of the Russian Orthodox Church," 78.

52. Ibid., 77–78; Mchedlov, *O sotsial'noi kontseptsii russkogo pravoslaviia,* 377.

53. Jubilee Bishops' Council, "Foundations of the Social Conception of the Russian Orthodox Church," 77.

54. Ibid., 72.

55. Ibid., 78; Mchedlov, *O sotsial'noi kontseptsii russkogo pravoslaviia,* 118.

56. See "Politicheskii rezonans Iubileinogo sobora," *Russkaia mysl'* (7–13 September 2000): 20.

57. Kyrlezhev, "Tserkov' i mir v sotsial'noi kontseptsii Russkoi Pravoslavnoi Tserkvi," 20.

58. Ibid.

59. Fr Maksim Kozlov, interview with author, 25 May 2001, Moscow.

60. Sergei Borisovich Filatov, interview with author, 4 June 2001, Moscow. The interview was conducted with the assistance of Vladimir Salov.

61. Jubilee Bishops' Council, "Foundations of the Social Conception of the Russian Orthodox Church," 74–75; Mchedlov, *O sotsial'noi kontseptsii russkogo pravoslaviia*, 374.

CHAPTER 6

1. Archbishop Gregory of Mozhaisk, Vicar of the Moscow diocese, "In Memory of Hegumenia Serafima (Chernaia)," archived at http:www.russian-orthodox-church.org.ru/ne912233 .htm; accessed on 28 July 2003.

2. Ibid.

3. Mother Serafima, interview with author, Moscow, 23 June 1997.

4. Sergei Borisovich Filatov, gen. ed., *Religiia i obshchestvo: ocherki religioznoi zhizni sovremennoi Rossii* (Moscow and St. Petersburg: Letnii sad, 2002). Filatov collaborated with the Keston Institute in Oxford, England, whose founder and director emeritus, Michael Bourdeaux, served as general supervisor for the project.

5. Sergei Borisovich Filatov, interview with author, Moscow, 4 June 2001. This interview was conducted with the assistance of Vladimir Salov and Georgii Bovt.

6. See Filatov, *Religiia i obshchestvo*, 447–49; Filatov, "Sovremennaia Rossiia i sekty," *Inostrannaia literatura* no. 8 (1996): 201–19, and Filatov, "Sects and New Religious Movements in Post-Soviet Russia," in Witte and Bourdeaux, *Proselytism and Orthodoxy*, 163–84.

7. Filatov, *Religiia i obshchestvo*, 480–81.

8. Ibid.; see also Sergei Filatov, "Protestantism in Postsoviet Russia: An Unacknowledged Triumph," *Religion, State, and Society* 28, no. 1 (March 2000): 93–104.

9. Sergei Borisovich Filatov, interview with author, Moscow, 4 June 2001.

10. Filatov's study brought out emphatically the great diversity of religious beliefs found in contemporary Russia. Surveying religious life in seventy-eight of the Russian Federation's eighty-nine regions, his work undermines the common notion, often projected in political propaganda, that Russian culture presents a homogeneous picture throughout the federation. See also Philip Walters, "The Encyclopedia of Religious Life in Russia Today: A Landmark Research Project," *Religion, State, and Society* 30, no. 2 (June 2002): 159.

11. Filatov, *Religiia i obshchestvo*, 54–57; Sergei Borisovich Filatov and Roman Lunkin, "Traditions of Lay Orthodoxy in the Russian North," *Religion, State, and Society* 28, no. 1 (March 2000): 35.

12. Fyodor Dostoevsky, *The Brothers Karamazov*, trans. and annotated by Richard Pevear and Larissa Volokhonsky (New York: Random House, 1991), 29.

13. Alexander N. Domrin, "Ten Years Later: Society, 'Civil Society,' and the Russian State," *Russian Review* 62, no. 2 (April 2003), 193.

14. Catherine II, *Catherine the Great's Instruction (Nakaz) to the Legislative Commission, 1767*, vol. 2 of *Russia under Catherine the Great*, ed. Paul Dukes (Newtonville, Mass.: Oriental Research Partners, 1977), 46.

15. Domrin, "Ten Years Later," 201.

16. Oleg Rumiantsev, quoted in ibid.

17. Kharkhordin, "Civil Society and Orthodox Christianity," 949–68.

18. Henry Bettenson, ed. and trans., *The Later Christian Fathers: A Selection from the Writings of the Fathers from St. Cyril of Jerusalem to St. Leo the Great* (Oxford: Oxford University Press, 1970), 130.

19. Semen Frank, *Dukhovnye osnovy obshchestva* (1930), quoted in Evert van der Zweerde, "'Civil Society' and 'Orthodox Christianity' in Russia: A Double Test-Case," *Religion, State, and Society* 27, no. 1 (1995): 35; emphasis in original.

20. The Civic Forum, held in the Kremlin and hosted by the Russian government on 20–21 November 2001, drew some thirty-five hundred representatives from Russian governmental and nongovernmental organizations (NGOs) to discuss problems of civil society. The conference produced few concrete results; nevertheless, in scope and substance, it represented a unique occurrence in society's relationship with the government in Russia. While some representatives approached the forum with cynicism and even disdain, the discussions that took place were significant; the NGO participants refused to be subordinate to Kremlin officials and insisted on partnership in the proceedings. The leadership the NGOs provided, especially on human rights and environmental issues, suggested a greater assertiveness and a much more active program than existed in earlier times. As Alexander Nikitin and Jane Buchanan have suggested, the discussion on civil society that developed in the Civic Forum is itself an important development; the forum "inspired an exceptional level of conversation on civil society, its definition, its development, and its very existence in Russia." The conversation signaled a desire for a dynamic interaction between the government and its citizens on some of the most important issues facing Russia in the twenty-first century. See Alexander Nikitin and Jane Buchanan, "The Kremlin's Civic Forum: Cooperation or Co-optation for Civil Society in Russia?" *Demokratizatsiya* 10, no. 2 (Spring 2002): 147–65, and, in the same issue, Marcie A. Weigle, "On the Road to the Civic Forum: State and Civil Society from Yeltsin to Putin," 117–46.

21. Filatov, *Religiia i obshchestvo,* 57.

22. George E. Hudson, "Civil Society in Russia: Models and Prospects for Development," *Russian Review* 62, no. 2 (April 2003): 212–22. See also Christopher Marsh's observations concerning Russia's social capital and its political processes, in "Social Capital and Democracy in Russia," *Communist and Post-Communist Studies* 33 (2000), 185–86, and Marsh, *Making Democracy Work: Social Capital, Economic Development, and Democratization* (Lewiston, N.Y.: Edwin Mellen Press, 2000), 128–31. The conference on Civil Society and Social Justice, held at Baylor University, 1–2 February 2001, added significantly to this discussion and reevaluation. See Marsh and Gvosdev, *Civil Society and the Search for Justice in Russia.*

23. Hudson, "Civil Society in Russia," 222.

24. Czeslaw Milosz, "Along This Rutted Path," *Harper's,* July 2001, 21; and Milosz, *To Begin Where I Am: Selected Essays,* ed. and with an introd. by Bogdana Carpenter and Madeline G. Levine (New York: Farrar, Straus and Giroux, 2001), 200. Milosz's essay, originally written in 1942 as "Letter to Jerzy Andrzejewski," was first published in 1990.

Bibliography

INTERVIEWS BY AUTHOR

Aksiuchits, Viktor Vladimorovich. Leader of Russian Christian Democratic Party, coeditor of *Vybor,* Moscow, 29 May 1991.

Chichagova, Varvara Vasil'evna (Mother Serafima). Novodevichy Monastery, Moscow, 3 June 1995, 23 June 1997.

Filatov, Sergei Borisovich. Scholar, Institute of USA-Canada, Russian Academy of Sciences, associate of Center of the Sociology of Religion, Russian Academy of Sciences, Moscow, 15 June 1994, 29 May 1995, 26 May 1997, 8 June 1997, 4 June 2001.

Furman, Dmitrii Efimovich. Scholar, director of the Center of the Sociology of Religion, Russian Academy of Sciences, Moscow, 6 June 1994, 26 May 1997.

Ivanova, Evgeniia Viktorovna. Scientific worker in the World Literature Institute, Russian Academy of Sciences, secretary of the commission on Father Pavel Florinsky, Moscow, 8 June 1994, 3 June 1995, 11 July 1997.

Kochetkov, Fr Georgii. Priest, Church of the Dormition of the Mother of God in Pechatniki (Uspeniia Bogoroditsy Tserkov' v Pechatnikakh), Moscow, 25 March 1995, 1 July 1995, 23 June 1997.

Kozlov, Fr Maksim. Priest, Church of the Sacred Martyr Tat'iana, Moscow University, Moscow, 6 June 1995, 25 May 2001.

Mitrokhin, Lev Nikolaevich. Scholar, Institute of Philosophy, Russian Academy of Sciences, 9 June 1994.

Osipov, Fr Andrei Il'ia. Professor of theology, Kafedra of Theology, Spiritual Academy of the Moscow Patriarchy, chief editor of *Bogoslovskii vestnik,* Sergiev Posad, 11 June 1994.

Paissy, Fr Vladimir. Priest, Oxford, England, 6 July 2000.

Pchelintsev, Anatolii Vasil'evich. Lawyer, director of the Institute of Religion and Law, Moscow, 3 June 1997.

Raushenbakh, Boris Viktorovich. Physicist, member, Russian Academy of Sciences, Moscow, 3 November 1994.

Rumiantseva, Mariia. Parishioner, Church of the Sacred Martyr Tat'iana, Moscow University, Moscow, 15 July 1995.

Shevchenko, Maksim Leonidovich. Journalist and chief editor, *Nezavisimaia gazeta—religiia,* Moscow, 26 June 1997, 2 July 1997.

Shusharin, Dmitrii. Journalist, *Segodnia,* Moscow, 22 May 1992.

Smyslova, Ekaterina Aleksandrova. Lawyer, Institute of Religion and Law, Moscow, 8 July 1997.

Vinogradov, Igor' Ivanovich. Chief editor, *Kontinent,* Moscow, 14 June 1994.

Vorontsova, Liudmila Mikhailovna. Scholar, Moscow, 29 May 1995.

Round Table Discussion.

Andrei Borisovich Zubov, professor of political studies at the University of International Affairs; Mikhail Petrovich Mchedlov, director of the Center for Religion in Contemporary Society; Archpriest Vsevolod Chaplin, vice chairman of the Department for External Church Relations of the Moscow Partriarchate; Aleksandr Il'ich Kurdriavtsev, director of the Department of Social and Religious Organizations, Russian Ministry of Justice; Professor Peter Berger, Boston University; Professor Christopher Marsh, Baylor University; and the author, Danilov Monastery, Moscow, 9 July 2003.

Primary Texts and Published Works

Adams, Arthur E. "Pobedonostsev's Religious Politics." *Church History* 22, no. 4 (December 1953): 314–26.

Akhmatova, Anna. *The Complete Poems.* Trans. Judith Hemschemeyer. Ed. and with an introd. by Roberta Reeder. Boston: Zephyr, 1997.

Alekseev, Valerii Arkad'evich. *Illiuzii i dogmy.* Moscow: Politizdat, 1991.

Aleksi II, Patriarch of Moscow and All Russia. "Appeal of the Patriarch Aleksi II of Moscow and All Russia to the Holy Synod of the Russian Orthodox Church and Hierarchs Who Came to the Trinity–St Sergius Lavra for the Commemoration Day of St Sergius of Radonezh." Trinity–St Sergius Lavra, 8 October 1993. In *Information Bulletin,* Department for External Church Relations, Moscow Patriarchate, no. 19 (18 October 1993): 12.

———. "Appeal of the Patriarch of Moscow and All Russia." Moscow, 29 September 1993. In *Information Bulletin,* Department for External Church Relations, Moscow Patriarchate, no. 19 (18 October 1993).

———. "Appeal of the Patriarch of Moscow and All Russia." San Francisco, 22 September 1993. In *Information Bulletin,* Department for External Church Relations, Moscow Patriarchate, no. 19 (18 October 1993): 7.

———. "Education and the Christian View of Man." *Russian Social Science Review* 35, no. 6 (November–December 1994): 45–48.

———. "Zaiavleniia Patriarkha Moskovskogo i Vseia Rusi." *Izvestiia,* 20 August 1991, 3.

Alimov, G., and G. Charodeev. "Faith without Deeds Is Dead—An Interview with Patriarch Aleksi II." Trans. Suzanne Oliver. *Religion in Communist Lands* 18, no. 3 (Autumn 1990): 262–75.

Anishchenko, Gleb. "'Beseda' v gostiakh y 'Vybora' (inerv'iu s Tat'ianoi Gorichevoi i Pavlom Rakom." *Vybor,* 1991, 25–41.

Anisimov, Evgenii Viktorovich. "Progress through Violence from Peter the Great to Lenin and Stalin." *Russian History/Histoire Russe* 17, no. 4 (Winter 1990): 409–18.

———. *The Reforms of Peter the Great: Progress through Coercion in Russia.* Trans. and with an introd. by John T. Alexander. Armonk, N.Y., and London: M. E. Sharpe, 1993.

"Antikhrist v Moskve." *Russkii vestnik* no. 2 (21 February 1994).

Antipin, G. G. *Khudozhestvennye nadgrobiia, 1914–1969.* Moscow: "Reklama," 1970.

Antonov, Mikhail. "Etika zhivogo khristianstva: problemy filosofii khoziaistva v trudakh S. N. Bulgakova." *Nash sovremennik* no. 12 (1990): 154–59.

Baedeker, Karl. *Russia, with Teheran, Port Arthur, and Peking: Handbook for Travelers.* Leipzig: Karl Baedeker, 1914.

Barsegian, Tamara Vasil'evna. "Tipologiia pravoslavnykh monastyrei Rossii." In *Monastyri v zhizni Rossii: materialy Nauchnoi Konferentsii posviashchennoi 600-letiiu prepodobnogo Pafnutiia Borovskogo i 550-letiiu osnovaniia im Rozhdestva Bogoroditsy Pafnut'ev-Borovskogo monastyria (19–20 aprelia 1994 goda),* comp. V. I. Osipov. Kaluga: Borovskii muzei, Filial

Kaluzhskogo kraevedcheskogo muzeia: Russkoe geografcheskoe obshchestvo, Obninskii otdel, 1997.

Batalden, Stephen K. "Printing the Bible in the Reign of Alexander I: Toward a Reinterpretation of the Imperial Russian Bible Society." In *Church, Nation, and State in Russia and Ukraine,* ed. Geoffrey A. Hosking, 65–78. London: Macmillan, 1991.

Berger, Peter L., and Richard John Neuhaus. *To Empower People: The Role of Mediating Structures in Public Policy.* Washington, D.C.: American Enterprise Institute for Public Policy Research, 1977.

Berman, Harold J. "Freedom of Religion in Russia: An Amicus for the Defendant." In *Proselytism and Orthodoxy in Russia: The New War for Souls,* ed. John Witte Jr. and Michael Bourdeaux, 265–83. Maryknoll, N.Y.: Orbis, 1999.

Bettenson, Henry, ed. and trans. *The Later Christian Fathers: A Selection from the Writings of the Fathers from St. Cyril of Jerusalem to St. Leo the Great.* London and New York: Oxford University Press, 1970.

Billington, James H. "The Case for Orthodoxy: Russia's New and Divided Lodestar." *New Republic,* 30 May 1994, 24–27.

———. *The Icon and the Axe: An Interpretive History of Russian Culture.* New York: Random House, 1966.

———. "Orthodox Christianity and the Russian Transformation." In *Proselytism and Orthodoxy in Russia: The New War for Souls,* ed. John Witte Jr. and Michael Bourdeaux, 51–65. Maryknoll, N.Y.: Orbis, 1999.

———. *Russia in Search of Itself.* Washington, D.C.: Woodrow Wilson Center Press, 2004.

———. "Russia's Fever Break." *Wilson Quarterly* 15, no. 4 (Autumn 1991): 58–65.

———. *Russia Transformed: Breakthrough to Hope: Moscow, August 1991.* New York: Free Press, 1992.

———. "The True Heroes of the Soviet Union." *New York Times,* 30 August 1991, 23(A).

Bogolepov, Aleksandr Aleksandrovich. *Church Reforms in Russia, 1905–1918.* In commemoration of the fiftieth anniversary of the All-Russian Church Council of 1917–18. Trans. A. E. Moorhouse. Bridgeport, Conn.: Publications Committee of the Metropolitan Council of the Russian Orthodox Church of America, 1966.

Bondarenko, Yuri Iakovlevich. "The Church Regains the Optina Monastery." *Religion in USSR* no. 2 (February 1988): 23–25

Borisov, Aleksandr. "Nekotorye zamechaniia o sovremennom sostoianii russkoi pravoslavnoi tserkvi." *Biulleten' Khristianskoi obshchestvennosti* no. 8 (May 1988): 109–13.

Bourdeaux, Michael. *Gorbachev, Glasnost, and the Gospel.* London: Hodder and Stoughton, 1990.

Bulgakov, Sergei Nikolaevich. *Avtobiografcheskie zametki.* Posmertnoe izdanie. Paris: YMCA Press, 1946.

Carter, Stephen L. *Civility: Manners, Morals, and the Etiquette of Democracy.* New York: Basic Books, 1998.

Catherine II. *Catherine the Great's Instruction (Nakaz) to the Legislative Commission, 1767.* Vol. 2 of *Russia under Catherine the Great,* ed. Paul Dukes. Newtonville, Mass.: Oriental Research Partners, 1977.

Chaplin, Vsevolod. "Active Neutrality." *Nezavisimaia gazeta—religii,* 10 November 1999. Archived at http://www.stetson.edu/~psteeves/relnews/9911a.html.

Cherepnina, Nadezhda Iur'evna, and Mikhail Vital'evich Shkarovskii, eds. *Sankt-Peterburgskaia eparkhiia v dvadtsatom veke v svete arkhivnykh materialov, 1917–1941: sbornik dokumentov.* St. Petersburg: "Liki Rossii," 2000.

Chernaia, Varrara Vasil'evna "Mitropolit Serafim (Chichagov)." *Zhurnal Moskovskoi Patriarkhii* no. 2 (1989): 13–18.

Chichagov, Leonid Mikhailovich. *Dnevnik prebyvaniia Tsaria-Osvoboditelia v Dunaiskoi armii v 1877 godu.* St. Petersburg: Satus', 1995.

———. *Kratkoe izlozhenie meditsinskikh besed.* Moscow: Tipo-lit. T-va "N. Kushnerev," 1891.

———. *Letopis' serafimo-diveevskogo monastyria.* 2nd ed. St. Petersburg: Tip. M. M. Stasiulevicha, 1903.

———. *Obrashchenie Preosviashchennogo Serafima, Episkopa Kininevskogo k dukhovenstvu eparkhii po voprosu o vozrozhdenii prikhodskoi zhizni.* Kishinev: Eparkhial'naia tipografiia, 1909.

———. See also Serafim, Mitropolit.

Chickering, Lawrence. *Beyond Left and Right: Breaking the Political Stalemate.* San Francisco: ICS Press, 1993.

Chinyaeva, Elena. "Russian Orthodox Church Forges a New Role." *Transitions* 2, no. 7 (5 April 1996): 14–19.

Chumachenko, Tat'iana Aleksandrovna. *Church and State in Soviet Russia: Russian Orthodoxy from World War II to the Khrushchev Years.* Ed. and trans. Edward E. Roslof. Armonk, N.Y.: M. E. Sharpe, 2002.

Claus, Claire Louise. "Die Russischen Frauenkloster um die Wende des 18. Jahrhunderts Ihre Karitatative Tatigkeit und Religiose Bedentang." *Kirche im Osten: Studien zur osteuropäischen Kirchengeschichte und Kirchenkunde,* vol. 4 (1961).

Cohen, Stephen F. "The Friends and Foes of Change: Soviet Reformism and Conservatism." In *Rethinking the Soviet Experience: Politics and History since 1917,* 128–57. Oxford and New York: Oxford University Press, 1985.

Cox, Harvey. "The 'Secular City' Twenty-five Years Later." Introduction to *The Secular City: Secularization and Urbanization in Theological Perspective.* New York: Macmillan, 1990.

Cracraft, James. *The Petrine Revolution in Russian Culture.* Cambridge, Mass., and London: Belknap Press of Harvard University, 2004.

Cunningham, James W. *A Vanquished Hope: The Movement for Church Renewal in Russia, 1905–06.* Crestwood, N.Y.: St. Vladimir's Seminary Press, 1981.

Curtiss, John Shelton. *The Russian Church and the Soviet State, 1917–1950.* Boston: Little, Brown, 1953.

Daniel, Wallace. "The New Religious Press in Russia." In *Christianity after Communism: Social, Political, and Cultural Struggle in Russia,* ed. Niels C. Nielson Jr., 47–62. Boulder, Colo.: Westview Press, 1994.

———. "Religion and Science: The Evolution of Soviet Debate." *Christian Century* 109, no. 4 (29 January 1992): 98–100.

———. "Religion and the Struggle for Russia's Future." *Religion, State, and Society* 24, no. 4 (December 1996): 367–383.

———. "Religion, Science, Russia: An Interview with Boris Raushenbakh." *Christian Century* 113, no. 7 (28 February 1996): 232–35.

———. "The Vanished Past: Russia's Search for Identity." *Christian Century* 110, no. 9 (17 March 1993): 293–96.

Davis, Derek H. "Editorial: Russia's New Law on Religion: Progress or Regress?" *Journal of Church and State* 39, no. 4 (Autumn 1997): 645–55.

Davis, Nathaniel. *A Long Walk to Church: A Contemporary History of Russian Orthodoxy.* 2nd ed. Boulder, Colo.: Westview Press, 2003.

Denisov, Leonid Ivanovich. *Pravoslavnye monastyri Rossiiskoi imperii: polnyi spisok vsiekh 1105 nynie sushchestvuiushchikh v 75 guberniiakh i oblastiakh Rossii (i 2 inostrannykh gosudarst-*

vakh) muzhskikh i zhenskikh monastyrei, arkhiereiskikh domov i zhenskikh obshchin. Moscow: Izdanie A. D. Stupina, 1908.

Dixon, Simon. "The Church's Social Role in St. Petersburg, 1880–1914." In *Church, Nation, and State in Russia and Ukraine,* ed. Geoffrey A. Hosking, 167–92. London: Macmillan Academic and Professional, 1991.

"Domovaia tserkov'." *Tat'ianin Den'* no. 3 (June 1995): 2.

Domrin, Alexander N. "Ten Years Later: Society, 'Civil Society,' and the Russian State." *Russian Review* 62, no. 2 (April 2003): 193–211.

Dostoevsky, Fyodor. *The Brothers Karamazov.* Trans. and annotated by Richard Pevear and Larissa Volokhonsky. New York: Random House, 1991.

Dubin, Boris Vladimirovich. "Religiia, tserkov', obshchestvennoe mnenie." *Svobodnaia mysl'* no. 11 (1997): 94–103. In English translation by Michael Vale, "Religion, the Church, and Public Opinion." *Russian Social Science Review* 39, no. 6 (November–December 1998): 51–66.

Dunlop, John B. "The Russian Orthodox Church and Nationalism after 1988." *Religion in Communist Lands* 18, no. 4 (Winter 1990): 292–305.

Durham, W. Cole, Jr., and Lauren B. Homer. "Russia's 1997 Law on Freedom of Conscience and Religious Associations: An Analytical Appraisal." *Emory International Law Review* 12, no. 1 (Winter 1998): 101–246.

Durham, W. Cole, Jr., Lauren B. Homer, Pieter van Dijk, and John Witte Jr. "The Future of Religious Liberty in Russia: Report of the De Burght Conference on Pending Russian Legislation Restricting Religious Liberty." *Emory International Law Review* 8, no. 1 (Spring 1994): 1–46.

Eberly, Don E., ed. *The Essential Civil Society Reader.* Boulder, Colo.: Rowman and Littlefield, 2000.

Edelshtein, Georgi. "The Election of a Patriarch—Crossroads or Dead-End?" *Religion in Communist Lands* 18, no. 3 (Autumn 1990): 268–71.

Ehrenberg, John. *Civil Society: The Critical History of an Idea.* New York and London: New York University Press, 1999.

Elliott, Mark, and Anita Deyneka. "Protestant Missionaries in the Former Soviet Union." In *Proselytism and Orthodoxy in Russia: The New War for Souls,* ed. John Witte Jr. and Michael Bourdeaux, 197–223. Maryknoll, N.Y.: Orbis, 1999.

Ellis, Jane. *The Russian Orthodox Church: A Contemporary History.* London and Sydney: Croom Helm, 1986.

———. *The Russian Orthodox Church: Triumphalism and Defensiveness.* New York: St. Martin's Press, 1996.

———. "USSR: The Christian Seminar." *Religion in Communist Lands* 8, no. 2 (Summer 1980): 92–112.

Eshenbakh, I. B. "Teoriia i opyt obshchinnoi zhizni." *Pravoslavnaia obshchina,* 1992, no. 1: 49–54.

Fedotov, George Petrovich. "The Christian Origins of Freedom." In *Ultimate Questions: An Anthology of Modern Russian Religious Thought,* ed. and with an introd. by Alexander Schmemann, 281–95. New York and Chicago: Holt, Rinehart and Winston, 1965.

Ferguson, Adam. *An Essay on the History of Civil Society.* Ed. Fania Oz-Salzberger. Cambridge Texts in the History of Political Thought. Cambridge: Cambridge University Press, 1995.

Figes, Orlando. *Natasha's Dance: A Cultural History of Russia.* New York: Henry Holt, 2002.

Filatov, Sergei Borisovich. *Katolitsizm v SShA: 60–80e gody.* Moscow: Nauka, 1993.

———. "The Prospects for Catholicism in Russia." *Religion, State, and Society* 22, no. 1 (1994): 69–72.

————. "Protestantism in Postsoviet Russia: An Unacknowledged Triumph." *Religion, State, and Society* 28, no. 1 (March 2000): 93–104.

————. "Russkaia Pravoslavnaia Tserkov' i politicheskaia elita." In *Religiia i politika v postkommunisticheskoi Rossii,* ed. L. N. Mitrokhin, 99–118. Moscow: Institut filosofii RAN, 1994.

————. "Sects and New Religious Movements in Post-Soviet Russia." In *Proselytism and Orthodoxy in Russia: The New War for Souls,* ed. John Witte Jr. and Michael Bourdeaux, 163–84. Maryknoll, N.Y.: Orbis Books, 1999.

————. "Sovremennaia Rossiia i sekty." *Inostrannaia literatura* no. 8 (1996): 201–19.

————, gen. ed. *Religiia i obshchestvo: Ocherki religioznoi zhizni sovremennoi Rossii.* Moscow and St. Petersburg: Letnii sad, 2002.

Filatov, Sergei Borisovich, and Dmitrii Efimovich Furman, eds. *Religiia i demokratiia: na puti k svobode sovesti.* Moscow: Progress-Kul'tura, 1993.

Filatov, Sergei Borisovich, and Roman Lunkin, "Traditions of Lay Orthodoxy in the Russian North." *Religion, State, and Society* 28, no. 1 (March 2000): 23–35.

Filatov, Sergei Borisovich, and Aleksandr Shchipkov. "Ural: prel'shchenie monetarizmom." *Druzhba narodov* no. 12 (1996): 132–45.

Fitzpatrick, Sheila. "Cultural Revolution as Class War." In *Cultural Revolution in Russia, 1928–1939,* ed. Sheila Fitzpatrick, 8–40. Bloomington and London: Indiana University Press, 1977.

————. *Education and Social Mobility in the Soviet Union, 1921–1934.* Cambridge, Eng., and New York: Cambridge University Press, 1979.

————. "Stalin and the Making of a New Elite, 1928–1939." *Slavic Review* 38, no. 3 (September 1979): 377–402.

Florovsky, Georges, "The Lost Scriptural Mind." In *Bible, Church, Tradition: An Eastern Orthodox View.* Vol. 1 of *The Collected Works of Fr Georges Florovsky,* 9–16. Belmont, Mass.: Nordland Publishing, 1972.

————. "St. Gregory Palamas and the Tradition of the Fathers." In *Bible, Church, Tradition: An Eastern Orthodox View."* Vol. 1 of *The Collected Works of Fr Georges Florovsky,* 105–20. Belmont, Mass.: Nordland Publishing, 1972.

————. "St. John Chrysostom: The Prophet of Charity." In *Aspects of Church History.* Vol. 4 of *The Collected Works of Fr Georges Florovsky,* 79–88. Belmont, Mass.: Nordland Publishing, 1975.

Frank, Semen Liudvigovich. *The Spiritual Foundations of Society: An Introduction to Social Philosophy.* Trans. Boris Jankin. Athens: Ohio University Press, 1987.

Freeze, Gregory L. "Counter-reformation in Russian Orthodoxy: Popular Response to Religious Innovation, 1922–1925." *Slavic Review* 54, no. 2 (Summer 1995): 305–39.

————. "Handmaiden of the State? The Church in Imperial Russia Reconsidered." *Journal of Ecclesiastical History* 36, no. 1 (January 1985): 82–102.

————. *The Parish Clergy in Nineteenth-Century Russia: Crisis, Reform, Counter-Reform.* Princeton, N.J.: Princeton University Press, 1983.

————. *The Russian Levites: Parish Clergy in the Eighteenth Century.* Cambridge, Mass.: Harvard University Press, 1977.

————. "Subversive Piety: Religion and the Political Crisis in Late Imperial Russia." *Journal of Modern History* 68, no. 2 (June 1996): 308–50.

Fukuyama, Francis. *Trust: The Social Virtues and the Creation of Prosperity.* New York: Simon and Schuster, 1995.

Furman, Dmitrii Efimovich. "Religiia, ateizm i perestroika." In *Na puti k svobode sovesti. Perestroika: Glasnost', Demokratiia, Sotsializm,* ed. D. E. Furman and Fr Mark (Smirnov), 7–18. Moscow: Progress, 1989.

————. "Stalinism i my s religiovedcheskoi tochki zreniia." In *Osmyslit' kul't Stalina,* ed. Kh. Kovo, 402–26. Moscow: Progress, 1989.

————. "Veruiushchie, ateisty i prochie: novoe issledovanie rossiiskoi religioznosti." *Svobodnaia mysl'* no. 1 (January 1997): 79–91.

Gellner, Ernest. *Conditions of Liberty: Civil Society and Its Rivals.* London and New York: Penguin, 1996.

Gordon, Michael R. "Russian Nationalist Woos Voters with Vows and Vodka and Gifts." *New York Times,* international ed., 12 February 1996.

Gorin, Dmitrii. "Silence of the Pastors." *Nezavisimaia gazeta—religii,* 3 November 1999. Archived at http://www.stetson.edu/~psteeves/relnews/gorin9910a.html.

Graham, Loren R. *Science, Philosophy, and Human Behavior in the Soviet Union.* New York: Columbia University Press, 1987.

Granin, Daniil Aleksandrovich. "O miloserdii." *Literaturnaia gazeta* no. 12 (18 March 1987).

Gregory, Archbishop of Mozhaisk, Vicar of the Moscow diocese, "In Memory of Hegumenia Serafima (Chernaia)." Archived at http://www.russian-orthodox-church.org.ru/ne912233 .htm.

Gubin, Dmitrii. "Simvol very." *Ogonek* no. 47 (18–23 November 1991): 1–2.

Gunn, T. Jeremy. "The Law of the Russian Federation on the Freedom of Conscience and Religious Association from a Human Rights Perspective." In *Proselytism and Orthodoxy in Russia: The New War for Souls,* ed. John Witte Jr. and Michael Bourdeaux, 239–64. Maryknoll, N.Y.: Orbis, 1999.

Gurevich, Pavel Semenovich. "Vse religii ravny, no est' bolee ravnye?" *Literaturnaia gazeta,* 22 September 1993.

Gvosdev, Nikolas K. *Emperors and Elections: Reconciling the Orthodox Tradition with Modern Politics.* Huntington, N.Y.: Troitsa Books, 2000.

————. "'Managed Pluralism' and Civil Religion in Post-Soviet Russia." In *Civil Society and the Search for Justice in Russia,* ed. Christopher Marsh and Nikolas K. Gvosdev, 75–88. Lanham, Md.: Lexington Books, 2002.

————. "The New Party Card? Orthodoxy and the Search for Post-Soviet Russian Identity." *Problems of Post-Communism* 47, no. 6 (November–December 2000): 29–38.

Haberman, Clyde. "Gorbachev Lauds Religion on Eve of Meeting Pope." *New York Times,* 1 December 1989, sec. 1.

Hampl, Patricia. *Virgin Time.* New York: Farrar, Straus and Giroux, 1992.

Havel, Václav. "Letter to Dr. Gustáv Husák, General Secretary of the Czechoslovak Communist Party." In *Living in Truth: Twenty-two Essays Published on the Occasion of the Award of the Erasmus Prize to Václav Havel,* ed. Jan Vladislav, 3–35. London and Boston: Faber and Faber, 1987.

————. "Paradise Lost." *New York Review of Books,* 9 April 1992, 6–8.

————. "Paying Back the West." *New York Review of Books,* 23 September 1999, 54.

————. "Politics, Morality, and Civility." In *The Essential Civil Society Reader,* ed. Don E. Eberly, 391–402. Boulder, Colo.: Rowman and Littlefield, 2000.

————. "The Power of the Powerless." In *Living in Truth: Twenty-two Essays Published on the Occasion of the Award of the Erasmus Prize to Václav Havel,* ed. Jan Vladislav, 36–122. London and Boston: Faber and Faber, 1987.

Hervieu-Léger, Danièle. *Religion as a Chain of Memory.* Trans. Simon Lee. Cambridge, Eng.: Polity Press, 2000.

Herzen, Aleksandr. *My Past and Thoughts: The Memoirs of Alexander Herzen.* Trans. Constance Garnett. Revised by Humphrey Higgens. Introd. by Isaiah Berlin. 4 vols. New York: Alfred A. Knopf, 1986.

Hilarion, Metropolitan. "Sermon on Law and Grace." In *Medieval Russia's Epics, Chronicles, and Tales,* ed. and trans. Serge A. Zenkovsky, 78–83. New York: E. P. Dutton, 1963.

Homer, Lauren B., and Lawrence A. Uzzell. "Federal and Provincial Religious Freedom in Russia: A Struggle for and Against Federalism and the Rule of Law." In *Proselytism and Orthodoxy in Russia: The New War for Souls,* ed. John Witte Jr. and Michael Bourdeaux, 284–320. Maryknoll, N.Y.: Orbis, 1999.

Hosking, Geoffrey A. *The Awakening of the Soviet Union.* Cambridge, Mass.: Harvard University Press, 1990.

———. *Russia: People and Empire, 1552–1917.* Cambridge, Mass.: Harvard University Press, 1997.

Howell, Jude, and Jenny Pearce. *Civil Society and Development: A Critical Exploration.* Boulder and London: Lynne Rienner, 2001.

Hudson, George E. "Civil Society in Russia: Models and Prospects for Development." *Russian Review* 62, no. 2 (April 2003): 212–22.

Husband, William B. *"Godless Communists": Atheism and Society in Soviet Russia, 1917–1932.* DeKalb: Northern Illinois University Press, 2000.

Iakovlev, A., M. Khromchenko, and V. Povoliaev, eds. *Tishaishie peregovory: 1–3 oktiabria 1993 g.: zapis' fonogrammy peregovorov v Sviato-Danilovom monastyre.* Moscow: "Magisterium," 1993.

Iakunin, Gleb. "The Moscow Patriarchate and Stalin's Cult of Personality." *Glasnost No. 13,* nos. 21–23 (March–May 1989): 8–15.

———. "V sluzhenii kul'tu (Moskovskaia Patriarkhiia i kul't lichnosti Stalina)." In *Na puti k svobode sovesti. Perestroika: Glasnost', Demokratiia, Sotsializm,* ed. D. E. Furman and Fr Mark (Smirnov), 172–207. Moscow: Progress, 1989.

Ignatieff, Michael. *The Russian Album.* New York and London: Penguin, 1988.

Innokentii, Igumen. "Deklaratsiia mitropolita Sergiia i sovremennaia tserkov'." *Nezavisimaia gazeta,* 29 July 1992. English translation in *Russian Studies in History* 32, no. 2 (Fall 1993): 82–88.

"An International Conference on Christianity on the Threshold of a New Millennium Opens in Moscow." Archived at http://www.russian-orthodox-church.org.ru/ne006204.htm.

Itkin, V. "Kto podnial ruki na sviashchennika?" In *Khronika neraskrytogo ubiistva,* ed. Sergei Bychkov, 3. Moscow: Russkoe reklamnoe izd-vo, 1996.

Iuvenali, Metropolitan of Krutitsy and Kolomna. "Address to His Holiness Aleksi II of Moscow and All Russia before the Prayer Service at the Vladimir Icon of the Mother of God." Cathedral of the Epiphany, Moscow, 3 October 1993. *Information Bulletin,* Department for External Church Relations, Moscow Patriarchate, no. 19 (18 October 1993): 20.

"Iz materialov Sviashchennogo Sobora Russkoi Pravoslavnoi Tserkvi, 1917–1918 gg." *Khristianskii vestnik,* 1994, nos. 3–4 (65–66): 12–13.

Jubilee Bishops' Council of the Russian Orthodox Church. "Bases of the Social Conception of the Russian Orthodox Church." Archived at http://www.russian-orthodox-church .org.ru/sd00e.htm.

Kääriänen, Kimmo. *Religion in Russia after the Collapse of Communism: Religious Renaissance or Secular State?* Lewiston, N.Y.: Edwin Mellen Press, 1998.

Kääriänen, Kimmo, and D. E. Furman. "Veruiushchie, ateisty i prochie [evoliutsiia rossisskoi religioznosti]." *Voprosy filosofii* no. 6 (1997): 35–52.

Kalymagin, Boris. "Father Kochetkov's Congregation Expelled Despite Official Exoneration." *Russian Religion News,* October 1997. Archived at http://www.stetson.edu/~psteeves/ relnews/9710a.html.

Karpov, A. "Personality and the Church: The Problem of Personality in the Light of Christian

Teaching." In *The Church of God: An Anglo-Russian Symposium,* ed. E. L. Mascall, with a preface by the Right Rev. W. H. Frere, 134–54. London: Society for Promoting Christian Knowledge, 1934.

Kartashev, Anton Vladimirovich. "Vremennoe pravitel'stvo i russkaia tserkov'." In *Iz istorii khristianskoi tserkvi na rodine i za rubezhom v XX stoletii: sbornik,* ed. A. V. Kartashev, I. A. Stratonov, and Metropolitan Elerferii (Bogoiavlenskii), 9–27. Moscow: Krutitskoe patriarshee podvor'e, 1995.

Kassow, Samuel D. *Students, Professors, and the State in Tsarist Russia.* Berkeley: University of California Press, 1989.

Kenez, Peter. *The Birth of the Propaganda State: Soviet Methods of Mass Mobilization, 1917–1929.* Cambridge and London: Cambridge University Press, 1985.

Kessler, Sanford. "Tocqueville on Civil Religion and Liberal Democracy." *Journal of Politics* 39, no. 1 (February 1977): 119–46.

"The KGB, the Moscow Patriarch, and the State of the Russian Orthodox Church." *Glasnost No. 13,* no. 5 (October 1988): 2–15.

Kharkhordin, Oleg. "Civil Society and Orthodox Christianity." *Europe-Asia Studies* 50, no. 6 (September 1998): 949–68.

Khomiakov, Aleksei Stepanovich. "On Humboldt." In *Russian Intellectual History: An Anthology,* 208–29. Ed. Marc Raeff. Introd. by Isaiah Berlin. New York: Harcourt, Brace and World, 1966.

Khram uspeniia presviatoi Bogoroditsy v Pechatnikakh na Sretinke, 1695–1995. Moscow: Prosvetitel'sko blagotvoritel'noe bratsvo "Sretenie," 1995.

Kireeva, R. A. "Luchshii obrazets russkoi istoricheskoi literatury." Introd. to Vasilii Osipovich Kliuchevskii, *O nravstvennosti i russkoi kul'ture.* Moscow: Institut rossiiskoi istorii RAN, 1998.

Kirill (Gundiaev), Metropolitan of Smolensk and Kaliningrad. "Called to One Hope—The Gospel in Diverse Cultures." Presented at World Council of Churches Conference on World Missions and Evangelism, November 1996, Salvador, Bahia, and Brazil. Reprinted in *Proselytism and Orthodoxy in Russia: The New War for Souls,* ed. John Witte Jr. and Michael Bourdeaux, 66–76. Maryknoll, N.Y.: Orbis, 1999.

———. "Called to One Hope—The Gospel in Diverse Cultures." Address to Conference on World Missions and Evangelism, World Council of Churches, Salvador, Bahia, Brazil, 24 November–3 December 1996. Mimeograph copy, Keston Institute, Oxford, Eng.

———. "Standard of Faith as Norm of Life." *Nezavisimaia gazeta,* 16–17 February 2000. Archived at http://www.russian-orthodox-church.org.ru/ne003161.htm.

———. "Test Everything: Hold Fast That Which Is Good." *Anthology, St. Filaret's Christian Institute,* August 2000. Archived at http://www.stetson.edu/~psteeves/relnews/0008e .html, under the third article, "Metropolitan Kirill Affirms Current Status of Fr Kochetkov."

———. "Tserkov' v otnoshenii k obshchestvu v usloviiakh perestroiki." *Zhurnal Moskovskoi Patriarkhii* no. 2 (February 1990): 32–38.

Kivelson, Valerie A., and Robert H. Greene, eds. *Orthodox Russia: Belief and Practice under the Tsars.* University Park: Pennsylvania State University Press, 2003.

Kizevetter, Aleksandr Aleksandrovich. *Moskovskii universitet i ego traditsii: rol' Moskovskogo universiteta v kul'turnoi zhizni Rossii.* Prague: Tip. "Politika," 1927.

Kliuchevskii, Vasilii Osipovich. "Monastyri v russkoi istorii." In *Russkie monastyri: tsentral'naia chast' Rossii,* ed. Anatolii A. Feoktistov, 18–26. Moscow: Izd-vo "Ocherovannyi strannik," 1995.

———. *O nravstvennosti i russkoi kul'ture.* Moscow: Institut rossiiskoi istorii RAN, 1998.

————. *Tri lektsii.* Paris: YMCA Press, 1969.

Knox, Zoe. "The Symphonic Ideal: The Moscow Patriarchate's Post-Soviet Leadership." *Europe-Asia Studies* 55, no. 4 (2003): 575–96.

Kochetkov, Georgii. "Indeed, I Can Affirm and Sign All of This." *Nezavisimaia gazeta—religii,* 28 June 2000. Archived at http//www.stetson.edu/~psteeves/relnews/0007a.html; accessed on 3 July 2000.

————. "Iz popovedei (aprel' 1991 g.)." *Pravoslavnaia obshchina,* 1993, nos. 4–6 (16–18): 29–30.

————. "Obshchina v pravoslavii." In *Obshchina v pravoslavii: sbornik materialov ezhegodnoi vstrechi Preobrazhenskogo bratsva (18–23 avgusta 1993 g.),* 47–52. Moscow: Moskovskaia vysshaia pravoslavno-khristianskaia shkola Bratsvo "Sretenie," 1994.

————. "Pravoslavnoe bogoslovskoe obrazovanie i sovremennost'." *Pravoslavnaia obshchina* no. 6 (24) (1994): 93–105.

————. "Preodolenie raskola mezhdu svetskim i dukhovnym v cheloveke i obshchestve." *Pravoslavnaia obshchina* no. 3 (21) (1994): 53–72.

————. "Prikhod, obshchina, bratstvo, tserkov' (Ob opyte zhizni missionersko-obshchinnykh prikhodov)." *Pravoslavnaia obshchina* no. 3 (9) (1992): 28–43.

————. "Prikhodskie obshchiny v pravoslavnoi tserkvi i problemy sovremennogo obshchestva v SSSR." *Pravoslavnaia obshchina* no. 1 (1991): 17–29.

————. "Russkaia kul'tura i Pravoslavie segodnia." *Pravoslavnaia obshchina* no. 3 (33) (1996): 65–74.

Kopylova, Elena. "Kamen'—v sobstvennuiu svobodu." *Moskovskie novosti,* 19 September 1993.

Korolev, Stanislav. "Pravoslavie i Velikaia Otechestvennaia Voina 1941–1945 godov." *Molodaia gvardiia* no. 5 (1990): 204–208.

Kozhatkina, Larisa. "Lechit'sia nado vsem." *Tverskaia* 13, no. 23 (5–11 June 1997): 4.

Kozlova, Maria. "Some More 'Witnesses' Have Burst into Moscow." *Nezavisimaia gazeta—religii,* 8 December 1999. Archived at http://www.stetson.edu/~psteeves/relnews/9912a .html.

Krasnov-Levitan, A. E. "Mitropolit-geroi Plevnoi." *Moskovskii Tserkovnyi vestnik* no. 17 (October 1991): 10–11.

"'Kruglyi stol': rol' pravoslavnoi tserkvi v istorii Rossii." *Voprosy istorii* no. 3 (1990): 84–106. Trans. and reprinted as "A 'Roundtable': The Role of the Orthodox Church in Russian History." *Russian Studies in History* (Fall 1993): 8–42.

"Kul'tura, nravstvennost', religiia: material 'kruglogo stola.'" *Voprosy filosofii* no. 1 (1989): 30–63.

Kyrlezhev, Aleksandr. "Ponimaet li bog po-russki? Spor o iazyke bogosluzheniia." *Nezavisimaia gazeta,* 21 April 1994.

————. "Religiia i obshchestvo." *Russkaia mysl'* (31 August–6 September 2000).

————. "Tserkov' i mir v sotsial'noi kontseptsii Russkoi Pravoslavnoi Tserkvi." *Russkaia mysl'* (21–27 September 2000).

Kyrlezhev, Aleksandr, and Konstantin Troitskii. "Rannekhristianskaia tserkov' i transformatsiia khristianskogo soznaniia." Pt. 2 of "Sovremennoe rossiiskoe Pravoslavie." *Kontinent* no. 76 (April–June 1993): 281–303.

————. "Tserkov' v oktiabre 1993 goda." *Nezavisimiia gazeta,* 2 November 1993.

Lapidus, Gail Warshovsky. "Educational Strategies and Cultural Revolution: The Politics of Soviet Development." In *Cultural Revolution in Russia, 1928–1939,* ed. Sheila Fitzpatrick, 78–104. Bloomington and London: Indiana University Press, 1977.

Lebedova, Elena. "Tretii Rim." *Tat'ianin Den'* no. 3 (June 1995).

Lezov, Sergei. "Est' li u russkogo pravoslaviia budushchee? (ocherki sovremennogo pravoslavnogo liberalizma)." *Znamia* no. 3 (March 1994): 171–90.

Likhachev, Dmitrii Sergeevich. "Further Remarks on the Problem of Old Russian Culture." In

The Development of the USSR: An Exchange of Views, ed. Donald W. Treadgold, 167–72. Seattle: University of Washington Press, 1964.

———. "Kreshchenie Rusi i gosudarstvo Rus'." *Novyi Mir* no. 6 (June 1988): 249–58. English translation in Dmitrii S. Likhachev, *Reflections on Russia,* 97–117. Ed. Nicolai N. Petro. Trans. Christina Sever. Foreword by S. Frederick Starr. Boulder, Colo.: Westview Press, 1991.

———. "Kul'turnoe odichanie." *Izvestiia,* 29 May 1991.

———. *Natsional'noe samosoznanie drevnei Rusi: Ocherki iz oblasti russkoi literatury, XI–XVII vv.* Moscow: Izd-vo Akademii nauk, 1945.

———. "Pamiat' preodolevaet vremia." *Nashe nasledie* no. 1 (1988): 1–4.

———. "Russkaia kul'tura: nasledie proshloe i real'naia sila segodnia." *Sem'ia* no. 24 (15 June 1988): 14–15.

Lorgus, Andrei. "'Kruglyi stol' po aktual'nym problemam tserkovnoi zhizni: vozrodit' zhizn' prikhoda." *Zhurnal Moskovskoi Patriarkhii* no. 6 (June 1990): 21–22.

———. "Prikhodskaia zhizn': tol'ko v ograde khrama." *Zhurnal Moskovskoi Patriarkhii* no. 6 (June 1990): 20.

Lowenthal, David. *The Past Is a Foreign Country.* Cambridge: Cambridge University Press, 1985.

Makhnach, V. L. "Prosvetitel'." *Tat'ianin Den'* no. 3 (June 1995): 4.

Malkin, Aleksandr. "Ne rydaite obo mne . . ." *Ogonek* no. 39 (22–29 September 1990): 33.

Marsh, Christopher. "The Challenge of Civil Society." In *Russia's Policy Challenges: Security, Stability, and Development,* ed. Stephen K. Wegren, 141–58. Armonk, N.Y.: M. E. Sharpe, 2000.

———. *Making Democracy Work: Social Capital, Economic Development, and Democratization.* Lewiston, N.Y.: Edwin Mellen Press, 2000.

———. *Russia at the Polls: Voters, Elections, and Democratization.* Washington, D.C.: CQ Press, 2002.

———. "Social Capital and Democracy in Russia." *Communist and Post-Communist Studies* 33, no. 2 (June 2000): 183–99.

———, ed. *Burden or Blessing? Russian Orthodoxy and the Construction of Civil Society and Democracy.* Boston: Institute on Culture, Religion, and World Affairs, 2004.

Marsh, Christopher, and Paul Froese. "The State of Freedom in Russia: A Regional Analysis of Freedom of Religion, Media, and Markets." *Religion, State, and Society* 32, no. 2 (June 2004): 137–49.

Marsh, Christopher, and Nikolas K. Gvosdev, eds. *Civil Society and the Search for Justice in Russia.* Lanham, Md.: Lexington Books, 2002.

Mashkov, Ivan Pavlovich. *Arkhitektura novo-devich'ego monastyria v Moskve.* Moscow: Izd-vo Akademii Arkhitektury SSSR, 1949.

Mchedlov, Miran Petrovich. "Vliianie religioznogo faktora na mirovozzrencheskie ustanovki rossiiskoi molodozhi." In *Obnovlenie Rossii: trudnyi poisk reshenii: godichnye nauchnye chteniia "Rossiia segodnia,"* ed. M. K. Gorshkov and M. P. Mchedlov, 106–17. Moscow: RNISiNP, 2001.

———, gen. ed. *O sotsial'noi kontseptsii russkogo pravoslaviia.* Moscow: Respublika, 2002.

Meehan, Brenda. *Holy Women of Russia: The Lives of Five Orthodox Women Offer Spiritual Guidance for Today.* New York: HarperCollins, 1993.

———. "Metropolitan Filaret (Drozdov) and the Reform of Russian Women's Monastic Communities." *Russian Review* 50, no. 3 (July 1991): 310–23.

———. "Russian Convents and the Secularization of Monastic Property." In *Russia and the World of the Eighteenth Century.* Proceedings of the Third International Conference Organized by the Study Group on Eighteenth-Century Russia, Bloomington, Indiana, September 1984, ed. R. P. Bartlett, A. G. Cross, and Karen Rasmussen, 112–24. Columbus, Ohio: Slavica, 1988.

Men', Aleksandr. *Byt' khristianinom.* Moscow: "Protestant," 1994.

———. *Istoriia religii: v poiskakh puti, istiny i zhizni.* Moscow: Izd-vo Sovetsko-Britanskogo sovmestnogo predpriiatiia "Slovo," 1991.

———. "Mozhno li reformirovat' pravoslavnuiu tserkov'? Neizvestnoe interv'iu Aleksandra Menia." *Nezavisimaia gazeta,* 2 January 1992.

———. "Problemy tserkvi iznutri." In *Kyl'tura i dukhovnoe voskhozhdenie,* ed. R. I. Al'bertkova and M. T. Rabotiaga, 440–45. Moscow: "Iskusstvo," 1992.

———. "Rol' tserkvi v sovremennom mire." Introd. by Sergei Bychkov. *Segodnia,* 10 September 1994.

———. "Russia in Crisis." In *Christianity for the Twenty-first Century: The Life and Work of Alexander Men,* ed. Elizabeth Roberts and Ann Shukman, 138–50. London: SCM Press, 1996.

———. "The Russian Orthodox Church Today." In *Christianity for the Twenty-first Century: The Life and Work of Alexander Men,* ed. Elizabeth Roberts and Ann Shukman, 164–70. London: SCM Press, 1996.

———. *Svet vo t'me svetit: propovedi.* Moscow: AO "Vita-Tsentr," 1991.

———. *Syn chelovecheskii.* Moscow: "Protestant," 1994.

———. *Tainstvo, slovo i obraz: bogosluzhenie Vostochnoi Tserkvi.* Leningrad: Ferro-Logos, 1991.

———. "Vozvrashchenie k istokam." In *Kyl'tura i dukhovnoe voskhozhdenie,* ed. R. I. Al'bertkova and M. T. Rabotiaga, 259–78. Moscow: "Iskusstvo," 1992.

Meyendorff, John. *The Byzantine Legacy in the Orthodox Church.* Crestwood, N.Y.: St. Vladimir's Seminary Press, 1982.

———. *Byzantine Theology: Historical Trends and Doctrinal Themes.* 2nd ed. New York: Fordham University Press, 1979.

Michnik, Adam. *The Church and the Left.* Ed., trans., and with an introd. by David Ost. Chicago and London: University of Chicago Press, 1993.

Mikhail (Gribanovskii), Ieromonakh. "V chem sostoit tserkovnost'?" *Pravoslavnaia obshchina* no. 1 (1991) : 12–13.

Miliukov, Paul. *Outlines of Russian Culture.* Vol. 1, *Religion and the Church.* Ed. Michael Karpovich. Trans. Valentine Ughet and Eleanor Davis. New York: A. S. Barnes, 1960.

Milner-Gulland, Robin R. *The Russians.* Oxford: Blackwell, 1997.

Milosz, Czeslaw. "Along This Rutted Path." *Harper's,* July 2001, 21.

———. *To Begin Where I Am: Selected Essays.* Ed. and with an introd. by Bogdana Carpenter and Madeline G. Levine. New York: Farrar, Straus and Giroux, 2001.

Minasian, Liana, and Anatolii Pchelintsev. "Poslednii prizyv nastupaet." *Literaturnaia gazeta,* 4 June 1997.

Ministerstvo kyl'tyry RSFSR, Akademiia nauk SSSR, and Gosudarstvennaia publichnaia biblioteka. *Sovetskoe gosudarstvo i russkaia pravoslavnaia tserkov': k istorii vzaimootnoshenii (Metodiko-bibliograficheskie materialy v pomoshch' rabote bibliotek-metodicheskikh tsentrov).* Moscow: Gosudarstvennaia publichnaia istoricheskaia biblioteka RSFSR, 1990.

Mitrokhin, Lev Nikolaevich. *Filosofiia religii (opyt istolkovaniia Marksova naslediia).* Moscow: "Respublika," 1993.

Mramornov, Oleg. "Prokliatye voprosy i suzhenie religioznogo prostranstva." *Nezavisimaia gazeta—religii,* 29 May 1997.

Muller, Alexander V., ed. and trans. *The Spiritual Regulation of Peter the Great.* Seattle and London: University of Washington Press, 1972.

Myachin, Ivan, and Vladimir Chernov. *Moscow.* Moscow: Novosti Press Agency Publishing House, 1967.

Nabokov, Vladimir. *Speak, Memory: An Autobiography Revisited.* New York: Random House, Vintage Books, 1989.

Nezhnii, Aleksandr. "The Fifteenth Patriarch." *Religion in Communist Dominated Areas* 29 (Winter 1990): 37; first published in *Moscow News,* no. 24, 1990.

———. "Zakon i sovest'." In *Ogonek-88: luchshie publikatsii goda,* ed. L. Gushkin, S. Kliakin, and V. Iumashev, 318–23. Moscow: Ogonek, 1989.

Nichols, Robert L. "The Friends of God: Nicholas II and Alexandra at the Canonization of Serafim of Sarov, July 1903." In *Religious and Secular Forces in Late Tsarist Russia: Essays in Honor of Donald W. Treadgold,* ed. Charles E. Timberlake, 206–29. Seattle and London: University of Washington Press, 1992.

———. "Orthodoxy and Russia's Enlightenment." In *Russian Orthodoxy under the Old Regime,* ed. Robert L. Nichols and Theofanis George Stavrou, 65–89. Minneapolis: University of Minnesota Press, 1978.

Nielsen, Niels C., Jr. *Revolutions in Eastern Europe: The Religious Roots.* Maryknoll, N.Y.: Orbis, 1991.

Nikitin, Alexander, and Jane Buchanan. "The Kremlin's Civic Forum: Cooperation or Cooptation for Civil Society in Russia?" *Demokratizatsiya* 10, no. 2 (Spring 2002): 147–65.

Nikitin, Valentin. "New Patriarch, New Problems." *Religion in Communist Lands* 18, no. 3 (Autumn 1990): 271–74. First published in *Russkaia mysl'* (29 June 1990).

Nikitin, Valentin, and Fr Mark (Smirnov). "The New Saints Come Marching In." *Moscow News,* June 1988.

Nikolaeva, Olesya Aleksandrovna. "The Story of Joseph and His Brethren in a New Key." *Nezavisimaia gazeta—religiia,* 4 October 1997. Archived at http://www.stetson.edu/~psteeves/relnews/nikolaeva0410.html.

Novak, Josef. "The Precarious Triumph of Civil Society." *Transitions* 3, no. 1 (10 January 1997): 11–13.

Odintsev, Mikhail Ivanovich. *Gosudarstvo i tserkov' v Rossii: XX vek.* Moscow: Izd-vo "Luch," 1994.

———. *Russkie patriarkhi XX veka: Sud'by Otechestva i Tserkvi na stranitsakh arhivnykh dokumentov.* Moscow: RAGS, 1999.

Ogorodnikov, Aleksandr Ioilovich. "Ot sostovitelei." *Obshchina* no. 2 (1978): 1.

Pafnutiia Borovovskogo i 550-letiiu osnovaniia im Rozhdestva Bogorodnitsy Pafnut'ev-Borovskogo monastyria (19–20 aprelia 1994 godu), 6–10. Kaluga-Borovsk: Russkoe geograficheskoe obshchestvo, obniaskii otdel, 1997.

Palamarchuk, Petr Georgievich. *Sorok sorokov: al'bom-ukazatel' vsekh moskovskikh tserkvei v chetyrekh tomakh,* ed. S. Zvonarev. Paris: YMCA Press, 1988–90.

"Participation of the Russian Orthodox Church in the Mediation Mission to Overcome the Political Crisis in Russia." Moscow, 29 September 1993. In *Information Bulletin,* Department for External Church Relations, Moscow Patriarchate, no. 19 (18 October 1993): 1.

Pascal, Pierre. *The Religion of the Russian People.* Trans. Rowan Williams. Crestwood, N.Y.: St. Vladimir's Seminary Press, 1976.

Pashkov, Anatolii Ignat'evich, ed. *Istoriia russkoi ekonomicheskoi mysli.* Vol. 1, *Epokhi feodalizma.* Pt. 1, 9–18 v.v. Moscow: Gos. izd-vo politicheskoi literatury, 1955.

Pavlovsky, Gleb. "The Prospects of a Civil Society in Russia." *Izvestiia,* 3 July 2002, WPS Monitoring Agency. Archived at http//www.wps.ru/e_index.html.

Pchelintsev, Anatolii Viktorovich. "Religiia i prava cheloveka." In *Religiia i prava cheloveka.* Vol. 3 of *Na puti k svobode sovesti,* ed. L. M. Vorontsova, A. V. Pchelintsev, and S. B. Filatov, 7–11. Moscow: "Nauka," 1996.

Peris, Daniel. "Commissars in Red Cassocks: Former Priests in the League of the Militant God-
    less." *Slavic Review* 54, no. 2 (Summer 1995): 340–64.
————. *Storming the Heavens: The Soviet League of the Militant Godless.* Ithaca, N.Y.: Cornell
    University Press, 1998.
Persits, M. M. "Zakonodatel'stvo oktiabr'skoi revoliutsii o svobode sovesti." *Voprosy istorii re-
    ligii i ateizma: sbornik statei.* Vol. 5. Moscow: Akademiia nauk SSSR, 1958.
Petrenko, Elena. "Kul'turnyi sdvig ili religioznyi bum?" *Moskovskie novosti,* 11 August 1991.
Petro, Nikolai N. *The Rebirth of Russian Democracy: An Interpretation of Political Culture.* Cam-
    bridge, Mass.: Harvard University Press, 1995.
Pipes, Richard. *Russia under the Old Regime.* New York: Charles Scribner's Sons, 1974.
Platonov, Andrei. "We Are Regarded as Deceivers, Yet We Are Genuine, as Dying, Yet We
    Live." *Nezavisimaia gazeta—religii,* 27 February 1998. Archived at http://www.stetson
    .edu/~psteeves/relnews/platonov9802b.html.
————, comp. "E. E. Golubinskii o reforme v Russkoi tserkvi." *Pravoslavnaia obshchina* no. 5
    (1991): 40–41.
Pobedonostsev, Konstantin Petrovich. *Reflections of a Russian Statesman.* Trans. Robert Crozier
    Long. Ann Arbor.: University of Michigan Press, 1965.
"Police Report by Sr. Lt. A. L. Rimsky (addressed to Patriarch Aleksi II)." *Radonezh,* 1 July 1997.
    Archived at http://www.stetson.edu/~psteeves/relnews/dormitiondocuments.
"Politicheskii rezonans Iubileinogo sobora." *Russkaia mysl'* (7–13 September 2000).
Polnyi pravoslavnyi bogoslovskii entsiklopedicheskii slovar'. 2 vols. London: Variorum Reprints, 1971.
Popkov, Viktor. "Tserkov' segodnia." *Russkaia mysl'* 15 December, 22 December, 24 November
    1989; 5 January, 19 January, 26 January 1990.
Poresh, Vladimir. "Secret Police Harass Poresh." *Religion in Communist Lands* 8, no. 2 (Sum-
    mer 1980): 103–106. This appeared originally in *Obshchina* no. 2 (1978): 149–58.
Pospielovsky, Dimitry V. *The Orthodox Church in the History of Russia.* Crestwood, N.Y.: St.
    Vladimir's Seminary Press, 1998.
————. *The Russian Church under the Soviet Regime.* 2 vols. Crestwood, N.Y.: St. Vladimir's
    Seminary Press, 1984.
Pozdniaev, Mikhail. "Ego partiia." *Stolitsa* no. 36 (1992): 1–7.
Pravdoliubov, Sergei. "Nashi vypuskniki: pamiati uchitelia." *Tat'ianin Den'* no. 3 (June 1995):
    10–13.
Pushkarev, Sergei. "The Role of the Orthodox Church in Russian History." In Sergei Push-
    karev, Vladimir Rusak, and Gleb Yakunin, *Christianity and Government in Russia and the
    Soviet Union: Reflections on the Millennium,* trans. Anne Mortensen, 1–44. Boulder, San
    Francisco, and London: Westview Press, 1989.
————. *Self-Government and Freedom in Russia.* Trans. Paul Bannes. Introd. by Nicholas V. Ri-
    asanovsky. Boulder and London: Westview Press, 1988.
Putnam, Robert D. *Bowling Alone: The Collapse and Revival of American Community.* New
    York: Simon and Schuster, 2000.
————. *Making Democracy Work: Civic Traditions in Modern Italy.* Princeton, N.J.: Princeton
    University Press, 2002.
Ramet, Sabrina Petra. "Religious Policy in the Era of Gorbachev." In *Religious Policy in the So-
    viet Union,* ed. Sabrina Petra Ramet, 31–52. London: Cambridge University Press, 1993.
Raushenbakh, Boris Viktorovich. "K ratsional'no-obraznoi kartine mira." *Kommunist* no. 8
    (May 1989): 89–97.
————. "Religiia i nravstvennost.'" *Znamia* no. 1 (January 1991): 204–16.
————. "Religioznoe vozrozhdenie ili nravstvennye iskaniia?" *Nauka i religiia* no. 7 (July
    1989): 15–16.

Reeder, Roberta. *Anna Akhmatova: Poet and Prophet.* New York: St. Martin's Press, 1994.

Remnick, David. *Lenin's Tomb: The Last Days of the Soviet Empire.* New York: Random House, 1993.

———. *Resurrection: The Struggle for a New Russia.* New York: Random House, 1997.

"Renovationists Have Resorted to Criminal Methods." *Radonezh,* 1 July 1997. Archived at http://www.stetson.edu/~psteeves/relnews/radonezh1107.html.

Riasanovsky, Nicholas V. *A History of Russia.* 6th ed. New York and Oxford: Oxford University Press, 2000.

Roberts, Elizabeth, and Ann Shukman, eds. *Christianity for the Twenty-first Century: The Life and Work of Alexander Men.* London: SCM Press, 1996.

Rogger, Hans. *National Consciousness in Eighteenth-Century Russia.* Cambridge: Harvard University Press, 1960.

Rosenthal, Bernice Glatzer. "The Search for an Orthodox Work Ethic." In *Between Tsar and People: Educated Society and the Quest for Public Identity in Late Imperial Russia,* ed. Edith W. Clowes, Samuel D. Kassow, and James L. West, 57–74. Princeton, N.J.: Princeton University Press, 1991.

Roslof, Edward E. "The Heresy of 'Bolshevik' Christianity: Orthodox Rejection of Religious Reform during NEP." *Slavic Review* 55, no. 3 (Fall 1996): 614–35.

———. "The Myth of Resurrection: Orthodox Church in Postcommunist Russia." *Christian Century* 110, no. 9 (17 March 1993): 290–93.

———. *Red Priests: Renovationism, Russian Orthodoxy, and Revolution, 1905–1946.* Bloomington: Indiana University Press, 2002.

"Russia: Russian Poll Measures Trust in Institutions." *Interfax,* 26 June 1997, reprinted in *FBIS Report,* Central Eurasia; Russia, FBIS-SOV-97–177, 27 June 1997.

Safonov, Dmitrii. "Theological Commission Continues Study of Fr Georgii Kochetkov's Works." http://www.strana.ru/society/religion/2001/03/12/984387599.html, 12 March 2001. English translation archived at http://www.stetson.edu/~psteeves/relnews/0103c.html.

Salmin, A. "Natsional'nyi vopros i religiia v kontekste gosudarstvennogo stroitel'stva v postkommunisticheskom mire." In *Liberalizm v Rossii: sbornik statei,* ed. Iu. V. Krasheninnikov, 21–45. Moscow: "Znak," 1993.

Schmemann, Serge. "An Awakened Church Finds Russia Searching for Its Soul." *New York Times,* 26 April 1992, sec. 4.

———. *Echoes of a Native Land: Two Centuries of a Russian Village.* New York: Alfred A. Knopf, 1997.

———. "Patriarch's Church Revives, but Will Spirituality?" *New York Times,* 9 November 1991, sec. 1.

———. "Russia, History and the Struggle Not to Repeat It." *New York Times,* 29 November 1992, sec. 5.

Seligman, Adam B. *The Idea of Civil Society.* Princeton, N.J.: Princeton University Press, 1995.

Serafim, Mitropolit [Chichagov, Leonid Mikhailovich]. *Da budet volia Tvoia.* Pt. 1: *Ishchite Tsarstviia Bozhiia.* Comp. Varvara Vasil'evna Chernaia-Chichagova. Moscow and St. Petersburg: "Palomnik," 1993.

———. *Doblesti russkikh voinov: rasskazy o podvigakh soldat i ofitserov v russko-turetskoi voine 1877–1878 gg.* Moscow: "Palomnik," 1996.

———. *Slova, besedy i rechi Preosviashchennogo Serafima, Episkopa Kishinevskogo i Khotinskogo s eparkhial'noi khronikoi i rasporiazheniiami ego.* Kishinev: Tip. V. V. Iakubovicha, 1910.

Shevchenko, Maksim. "Denunciation at Beginning of Century." *Nevavisimaia gazeta—religii* 26 January 2000. Archived at http://www.stetson.edu/~psteeves/relnews/0001d.html.

————. "Kanonizatsiia Nikolaia Romanova ne sostoialas.'" *Nezavisimaia gazeta,* 20 February 1997.

————. "Kochetkova budut obsuzhdat' po-tserkovnomu." *Nezavisimaia gazeta—religiia,* 14 March 2001. Archived at http://religion.ng.ru/printed/provoslav/2001–03–14/4_kochetkov.html.

————. "Tseli." *Nezavisimaia gazeta-religii,* 30 January 1997.

Shevchenko, Maksim, and Oleg Mramornov. "The Largest Moscow Parish Remains without Its Beloved Rector." *Nezavisimaia gazeta—religii,* 24 July 1997. Archived at http://www.stetson.edu/~psteeves/relnews/kochetkov2407.html.

Shevkunov, Tikhon. "This Carthaginian Lie Must Be Destroyed." *Radonezh,* 1 July 1997. Archived at http://www.stetson.edu/~psteeves/relnews/radonezh1197html.

Shkarovskii, Mikhail Vital'evich. *Obnovlencheskoe dvizhenie v russkoi pravoslavnoi tserkvi XX veka.* St. Petersburg: "Nestor," 1999.

————. *Russkaia Pravoslavnaia Tserkov' i sovetskoe gosudarstvo v 1943–1964 godakh: ot "peremiriia" k novoi voine.* St. Petersburg: DEAN+ADIA-M, 1995.

Sinel, Allen. *The Classroom and the Chancellery: State Educational Reform in Russia under Count Dmitry Tolstoi.* Cambridge, Mass.: Harvard University Press, 1973.

Skrynnikov, Ruslan Grigor'evich. *Ivan the Terrible.* Ed. and trans. Hugh H. Graham. Gulf Breeze, Fla.: Academic International Press, 1981.

————. *Tsarstvo terrora.* St. Petersburg: "Nauka," St. Peterburgskoe otdelenie, 1992.

Slater, Wendy. "The Church's Attempts to Mediate in the Russian Crisis." *RFE/RL Research Report* 2, no. 42 (29 October 1993): 6–10.

Slater, Wendy, and Kjell Engelbrekt. "Eastern Orthodoxy Defends Its Position." *RFE/RC Research Report* 2, no. 35 (3 September 1993): 48–58.

Smirnov, Dmitrii. "Bibleiskie 'skazki.'" *Tat'ianin Den'* no. 2 (March 1995): 12–13.

Smirnov, S. "Storozh! Skol'ko nochi? . . . (Iz interv'iu s o. Georgiem Kochetkovym)." *Khristianskii vestnik* (1997): 56–61.

Snegirev, Ivan Alekseevich. *Moskva: podrobnoe istoricheskoe i arkheologicheskoe opisanie goroda.* 2nd. ed. Moscow: Izdanie A. Martynova, 1875.

Sogrin, Vladimir Viktorovich. "Novaia ideologiia dlia Rossii: drama iz sovremennoi istorii." *Obshchestvennye nauki i sovremennost'* (1993): 5–16.

Sokolinskii, Roman. "Khram Uspeniia Presviatoi Bogoroditsy v Pechatnikakh." *Pravoslavnoe bratstvo Sretenie* no. 2 (1995): 27–28.

Solzhenitsyn, Alexander, et al. *From under the Rubble.* Trans. A. M. Brock et al. Boston: Little, Brown, 1975.

Sontag, Susan. *On Photography.* New York: Farrar, Straus and Giroux, 1973.

Spinka, Matthew. *The Church and the Russian Revolution.* New York: Macmillan, 1927.

————. *The Church in Soviet Russia.* New York: Oxford University Press, 1956.

Steele, Jonathan. *Eternal Russia: Yeltsin, Gorbachev, and the Mirage of Democracy.* Cambridge, Mass.: Harvard University Press, 1994.

Stolovich, Leonid. "Religioznoe vozrozhdenie ili nravstvennye iskaniia?" *Nauka i religiia* no. 7 (July 1989): 15–17.

Struve, Nikita A. *Christians in Contemporary Russia.* Trans. Lancelot Sheppard and A. Manson. 2nd rev. ed. New York: Charles Scribner's Sons, 1967.

————. "Orthodox Witch Hunt." *Nezavisimaia gazeta—religii,* 13 September 2000. Archived at http://www.stetson.edu/~psteeves/relnews/0106a.html.

————. *Pravoslavie i kul'tura.* Moscow: Khristianskoe izd-vo, 1992.

Sumner, B. H. *A Short History of Russia.* New York: Reynal and Hitchcock, 1943.

"Symposium on Church and Society—2000." Archived at http://www.russian-orthodox-church.org.ru/ne006143.htm.

Taylor, Charles. "Modes of Civil Society." *Public Culture* 3, no. 1 (Fall 1990): 95–118.

"Text of the Law of the USSR on Freedom of Conscience and Religious Organizations." *Pravda*, 9 October 1990. English language text and commentary by Giovanni Codevilla. In *Religion in Communist Lands* 19, nos. 1–2 (Summer 1991): 119–45.

Tikhon, Bronitskii. "Milost' serdtsa." *Rus' pravoslavnaia,* supplement to *Sovetskaia Rossiia* no. 37 (30 March 1997).

Tocqueville, Alexis de. *Democracy in America.* Trans. George L. Lawrence. Ed. J. P. Meyer. Garden City, N.Y.: Doubleday, Anchor Books, 1969.

Tolz, Vera. "The Moscow Crisis and the Future of Democracy in Russia." *RFE/RL Research Report* 2, no. 42 (22 October 1993): 1–9.

Treadgold, Donald. "Russian Orthodoxy and Society." In *Russian Orthodoxy under the Old Regime,* ed. Robert L. Nichols and Theofanis George Stavrou, 21–43. Minneapolis, Minnesota: University of Minnesota Press, 1978.

Trepanier, Lee, "Nationalism and Religion in Russian Civil Society: An Inquiry into the 1997 Law 'On Freedom of Conscience.'" In *Civil Society and the Search for Justice in Russia,* ed. Christopher Marsh and Nikolas K. Gvosdev, 57–73. Lanham, Md.: Lexington Books, 2002.

"Tserkov' protiv modernizma." *Russkii vestnik* nos. 3–6 (28 February 1994).

Tsiurik, Lev Vladimirovich. *Novodevichii monastyr': al'bom putevoditel.'* Moscow: Izd-vo "Sovetskaia Rossiia," 1970.

Vasilevskii, Iurii Leonidovich. "Veriat, ishchut, ostaiutsia ateistami." *Nezavisimaia gazeta—religii,* 26 April 1997.

Vinogradov, Igor', and Sergei Iurov. "Vstrecha v redaktsii 'Kontinent.'" *Kontinent* no. 3 (1994): 207–19.

Vladimir, Fr. "Ne khlebom edinym." *Nash sovremennik* no. 6 (1990): 55–56.

Volgin, Igor.' "'V tochke samoubiistva. . . .'" *Nedelia,* 4 January 1995.

Volodin, Eduard. "Vozvrashchenie k istokam." *Nash sovremennik* no. 4 (1991): 191–92.

Vorontsova, Liudmila Mikhailovna, and Sergei Borisovich Filatov. "Russkii put' i grazhdanskoe obshchestvo." *Svobodnaia mysl'* no. 1 (1995): 58–68.

Walters, Philip. "Current Developments in Russia and the Response of the Russian Orthodox Church." In *Christianity after Communism: Social, Political, and Cultural Struggle in Russia,* ed. Niels C. Nielsen Jr., 85–102. Boulder, Colo., and Oxford: Westview Press, 1994.

———. "The Encyclopedia of Religious Life in Russia Today: A Landmark Research Project." *Religion, State, and Society* 30, no. 2 (June 2002): 157–60.

———. "The Ideas of the Christian Seminar." *Religion in Communist Lands* 9, nos. 3–4 (Autumn 1981): 111–22.

Walzer, Michael. "The Idea of Civil Society." *Dissent* (Spring 1991): 293–304.

———, ed. *Toward a Global Civil Society.* Providence, R.I.: Berghahn Books, 1995.

Ware, Kallistos [née Timothy]. *The Orthodox Church.* New York: Penguin, 1963.

———. *The Orthodox Way.* New rev. ed. Crestwood, N.Y.: St. Vladimir's Press, 1999.

Weigle, Marcie A. "On the Road to the Civic Forum: State and Civil Society from Yeltsin to Putin." *Demokratizatsiya* 10, no. 2 (Spring 2002): 117–46.

Wines, Michael. "Putin Describes an Ill Russia and Prescribes Strong Democracy." *New York Times,* 9 July 2000.

Witte, John, Jr. Introduction to *Proselytism and Orthodoxy in Russia: The New War for Souls.* Ed. John Witte Jr. and Michael Bourdeaux. Maryknoll, N.Y.: Orbis, 1999.

Witte, John, Jr., and Michael Bourdeaux, eds. *Proselytism and Orthodoxy in Russia: The New War for Souls.* Maryknoll, N.Y.: Orbis, 1999.

"Yeltsin Attends Sunday Church Services." *Summary of World Broadcasts,* 1408 B/1, 16 June 1992.

Yeltsin, Boris. "Obrashchenie k grazhdanam Rossii Prezidenta Rossiiskoi federatsii B. N. Yel'tsina v sviazi s otkloneniem federal'nogo zakona 'O svobode sovesti i o religioznykh ob'edineniiakh.'" Press release, mimeographed copy. Moscow, 22 July 1997.

Zacek, Judith C. "Champion of the Past: Count D. A. Tolstoi as Minister of the Interior, 1882–89." *Historian* 30, no. 3 (May 1968): 412–38.

Zernov, Nicholas. *The Russian Religious Renaissance of the Twentieth Century.* New York and Evanston: Harper and Row, 1963.

Zinoviev, Alexander. *Homo Sovieticus.* Trans. Charles Janson. Boston and New York: Atlantic Monthly Press, 1982.

———. *Kommunizm kak real'nost: krizis kommunizma.* Moscow: Tsentrpoligraf, 1994.

———. *My i zapad: stat'i, interv'iu, vystupleniia, 1979–1980.* Lausanne: L'Age d'Homme, 1981.

Zolotov, Andrei. "Ten Years after Coup, Putin Seeks Inspiration from Russia's Christian Roots." *Christianity Today,* 27 August 2001. Archived at http://www.christianitytoday.com/ct/2001/135/23.0.html.

Zverinskii, Vasilii Vasil'evich. *Materialy dlia istoriko-topograficheskogo issledovaniia o pravo-slavnykh monastyriakh v Rossiiskoi Imperii, s bibliograficheskim ukazatelem.* 2 vols. St. Petersburg: Tip. V. Bezobrazova i komp., 1890–97.

———, comp. *Statisticheskii vremennik Rossiiskoi Imperii,* ser. 3, no. 18: *Monastyri v Rossiiskoi Imperii.* St. Petersburg: Izd. Tsentral'nogo statisticheskogo komiteta ministerstva vnu-trennikh del, 1887.

Zviglyanich, Vladimir A. *The Morphology of Russian Mentality: A Philosophical Inquiry into Conservatism and Pragmatism.* Lewiston, N.Y.: Edwin Mellen Press, 1993.

Zweerde, Evert van der. "'Civil Society' and 'Orthodox Christianity' in Russia: A Double Test-Case." *Religion, State, and Society* 27, no. 1 (1999): 23–45.

JOURNALS AND NEWSPAPERS

Biulleten' Khristianskoi obshchestvennosti
The Christian Century
Communist and Post-Communist Studies
Domashnii advokat
The Economist
Emory International Review
Foreign Affairs
Glasnost No. 13
Izvestiia
Journal of Church and State
Khristianskii vestnik
Kommunist
Kontinent
Literaturnaia gazeta
Molodaia gvardiia
Moscow News

Moskovskie novosti
Moskovskii Tserkovnyi vestnik
Moskovskii zhurnal
Nash sovremennik
Nauka i religiia
Nauka i zhizn'
New Republic
New York Review of Books
New York Times
Nezavisimaia gazeta
Nezavisimaia gazeta—religii
Nezavisimaia gazeta—stsenarii
Obshchestvennye nauki i sovremennost
Ogonek
Pravoslavnaia obshchina
Pravoslavnaia Rus', supplement to *Sovetskaia Rossiia*
Protestant
Religiia i pravo
Religion in Communist Lands
Religion, State, and Society
Religion in USSR
Russian Studies in History
Russkaia mysl'
Segodnia
Sem'ia
Slovo
Sovetskaia bibliografiia
Stolitsa
Svobodnaia mysl'
Times (London)
Transitions
Tverskaia 13
Vybor
Zhurnal Moskovskoi Patriarkhii
Znamia

Index

Page numbers in *italic* type refer to illustrations.

ISBN-13: 978-1-58544-523-3
ISBN-10: 1-58544-523-1